SolidWorks 2014
Part I - Basic Tools

Introductory Level Tutorials
Parts, Assemblies and Drawings

Written by: Sr. Certified SolidWorks Instructor
Paul Tran, CSWE, CSWI

SDC Publications
P.O. Box 1334
Mission, KS 66222
913-262-2664
www.SDCpublications.com
Publisher: Stephen Schroff

ISBN-13: 978-1-58503-853-4
ISBN-10: 1-58503-853-9

Printed and bound in the United States of America.

Acknowledgments

Thanks as always to my wife Vivian for always being there and providing support and honest feedback on all the chapters in the textbook.

I would like to give a special thanks to Karla Werner and Rachel Schroff for their technical editing and corrections. Additionally thanks to Kevin Douglas, Peter Douglas and Dave Worcester for writing the forewords.

I also have to thank SDC Corp. and the staff for its continuing encouragement and support for this edition of **SolidWorks 2014 Part I – Basic Tools**. Thanks also to Zach Werner for putting together such a beautiful cover design.

Finally, I would like to thank you, our readers, for your continued support. It is with your consistent feedback that we were able to create the lessons and exercises in this book with more detailed and useful information.

Foreword

For more than two decades, I have been fortunate to have worked in the fast-paced, highly dynamic world of mechanical product development providing computer-aided design and manufacturing solutions to thousands of designers, engineers and manufacturing experts in the western US. The organization where I began this career was US CAD in Orange County CA, one of the most successful SolidWorks Resellers in the world. My first several years were spent in the sales organization prior to moving into middle management and ultimately President of the firm. In the mid 1990's is when I met Paul Tran, a young, enthusiastic Instructor who had just joined our team.

Paul began teaching SolidWorks to engineers and designers of medical devices, automotive and aerospace products, high tech electronics, consumer goods, complex machinery and more. After a few months of watching him teach and interacting with students during and after class, it was becoming pretty clear – Paul not only loved to teach, but his students were the most excited with their learning experience than I could ever recall from previous years in the business. As the years began to pass and thousands of students had cycled through Paul's courses, what was eye opening was Paul's continued passion to educate as if it were his first class and students in every class, without exception, loved the course.

Great teachers not only love their subject, but they love to share that joy with students – this is what separates Paul from others in the world of SolidWorks Instruction. He always has gone well beyond learning the picks & clicks of using the software, to best practice approaches to creating intelligent, innovative and efficient designs that are easily grasped by his students. This effective approach to teaching SolidWorks has translated directly into Paul's many published books on the subject. His latest effort with SolidWorks 2014 is no different. Students that apply the practical lessons from basics to advanced concepts will not only learn how to apply SolidWorks to real world design challenges more quickly, but will gain a competitive edge over others that have followed more traditional approaches to learning this type of technology. As the pressure continues to rise on U.S. workers and their organizations to remain competitive in the global economy, raising not only education levels but technical skills are paramount to a successful professional career and business. Investing in a learning process towards the mastery of SolidWorks through the tutelage of the most accomplished and decorated educator and author in Paul Tran will provide a crucial competitive edge in this dynamic market space.

Kevin Douglas
Vice President Sales/Board of Advisors, GoEngineer

Foreword

I first met Paul Tran when I was busy creating another challenge in my life. I needed to take a vision from one man's mind, understand what the vision looked like, how it was going to work and comprehend the scale of his idea. My challenge was I was missing one very important ingredient, a tool that would create a picture with all the moving parts.

Research led me to discover a great tool, SolidWorks. It claimed to allow one to make 3D components, in picture quality, on a computer, add in all moving parts, assemble it and make it run, all before money was spent on bending steel and buying parts that may not fit together. I needed to design and build a product with thousands of parts, make them all fit and work in harmony with millimeters tolerance. The possible cost implications of failed experimentation were daunting.

To my good fortune, one company's marketing strategy of selling a product without an instruction manual and requiring one to attend an instructional class to get it, led me to meet a communicator who made it all seem so simple.

Paul Tran has worked with and taught SolidWorks as his profession for nearly 30 years. Paul knows the SolidWorks product and manipulates it like a fine musical instrument. I watched Paul explain the unexplainable to baffled students with great skill and clarity. He taught me how to navigate the intricacies of the product so that I could use it as a communication tool with skilled engineers. *He teaches the teachers*.

I hired Paul as a design engineering consultant to create the thousands of parts for my company's product. Paul Tran's knowledge and teaching skill has added immeasurable value to my company. When I read through the pages of these manuals, I now have an "instant replay" of his communication skill with the clarity of having him looking over my shoulder - *continuously*. We can now design, prove and build our product and know it will always work and not fail. Most important of all, Paul Tran helped me turn a blind man's vision into reality and a monument to his dream.

Thanks Paul.

These books will make dreams come true and help visionaries change the world.

Peter J. Douglas

CEO, Cake Energy, LLC

Images courtesy of C.A.K.E. Energy Corp., designed by Paul Tran

Preface

The modern world of engineering design and analysis requires an intense knowledge of Computer Aided Design (CAD) tools. To gain this deep understanding of unique CAD requirements one must commit the time, energy, and use of study guides. Paul Tran has invested countless hours and the wealth of his career to provide a path of easy to understand and follow instructional books. Each chapter is designed to build on the next and supplies users with the building blocks required to easily navigate SolidWorks 2014. I challenge you to find a finer educational tool whether you are new to this industry or a seasoned SolidWorks veteran.

I have been a part of the CAD industry for over twenty five years and read my share of instructional manuals. I can tell you Paul Tran's SolidWorks books do what most promise; however what others don't deliver. This book surpasses any CAD instructional tool I have used during my career. Paul's education and vast experience provides a finely tuned combination, producing instructional material that supports industry standards and most importantly, industry requirements.

Anyone interested in gaining the basics of SolidWorks to an in-depth approach should continue to engage the following chapters. All users at every level of SolidWorks knowledge will gain tremendous benefit from within these pages.

Dave Worcester
System Administer
Advanced Sterilization Products - A Johnson & Johnson Company

Author's Note

SolidWorks 2014 Basic Tools and Advanced Techniques are comprised of lessons and exercises based on the author's extensive knowledge on this software. Paul has nearly 30 years of experience in the fields of mechanical and manufacturing engineering; 18 years were in teaching and supporting the SolidWorks software and its add-ins. As an active Sr. SolidWorks instructor and design engineer, Paul has worked and consulted with hundreds of reputable companies including; IBM, Intel, NASA, US-Navy, Boeing, Disneyland, Medtronic, Guidant, Terumo, Kingston and many more. Today, he has trained more than 7000 engineering professionals, and given guidance to nearly ½ of the number of Certified SolidWorks Professionals and Certified SolidWorks Expert (CSWP & CSWE) in the state of California.

Every lesson and exercise in this book was created based on real world projects. Each of these projects have been broken down and developed into easy and comprehendible steps for the reader. Learn the fundamentals of SolidWorks at your own pace, as you progress form simple to more complex design challenges. Furthermore, at the end of every chapter, there are self test questionnaires to ensure that the reader has gained sufficient knowledge from each section before moving on to more advanced lessons.

Paul believes that the most effective way to learn the "world's most sophisticated software" is to learn it inside and out, create everything from the beginning, and take it step by step. This is what the **SolidWorks 2014 Basic Tools & Advanced Techniques** manuals are all about.

About the Training Files

The files for this textbook are available for download on the publisher's website at **www.SDCpublications.com/downloads/978-1-58503-853-4**. They are organized by the chapter numbers and the file names that are normally mentioned at the beginning of each chapter or exercise. In the Built Parts folder you will also find copies of the parts, assemblies and drawings that were created for cross references or reviewing purposes.

It would be best to make a copy of the content to your local hard drive and work from these documents; you can always go back to the original training files location at anytime in the future, if needed.

Who this book is for

This book is for the mid-level user, who is already familiar with the SolidWorks program. It is also a great resource for the more CAD literate individuals who want to expand their knowledge of the different features that SolidWorks 2014 has to offer.

The organization of the book

The chapters in this book are organized in the logical order in which you would learn the SolidWorks 2014 program. Each chapter will guide you through some different tasks, from navigating through the user interface, to exploring the toolbars, from some simple 3D modeling and move on to more complex tasks that are common to all SolidWorks releases. There is also a self-test questionnaire at the end of each chapter to ensure that you have gained sufficient knowledge before moving on to the next chapter.

The conventions in this book

This book uses the following conventions to describe the actions you perform when using the keyboard and mouse to work in SolidWorks 2014:

Click: means to press and release the mouse button. A click of a mouse button is used to select a command or an item on the screen.

Double Click: means to quickly press and release the left mouse button twice. A double mouse click is used to open a program, or showing the dimensions of a feature.

Right Click: means to press and release the right mouse button. A right mouse click is used to display a list of commands, a list of shortcuts that is related to the selected item.

Click and Drag: means to position the mouse cursor over an item on the screen and then press and hold down the left mouse button; still holding down the left button, move the mouse to the new destination and release the mouse button. Drag and drop makes it easy to move things around within a SolidWorks document.

Bolded words: indicated the action items that you need to perform.

Italic words: Side notes and tips that give you additional information, or to explain special conditions that may occur during the course of the task.

Numbered Steps: indicates that you should follow these steps in order to successfully perform the task.

Icons: indicates the buttons or commands that you need to press.

SolidWorks 2014

SolidWorks 2014 is program suite, or a collection of engineering programs that can help you design better products faster. SolidWorks 2014 contains different combinations of programs; some of the programs used in this book may not be available in your suites.

Start and exit SolidWorks

SolidWorks allows you to start its program in several ways. You can either double click on its shortcut icon on the desktop, or go to the Start menu and select the following: All Programs / SolidWorks 2014 / SolidWorks, or drag a SolidWorks document and drop it on the SolidWorks shortcut icon.

Before exiting SolidWorks, be sure to save any open documents, and then click File / Exit; you can also click the X button on the top right of your screen to exit the program.

Using the Toolbars

You can use toolbars to select commands in SolidWorks rather than using the drop down menus. Using the toolbars is normally faster. The toolbars come with commonly used commands in SolidWorks, but they can be customized to help you work more efficiently.

To access the toolbars, either right click in an empty spot on the top right of your screen or select View / Toolbars.

To customize the toolbars, select Tools / Customize. When the dialog pops up, click on the Commands tab, select a Category, and then drag an icon out of the dialog box and drop it on a toolbar that you want to customize. To remove an icon from a toolbar, drag an icon out of the toolbar and drop it into the dialog box.

Using the task pane

The task pane is normally kept on the right side of your screen. It display various options like SolidWorks resources, Design library, File explorer, Search, View palette, Appearances and Scenes, Custom properties, Built-in libraries, Technical alerts and news, etc,.

The task pane provides quick access to any of the mentioned items by offering the drag and drop function to all of its contents. You can see a large preview of a SolidWorks document before opening it. New documents can be saved in the task pane at anytime, and existing documents can also be edited and re-saved. The task pane can be resized, close or move to different location on your screen if needed.

Table of Contents

Setting the System Parameters

Basic Modeling Topics

Bottom Up Assembly Topics

Chapter 15: Assembly Drawings – Links Assembly   15-1

Assembly Drawing – Alternate Position View   15-23

SolidWorks 2014 Quick-Guides:

Quick Reference Guide to SolidWorks 2014 Command Icons and Toolbars.

Created with Solidworks 2014-SP0

Introduction

SolidWorks User Interface

The SolidWorks 2014 User Interface

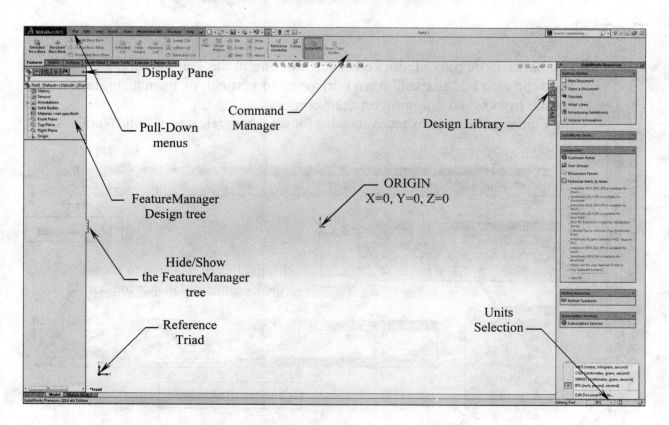

The 3 reference planes:

The Front, Top and the Right plane are

90°apart. They share the same center point called the Origin.

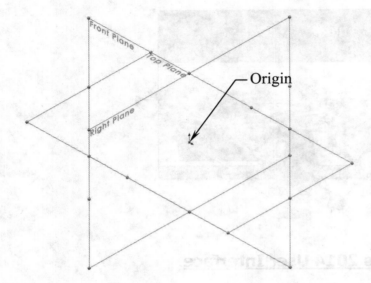

Origin

Y

Z X

6 Degrees of Freedom

The Toolbars:

- Toolbars can be moved, docked or left floating in the graphics area.
- They can also be "shaped" from horizontal to vertical, or from a single to double rows when dragging on their corners.
- The CommandManager is recommended for the newer releases of SolidWorks.

Drag corner

Right click in this area to access the CommandManager toolbar

CommandManager

- If CommandManager is not used, toolbars can be docked or left floating.

- Toolbars can be toggled off or on by activating or de-activating their check boxes:

- Select **Tools / Customize / Toolbars** tab.

- The icons in the toolbars can be enlarged when its check box is selected ☐ Large icons

The View ports: You can view or work with SolidWorks model or an assembly using one, two or four view ports.

View Orientation

- Some of the **System Feedback symbols** (Inference pointers):

Snap to Vertex (endpoint)   Snap to Intersection

Snap to Edge (curve)   Horizontal Line

Snap to Mid-point   Vertical Line

The Status Bar: (View / Status Bar)

Displays the status of the sketch entity using different colors to indicate:

Green = Selected

2D Sketch examples:

Click-Drag-Release: Single entity.

(Click Point 1, hold the mouse button, drag to point 2 and release).

Click-Release: Continuous multiple entities.

(The Inference Lines appear when the sketch entities are Parallel, Perpendicular or Tangent with each other).

Click-Drag-Release: Single Rectangle

(Click point 1, hold the mouse button, drag to Point 2 and release).

Click-Drag-Release: Single Centerpoint Arc

(Click point 1, hold the mouse button and drag to Point 2, release; then drag to Point 3 and release).

Click-Drag-Release: Single Circle

(Click point 1 [center of circle], hold the mouse button, drag to Point 2 [Radius] and release).

3D Feature examples:

Extrude

2D sketch   3D feature

Revolve

2D sketch   3D feature

Sweep

2D sketch   3D feature

Loft

2D sketch   3D feature

Box-Select: Use the Select Pointer to drag a selection box around items.

Box-Select from LEFT to RIGHT

Only items within the box are selected.

Entities NOT selected

Box-Select from RIGHT to LEFT

All items crossing the box boundary are selected.

ALL Entities selected

The default geometry type selected is as follows:

* Part documents – edges * Assembly documents – components * Drawing documents - sketch entities,
dims & annotations. * To select multiple entities, hold down **Ctrl** while selecting after the first selection.

The <u>Mouse Gestures</u> for Sketches, Drawings and Parts

- Similar to a keyboard shortcut, you can use a Mouse Gesture to execute a command. A total of 8 keyboard shortcuts can be independently mapped and stored in the Mouse Gesture Guides.

- To activate the Mouse Gesture Guide, **right-click-and-drag** to see the current eight-gestures, then simply select the command that you want to use.

Mouse Gestures for Sketches

Mouse Gestures for Parts & Assemblies

Mouse Gestures for Drawings

- To customize the Mouse Gestures and include your favorite shortcuts, go to:

Tools / Customize.

- From the **Mouse Gestures** tab, select **All Commands** and enable the **Show only commands with Mouse Gestures assigned** checkbox.

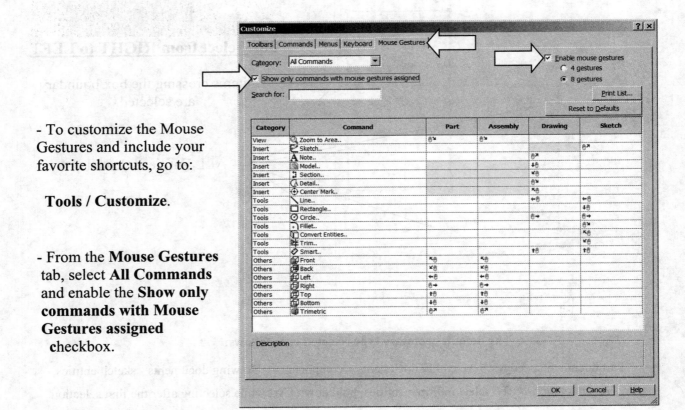

Fit to Left display — — Fit to Right display

Dual monitors display

Text and images created using Windows 7 SP1 and SolidWorks 2014 64bit SP0

CHAPTER 1

System Options

Setting Up The System Options

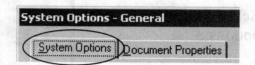

One of the first things to do after installing the SolidWorks software is to setup the system options to use as the default settings for all documents.

System Options such as:

- Input dimension value, Face highlighting…

- Drawing views controls, edge and hatch display.

- System colors, errors, sketch, text, grid, etc.

- Sketch display, Automatic relation.

- Edges display and selection controls.

- Performance and Large assembly mode.

- Area hatch/fill and hatch patterns.

- Feature Manager and Spin Box increment controls.

- View rotation and animation.

- Backup files and locations, etc.

The settings are all set and saved in the **system registry**. While not part of the document itself, these settings affect all documents, including current and future documents.

This chapter will guide you through some of the options settings for use with this textbook; you may need to modify them to ensure full compatibility with your applications or company's standards.

System Options

The **General** Options

- To start setting up the system options, go to: **Tools / Options.**

- Select the **General** options.

- Select only the check boxes as shown in the General Options dialog box.

- Go down the list and select the **Drawings** Options.

System Options

The **Drawings** Options

- Enable only the check boxes as indicated in this dialog box.

(These settings are intended for use with this training manual only, you may need to change them to meet your company's requirements).

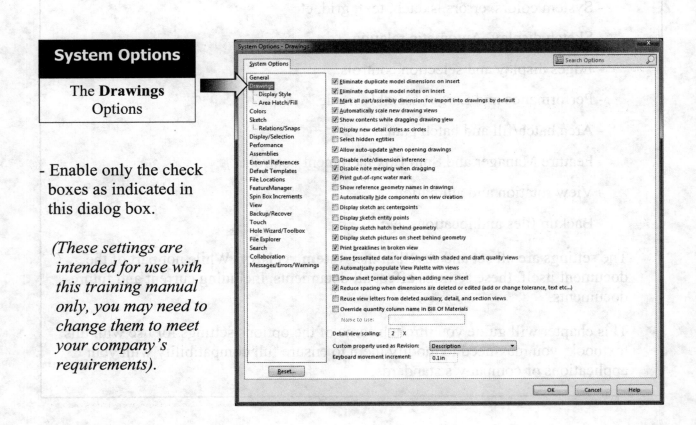

System Options

The **Display Style** Options

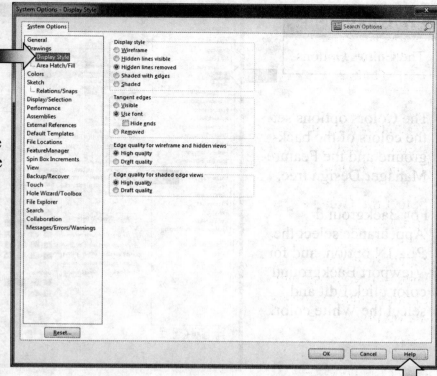

- Continue going down the list and follow the sample settings shown in the dialog boxes to setup your System Options.

- For more information on these settings click the Help button at the lower right corner of the dialog box (arrow).

System Options

The **Area Hatch/Fill** Options

- The Area Hatch/Fills option sets the hatch pattern and Spacing (Scale).

System Options

The **Colors** Options

- The Colors options set the colors of the background and the Feature-Manager Design tree.

- For Background-Appearance select the PLAIN option, and for Viewport Background color click Edit and select the White color.

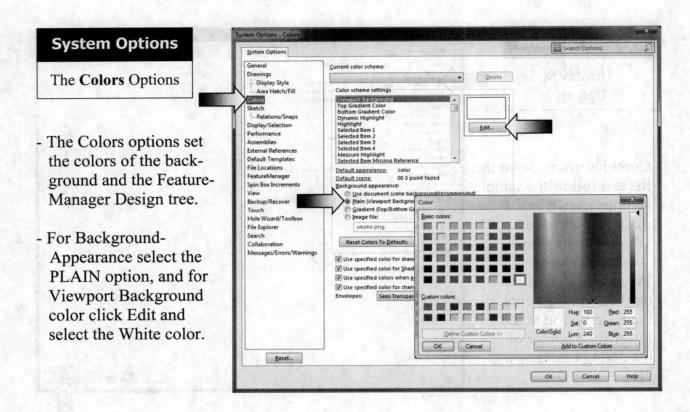

System Options

The **Sketch** Options

- The Sketch options control the displays of the sketch entities and their orientation.

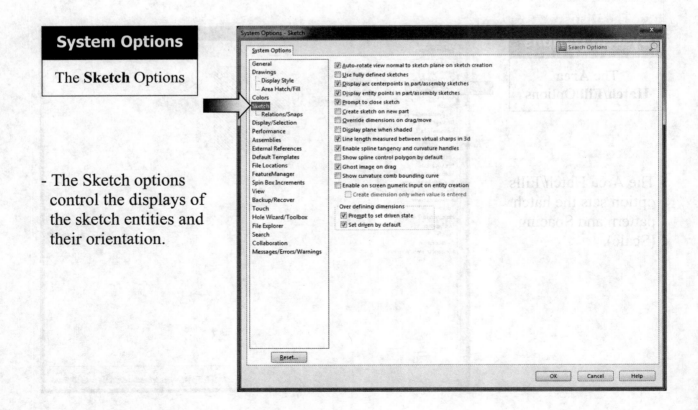

System Options

The **Relations / Snaps** Options

- Enable all Automatic-Relation options, except for the Grid and Angle options.

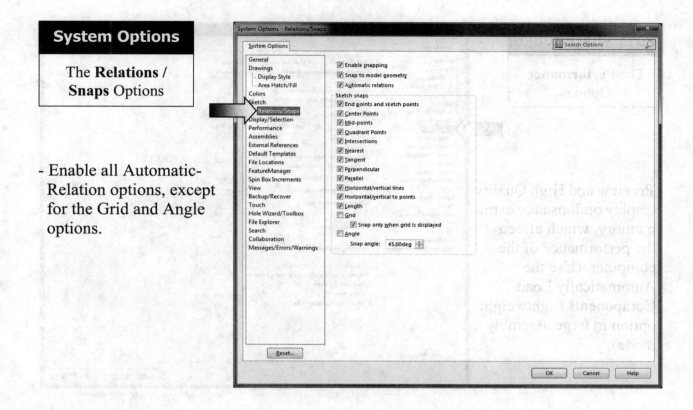

System Options

The **Display / Selection** Options

- The controls for Display and Selection options in the Part, Assembly, and Drawings modes.

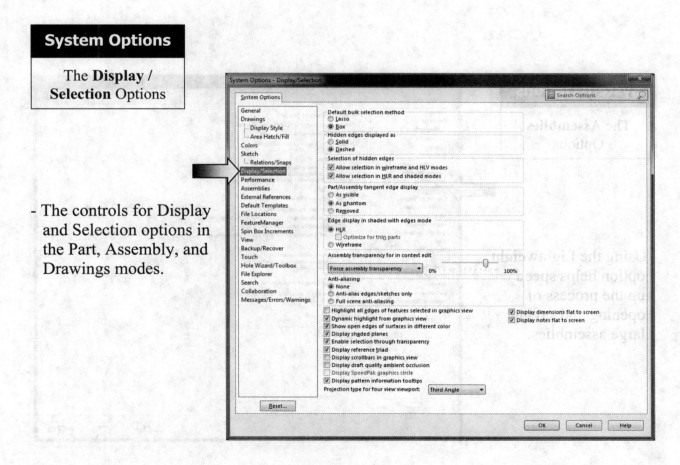

System Options

The **Performance** Options

- Preview and High Quality display options take extra memory, which effects the performance of the computer. (Use the Automatically Load Components Lightweight option in large assembly mode).

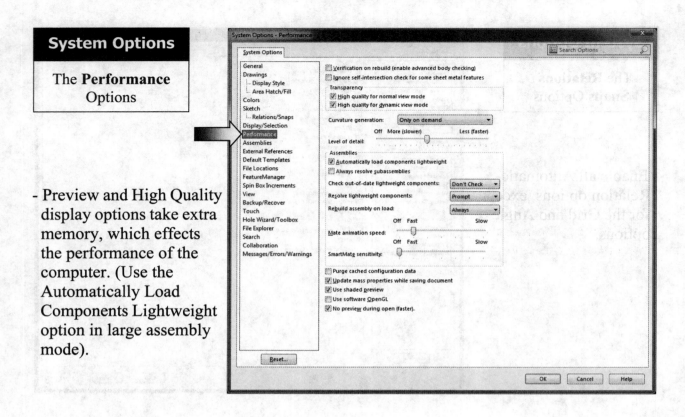

System Options

The **Assemblies** Options

- Using the Lightweight option helps speed up the process of opening and saving large assemblies.

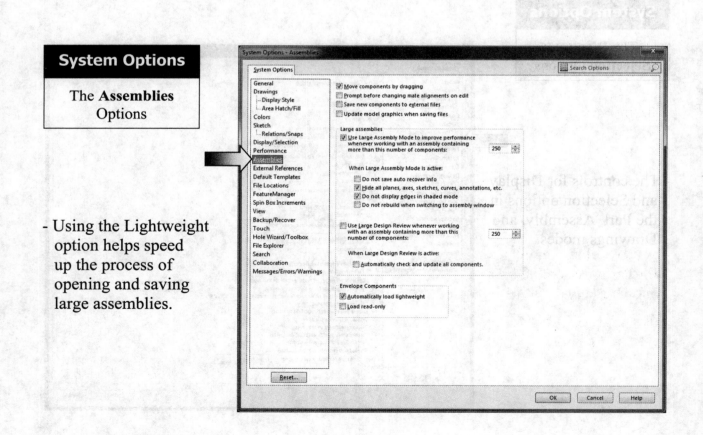

System Options

The **External References** Options

- Select the options that help locate file references and update component names.

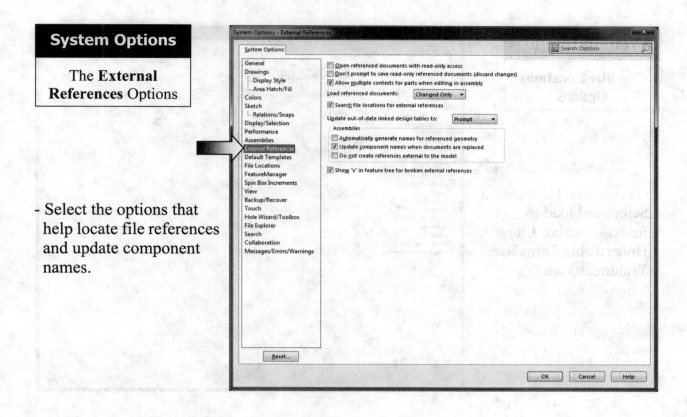

System Options

The **Default Templates** Options

- Set the default templates for Parts, Assemblies, and Drawings.

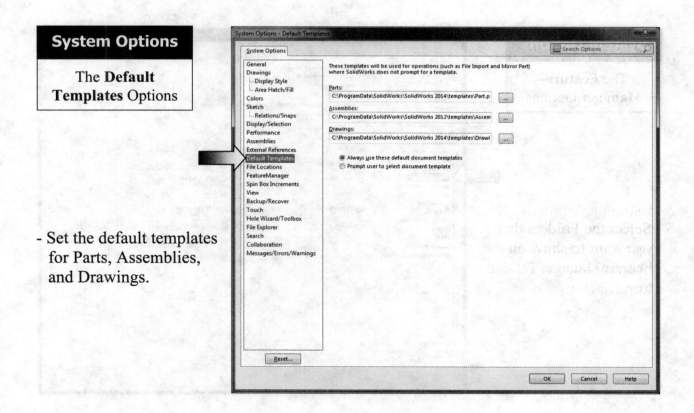

System Options

The **File Locations** Options

- Select and load the folders: Design Library, Holes Table Templates, Weldments, etc.

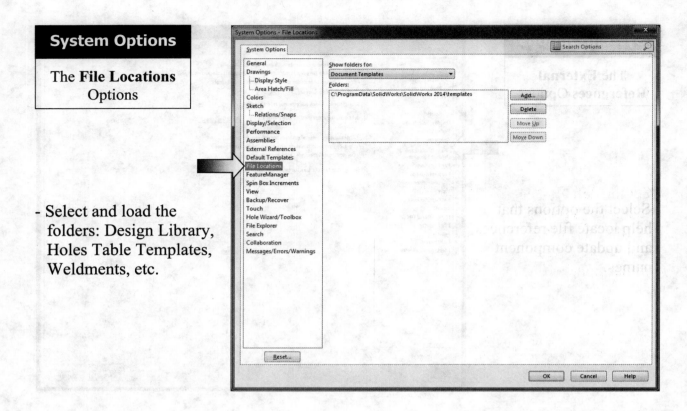

System Options

The **Feature-Manager** Options

- Select the Folders that you want to show on the FeatureManager Design tree.

System Options

The **Spin Box Increments** Options

- Set the default increments for the Modify Spin Box (when creating or editing dimensions).

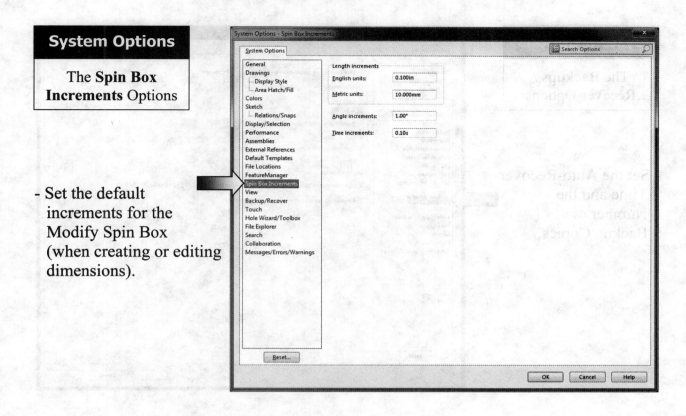

System Options

The **View** Options

- Set the Rotation, Mouse Speed, and Transitions of the view.

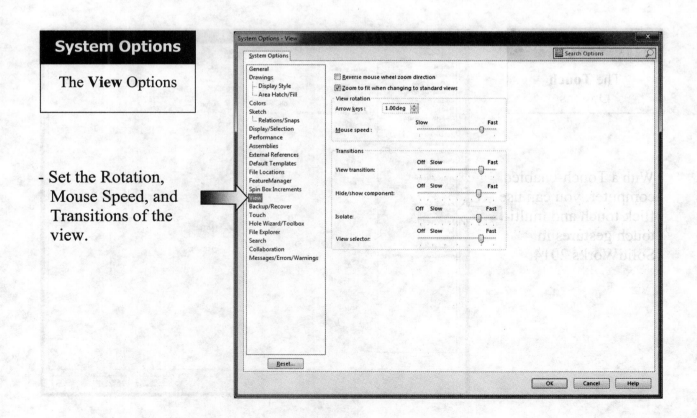

System Options

The **Backups /
Recover** Options

- Set the Auto-Recover-
Time and the
Number of
Backup Copies.

System Options

The **Touch**
Options

- With a Touch-enabled
computer, you can use
flick touch and multi-
touch gestures in
SolidWorks 2014.

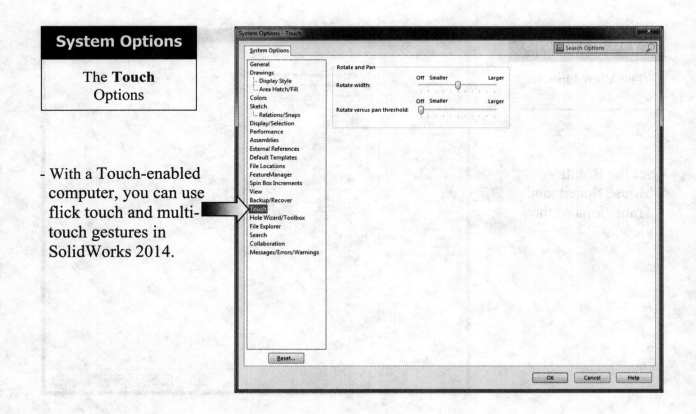

System Options

The **Hole-Wizard/Toolbox** Options

- Locate the Hole Wizard and Toolbox folder.

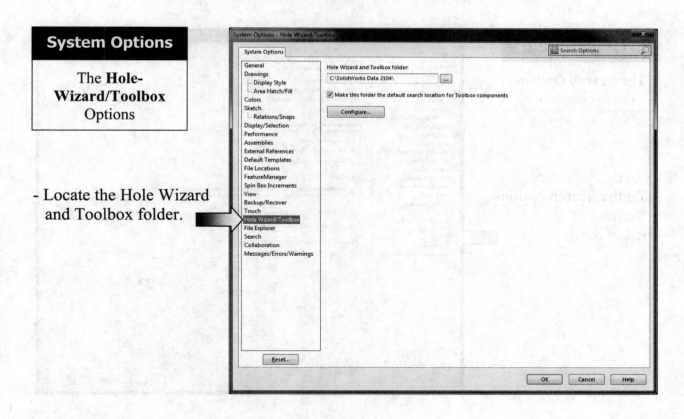

System Options

The **File Explorer** Options

- Enable the File Locations for accessing the SW documents.

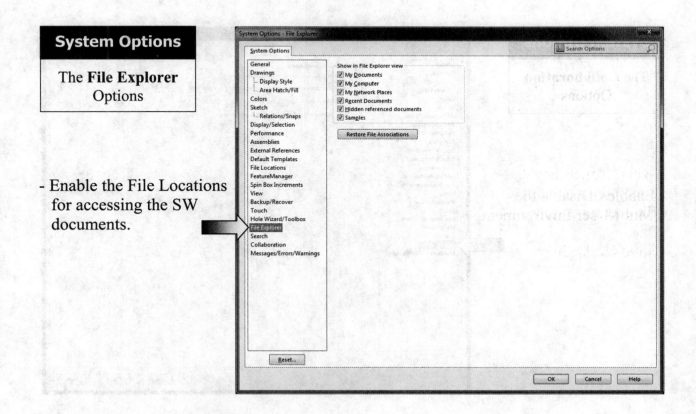

System Options

The **Search** Options

- Set the Search options.

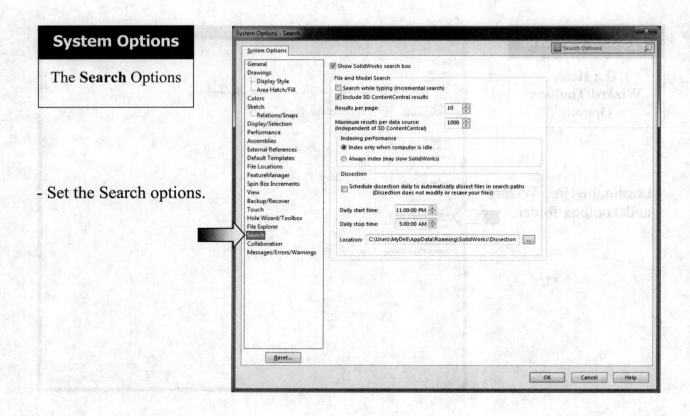

System Options

The **Collaboration**
Options

- Enable / Disable the
Multi-User Environment.

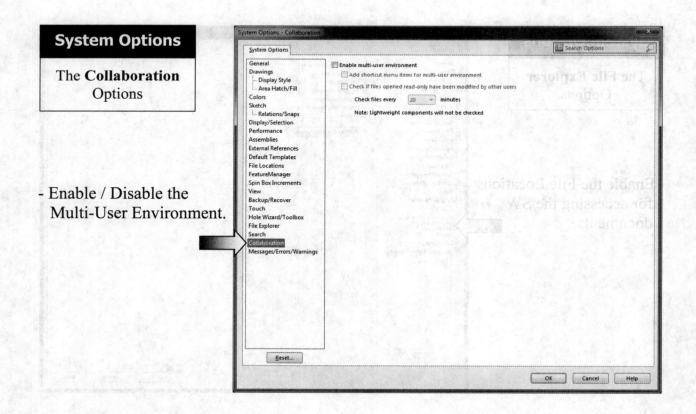

System Options

The **Advanced**
Options

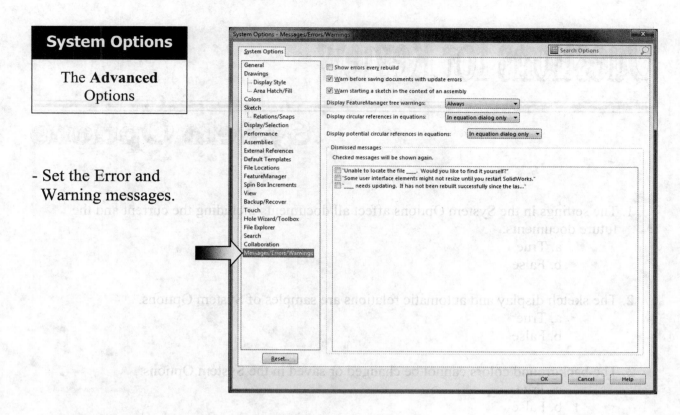

- Set the Error and
Warning messages.

- Continue to setup the Document Properties in Chapter 2...

Questions for Review

System Options

1. The settings in the System Options affect all documents including the current and the future documents.
   - a. True
   - b. False

2. The sketch display and automatic relations are samples of System Options.
   - a. True
   - b. False

3. The background colors cannot be changed or saved in the System Options.
   - a. True
   - b. False

4. The mouse wheel zoom direction can be reverse and saved.
   - a. True
   - b. False

5. Default document templates can be selected and saved in the System Options.
   - a. True
   - b. False

6. The spin box increment is fixed in the System Options; its value cannot be changed.
   - a. True
   - b. False

7. The number of backup copies for a document can be specified and saved in the System Options.
   - a. True
   - b. False

8. The System Options can be copied using the SolidWorks Utility / Copy Settings Wizard.
   - a. True
   - b. False

1. TRUE   2. TRUE
3. FALSE   4. TRUE
5. FALSE   6. FALSE
7. TRUE   8. TRUE

CHAPTER 2

Document Templates

Setting Up The Document Properties

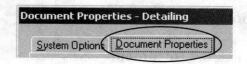

After setting up the System Options, the next task is to setup a document template, where drafting standards and other settings can be set, saved and used over and over again as a template. The Document Properties such as:

- Drafting Standard (ANSI, ISO, DIN, JIS, etc.).

- Dimension, Note, Balloon, and Fonts Sizes.

- Arrowhead sizes.

- Annotation display.

- Grid spacing and grid display.

- Units (Inches, Millimeters, etc.) and Decimal places.

- Feature Colors, Wireframe, and Shading colors.

- Material Properties.

- Image quality controls.

- Plane display controls.

These settings are all set and saved in the templates, all settings affect only the **current document** (C:\Program Files\SolidWorks Corp\SolidWorks Data\ Templates) OR (C:\Program Files\SolidWorks Corp\SolidWorks\Lang\English\ Tutorial).

The following are examples of various document settings which are intended for use with this textbook only; you may need to modify them to ensure full compatibility with your applications.

Document Properties

The **Drafting Standard** options

- Begin with a new document:

- Select: **File / New / Part.**

- Go to: **Tools / Options /**

- Click the **Document-Properties** tab.

- Click **Drafting Standard**.

- Set the Overall Drafting Standard to **ANSI**.

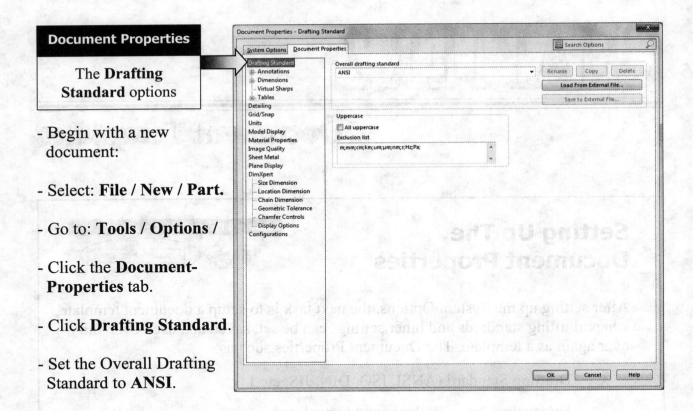

Note: If your Units is in Millimeter, skip to the Units options on page 2-13 and set your units to IPS, then return to where you left off and continue with your template settings.

Document Properties

The **Annotations** options

- Set the Annotations Option as shown. (detailed information such as Arrow Size, Font Height, Bent Leader Length, etc., can be verified from the Drawing Requirements Manual or DRM).

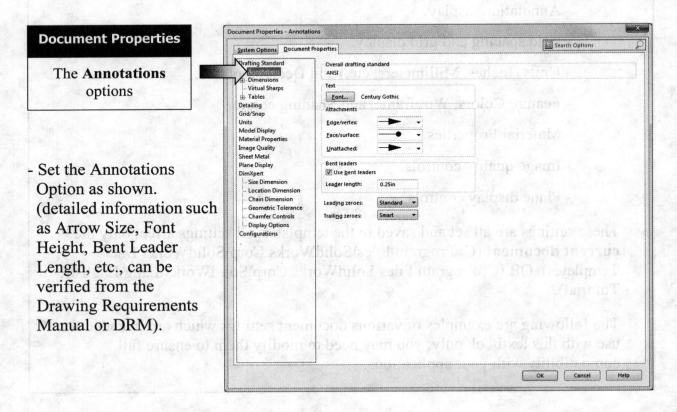

Document Properties

The **Annotations / Balloons** options

- Set the Balloons standard to ANSI and the other options as shown.

- Click on the Help button at any time to access the information on these topics.

Document Properties

The **Annotations / Datums** options

- Set the Datums standard to ANSI and other options as shown.

Note:

1982 Datum symbol – A –

1994 Datum symbol A

Document Properties

The **Annotations / Geo. Tol.** options

- Set the Geometric-Tolerance standard to ANSI.

- The Font selection should match the other options for all annotations.

Document Properties

The **Annotations / Notes** options

- Set the Notes standard to ANSI.

- Use the same settings for Font and Leader display.

Document Properties

The **Revision Clouds** options

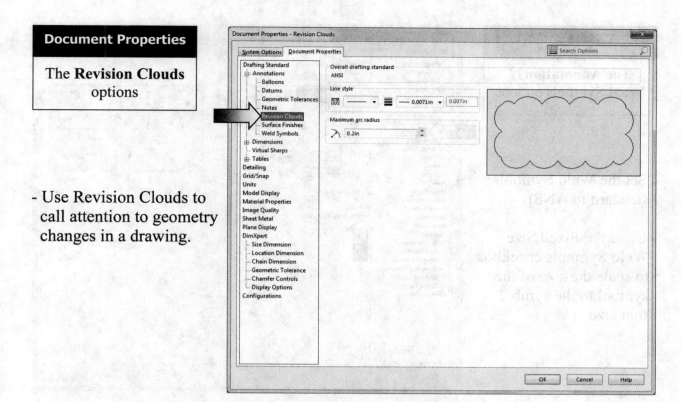

- Use Revision Clouds to call attention to geometry changes in a drawing.

Document Properties

The **Surface Finishes** options

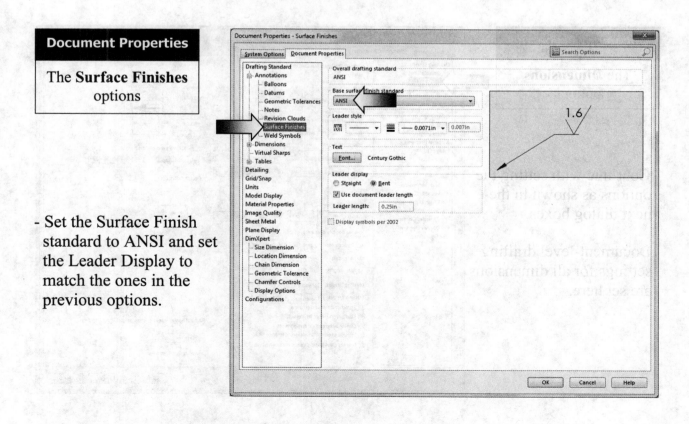

- Set the Surface Finish standard to ANSI and set the Leader Display to match the ones in the previous options.

Document Properties

The **Annotations / Weld Symbols** options

- Set the Weld Symbols standard to ANSI.

- Clear the Fixed Size Weld Symbols checkbox to scale the size of the symbol to the symbol font size.

Document Properties

The **Dimensions** options

- Continue with setting the options as shown in the next dialog boxes.

- Document-level drafting settings for all dimensions are set here.

Document Properties

The **Dimensions /
Angle** options

- Set the Angle Dimension
standard to ANSI and set
the other options shown.

Document Properties

The **Angular
Running** options

- A set of dimensions
measured from a zero-
degree dimension in a
sketch or drawing.

Document Properties

The **Dimensions /
Arc Length** options

- Set the Arc Length
Dimension standard to
ANSI, Primary Precision
to 3 decimals, and Dual
Precision to 2 decimals.

- The Arc Length
dimension is created by
holding the Control key
and clicking the arc and
both of its endpoints.

Document Properties

The **Dimensions /
Chamfer** options

- Set the Chamfer-
Dimension standard to
ANSI and the Primary-
Precision to 3 decimals.

Document Properties

The **Dimensions /
Diameter** options

- Set the Diameter-
Dimension standard to
ANSI.

- Set the Leader Style and
thickness here.

Document Properties

The **Dimensions /
Hole Callout** options

- Set the Hole Callout
Dimension standard
to ANSI.

- Set the Text justification
positions to Center and
Middle.

Document Properties

The **Dimensions / Linear** options

- Set the Linear Dimension standard to ANSI.

- Enable the Use Bent-Leader checkbox.

Document Properties

The **Dimensions / Ordinate** options

- Set the Ordinate-Dimension standard to ANSI.

- Enable the Automatically Jog Ordinates, when dimensions overlapping or too close to one another.

Document Properties

The **Dimensions** /
Radius options

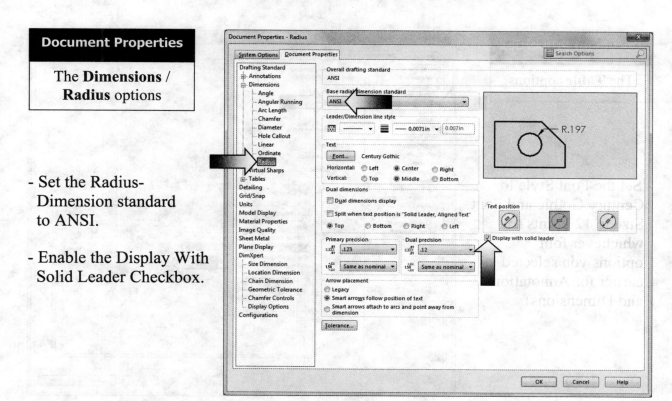

- Set the Radius-
Dimension standard
to ANSI.

- Enable the Display With
Solid Leader Checkbox.

Document Properties

The **Virtual Sharps**
options

- Select the Plus
symbol for Virtual
Sharp (the intersection
between the two
entities).

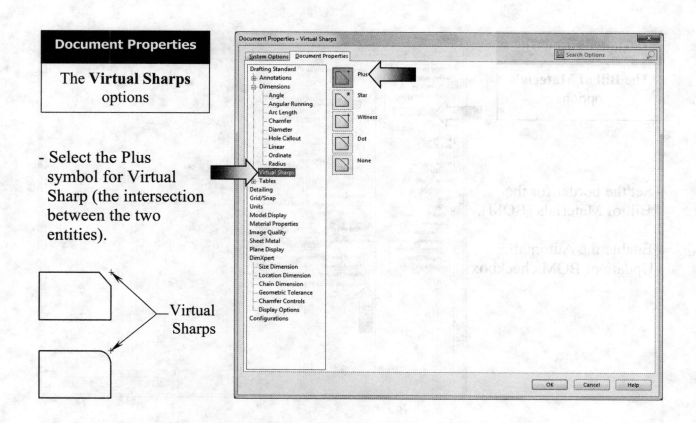

Virtual
Sharps

Document Properties

The **Tables** options

- Set the Font Style to Century Gothic and Font Size to 12 Points (or whichever font options you selected earlier for Annotations and Dimensions).

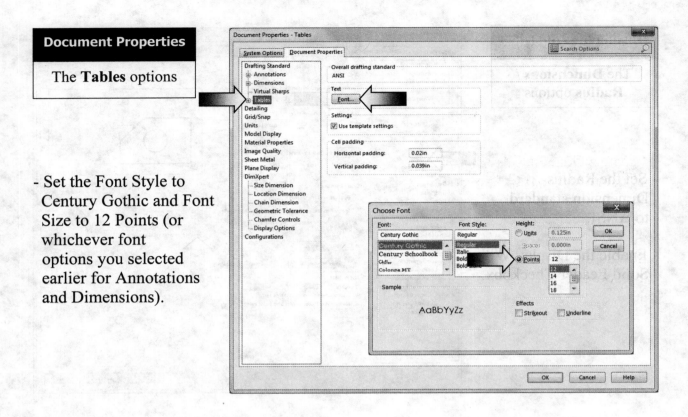

Document Properties

The **Bill of Materials** options

- Set the border for the Bill of Materials (BOM).

- Enable the Automatic Update of BOM checkbox.

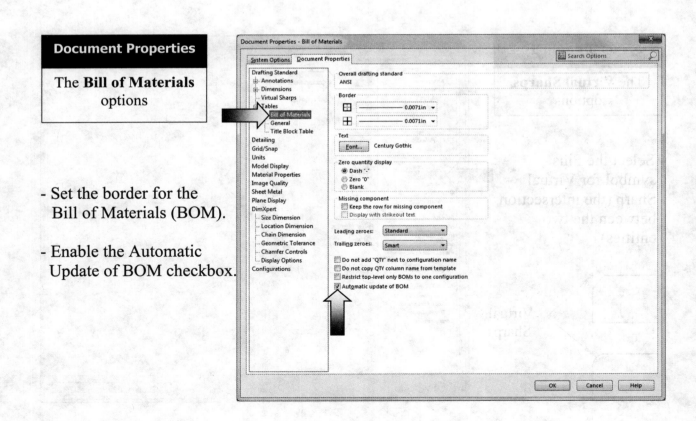

Document Properties

The **General** options

- Create a General Table to use in a drawing. The user inputs data in the cell manually.

- Set the line thickness for the border of the table here.

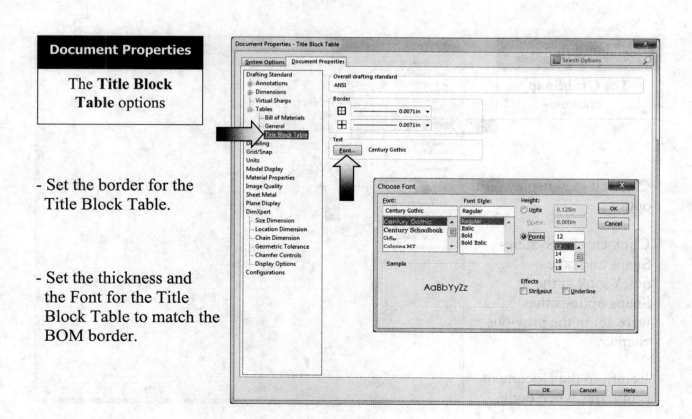

Document Properties

The **Title Block Table** options

- Set the border for the Title Block Table.

- Set the thickness and the Font for the Title Block Table to match the BOM border.

Document Properties

The **Detailing** options

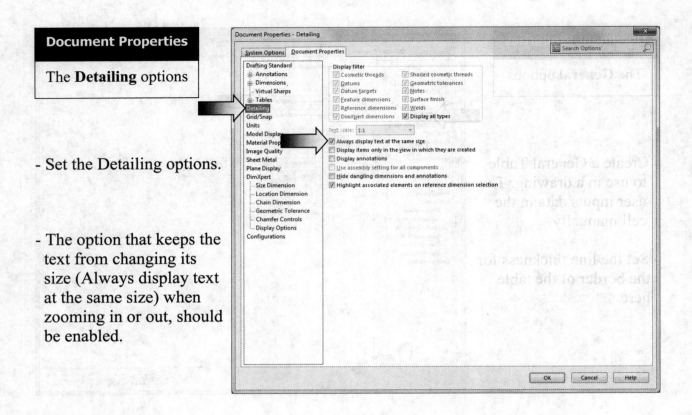

- Set the Detailing options.

- The option that keeps the text from changing its size (Always display text at the same size) when zooming in or out, should be enabled.

Document Properties

The **Grid/Snap** options

- Clear all the Display Grid options.

- Click Go-To-System-Snaps and take a quick look at the Snaps options that were set in the previous chapter.

- Return to the Document-Properties when done.

Document Properties

The **Units** options

- Set the Unit options to IPS, and the number of decimals as indicated.

(The Dual Dimension options are set in the Dimension section).

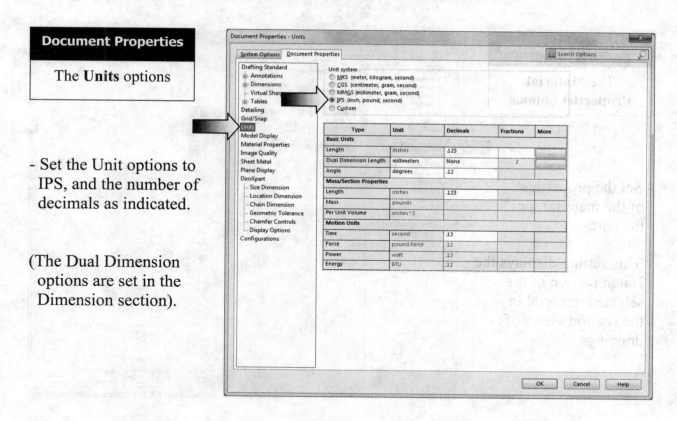

Document Properties

The **Model Display** options

- Keep all default Colors as they are, do not change.

- Uncheck the Store Appearance, Decal, and Scene… to reduce the file size.

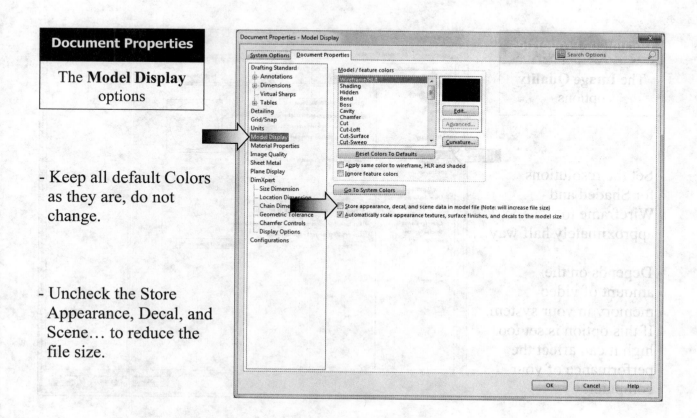

Document Properties

The **Material Properties** options

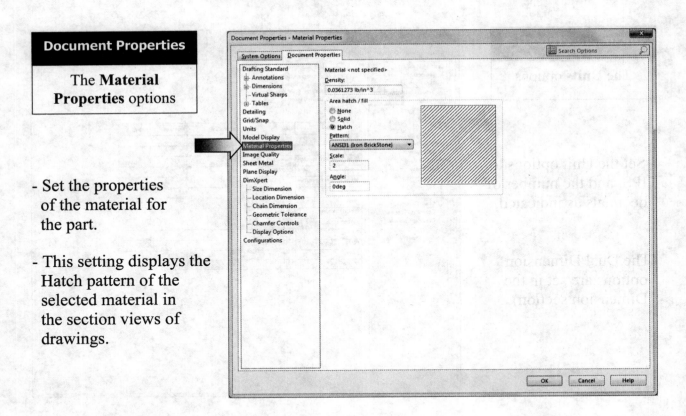

- Set the properties of the material for the part.

- This setting displays the Hatch pattern of the selected material in the section views of drawings.

Document Properties

The **Image Quality** options

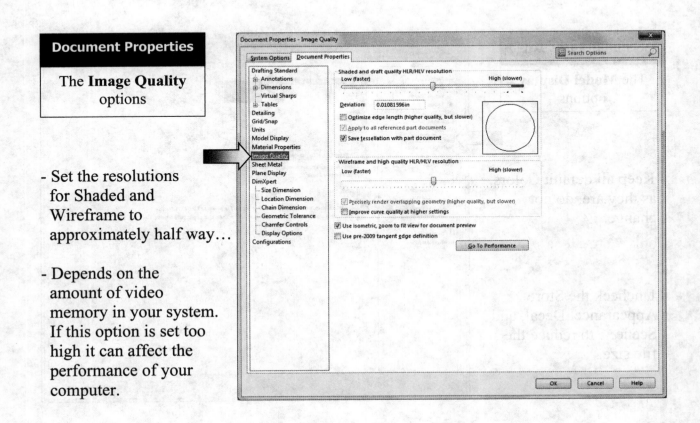

- Set the resolutions for Shaded and Wireframe to approximately half way…

- Depends on the amount of video memory in your system. If this option is set too high it can affect the performance of your computer.

Document Properties

The **Sheet Metal** options

- Set the Sheet Metal options as shown.

- These options vary depending on whether you are working with a part, assembly, or drawing. Click the Help button for more information about these settings.

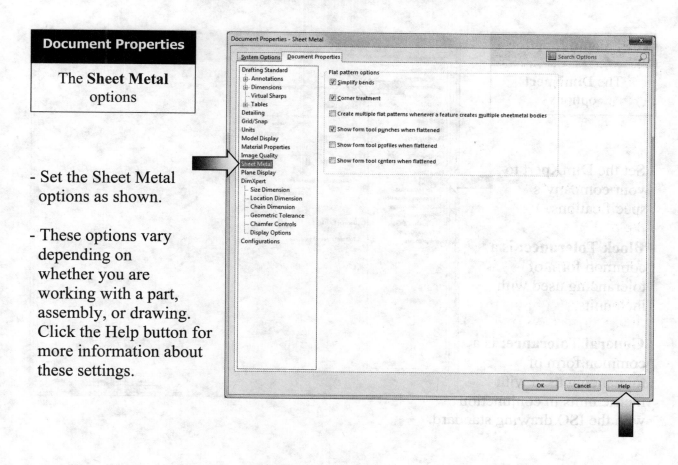

Document Properties

The **Plane Display** options

- Change the Plane colors and its transparency only as needed.

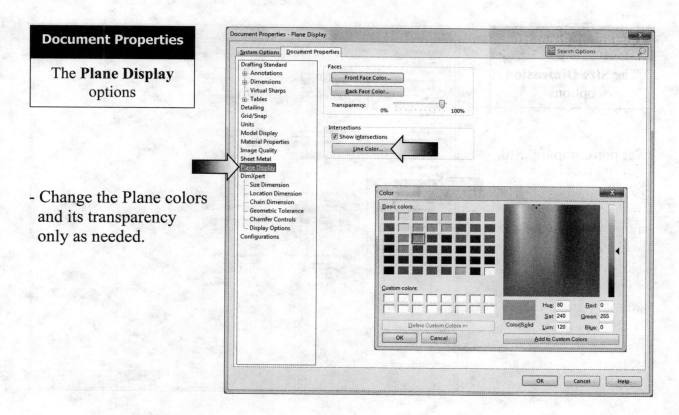

Document Properties

The **DimXpert** options

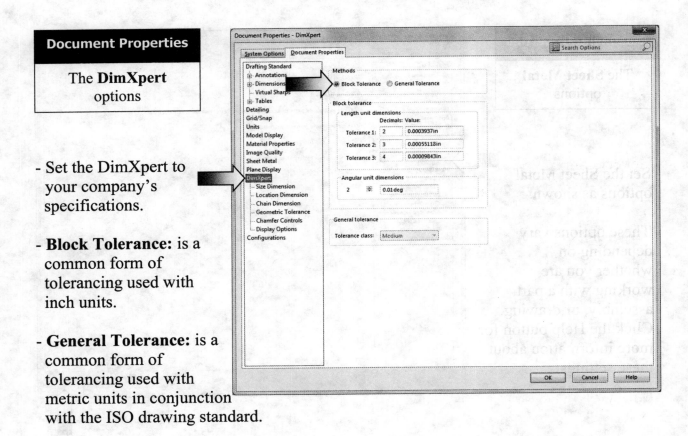

- Set the DimXpert to your company's specifications.

- **Block Tolerance:** is a common form of tolerancing used with inch units.

- **General Tolerance:** is a common form of tolerancing used with metric units in conjunction with the ISO drawing standard.

Document Properties

The **Size Dimension** options

- Set per company Std.

Document Properties

The **Location-Dimension** options

- Set per company Std.

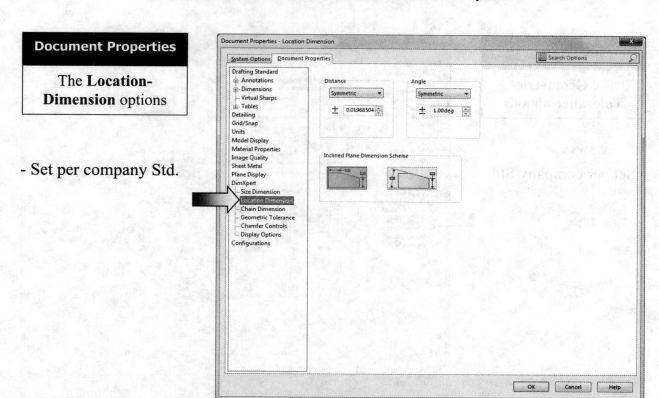

Document Properties

The **Chain Dimension** options

- Set per company Std.

Document Properties

The **Geometric-Tolerance** options

- Set per company Std.

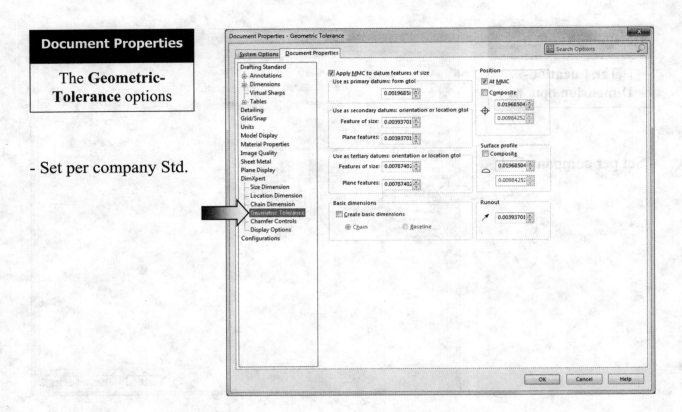

Document Properties

The **Chamfer-Controls** options

- Set per company Std.

Document Properties

The **Display** options

- Set per company Std.

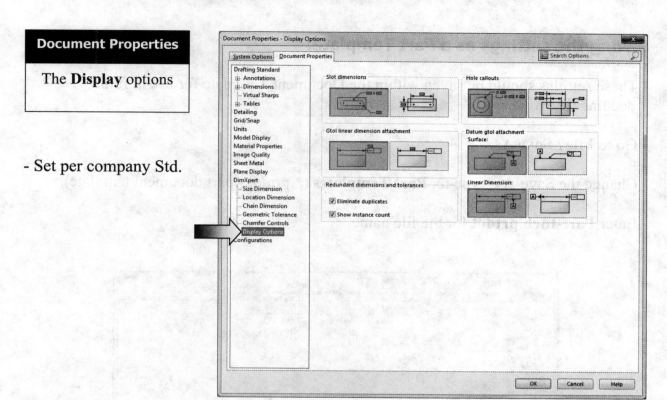

Document Properties

The **Configurations**
option

- Add a Rebuild or Save
icon next to the name of
configuration.

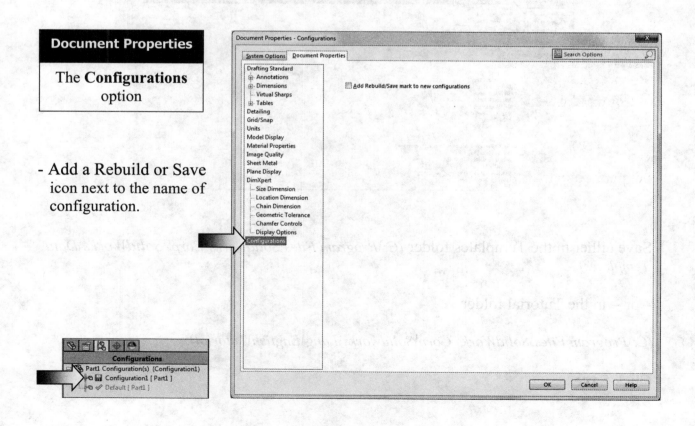

Saving the settings as a Part Template:

- These settings should be saved within the Document Template for use in future documents.

- Go to **File / Save As.**

- Change the Save-As-Type to: **Part Templates** (*.prtdot - part document template).

- Enter **Part-Inch.prtdot** for the file name.

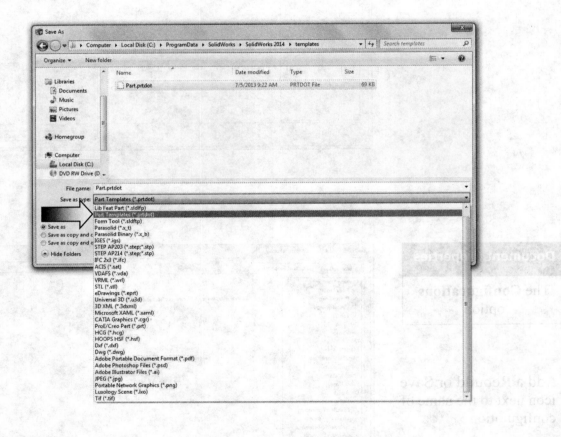

- Save either in the Templates folder *(C:\Program Files\Solidworks Corp\ SolidWorks\Data\ Templates).*

– or – in the Tutorial folder

(C:\Program Files\SolidWorks Corp\Solidworks\Lang\English\Tutorial).

- Click **Save**.

Questions for Review

Document Templates

1. The ANSI dimensioning standard (American National Standards Institute) can be set and saved in the System Options.
   - a. True
   - b. False

2. The size of dimension arrows can be controlled globally from the Document Templates.
   - a. True
   - b. False

3. The balloon's size and shape can be set and saved in the Document Templates.
   - a. True
   - b. False

4. Dimension and note fonts can be changed and edited both locally and globally.
   - a. True
   - b. False

5. The Grid option is only available in the drawing environment, not in the part or assembly.
   - a. True
   - b. False

6. The number of decimal places can be set up to 10 digits.
   - a. True
   - b. False

7. The feature colors can be pre-set and saved in the Document Templates.
   - a. True
   - b. False

8. The display quality of the model can be adjusted using the settings in the Image Quality option.
   - a. True
   - b. False

9. The plane colors and transparency can be set and saved in the Document Templates.
   - a. True
   - b. False

9. TRUE
7. TRUE
5. FALSE
3. TRUE
1. FALSE

8. TRUE
6. FALSE
4. TRUE
2. TRUE

CHAPTER 3

Basic Solid Modeling

Basic Solid Modeling
Extrude Options

- Upon successful completion of this lesson, you will be able to:

* Sketch on planes and/or planar surfaces.

* Use the sketch tools to construct geometry.

* Add the geometric relations or constraints.

* Add/modify dimensions.

* Explore the different extrude options.

- The following 5 basic steps will be demonstrated throughout this exercise:

* Select the sketch plane.

* Activate Sketch pencil .

* Sketch the profile using the sketch tools .

* Define the profile with dimensions or relations .

* Extrude the profile .

- Be sure to review the self-test questionnaires at the end of the lesson, prior to moving to the next chapter.

Basic Solid Modeling
Extrude Options

View Orientation Hot Keys:

Ctrl + 1 = Front View
Ctrl + 2 = Back View
Ctrl + 3 = Left View
Ctrl + 4 = Right View
Ctrl + 5 = Top View
Ctrl + 6 = Bottom View
Ctrl + 7 = Isometric View
Ctrl + 8 = Normal To
                    Selection

Dimensioning Standards: **ANSI**

Units: **INCHES** – 3 Decimals

Tools Needed:

 Insert Sketch

 Line

 Circle

 Add Geometric Relations

 Dimension

 Sketch Fillet

 Trim Entities

 Boss / Base Extrude

1. Starting a new Part:

- From the **File** menu, select **New / Part,** or click the **New** icon.

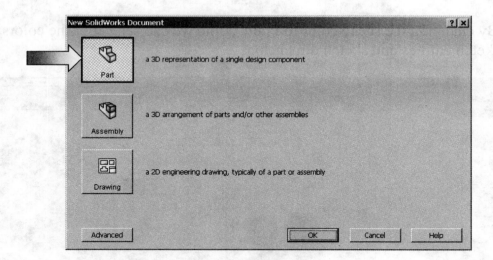

- Select the **Part** template from either the Templates or Tutorial folders.

- Click **OK** ; a new part template is opened.

2. Changing the Scene:

- From the View (Heads-up) toolbar, click the Apply Scene button (arrow) and select the Plain White option (arrow).

- By changing the scene color to Plain White we can see better the colors of the sketch entities and sketch dimensions.

- To show the Origin, click the **View** dropdown menu and select Origins.

- The Blue Origin is the Zero position of the part and the Red Origin is the Zero position of a sketch.

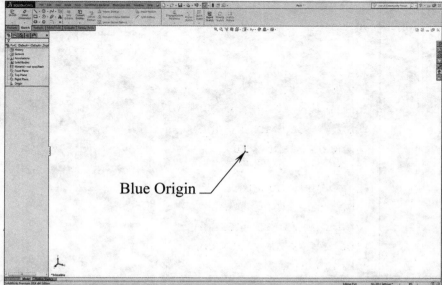

Blue Origin

3. Starting a new Sketch:

- Select the Front plane from the Feature-Manager tree and click the Pencil icon to start a new sketch.

- A sketch is normally created first, relations and dimensions are added after, and then it gets extruded into a 3D feature.

- From the Command-Manager toolbar, select the **Line** command.

Command Manager Toolbar

Mouse Gesture

OPTION:
Right-Drag to display the Mouse Gesture guide and select the Line command from it. (See the Introduction section, page XVIII for details on customizing the Mouse Gesture).

- Position the mouse cursor at the Red Origin point, a yellow feedback symbol appears to indicate a relation (Coincident) is going to be added automatically to the 1st endpoint of the line. This endpoint will be locked at the zero position.

Auto-Relation feedback symbol

4. Using the Click + Hold + Drag technique:

- Click at the Origin point and *hold* the mouse button to start the line at point 1, *drag upwards* to point 2, then release the mouse button.

Start the line from Point **1**
and drag to Point **2**

> ### The Base Sketch
>
> The Base Sketch is the parent sketch of a part and is also the very first sketch in a part document. It should primarily describe the basic shape of the part, before other features can be added.

- Continue adding other lines using the *Click-Hold-Drag* technique.

- The relations like Horizontal and Vertical are added automatically to each sketch line. Other relations like Collinear and Equal are added manually.

- The size and shape of the profile will be corrected in the next few steps.

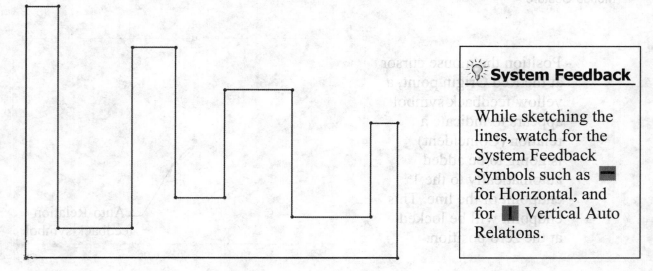

> ### System Feedback
>
> While sketching the lines, watch for the System Feedback Symbols such as ▬ for Horizontal, and for ▮ Vertical Auto Relations.

5. Adding Geometric Relations*:

- Click **Add Relation** under Display/Delete Relations - OR - select **Tools / Relations / Add**.

- Select the 4 lines shown below.

- Click **Equal** from the Add Geometric Relation dialog box. This relation makes the length of the two selected lines equal.

* Geometric relations are one of the most powerful features in SolidWorks. They're used in the sketch level to control the behaviors of the sketch entities when they are moved or rotated and to keep the associations between one another.

When applying geometric relations between entities, one of them should be a 2D entity and the other can either be a 2D sketch entity or a model edge, a plane, an axis, or a curve, etc.

💡 **Equal Relations**

Adding the EQUAL relations to these lines eliminates the need to dimension each line.

Geometric relations can be created manually or automatically. The next few steps in this chapter will demonstrate how geometric relations are added manually.

Select the top 4 lines and click Equal relation

The top 4 lines are now Equal in size.

6. Adding a Collinear relation**:

      - Select the **Add Relation** � command again.

      - Select the 3 lines as shown below.

      - Click **Collinear** from the Add Geometric Relations dialog box.

      - Click **OK** ✅.

Select the bottom 3 lines and click Collinear relation

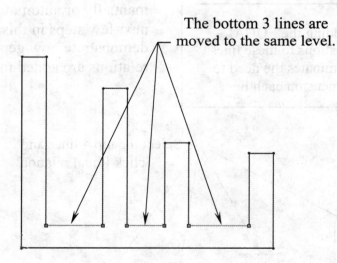

The bottom 3 lines are moved to the same level.

Collinear Relations

Adding a Collinear relation to these lines puts them on the same height level; only one dimension is needed to drive the height of all 3 lines.

** Collinear relations can be used to constrain the geometry as follow:

      - Collinear between a line and another line(s) (2D and 2D).

      - Collinear between a line(s) to an edge of a model (2D and 3D).

Geometric Relations Examples

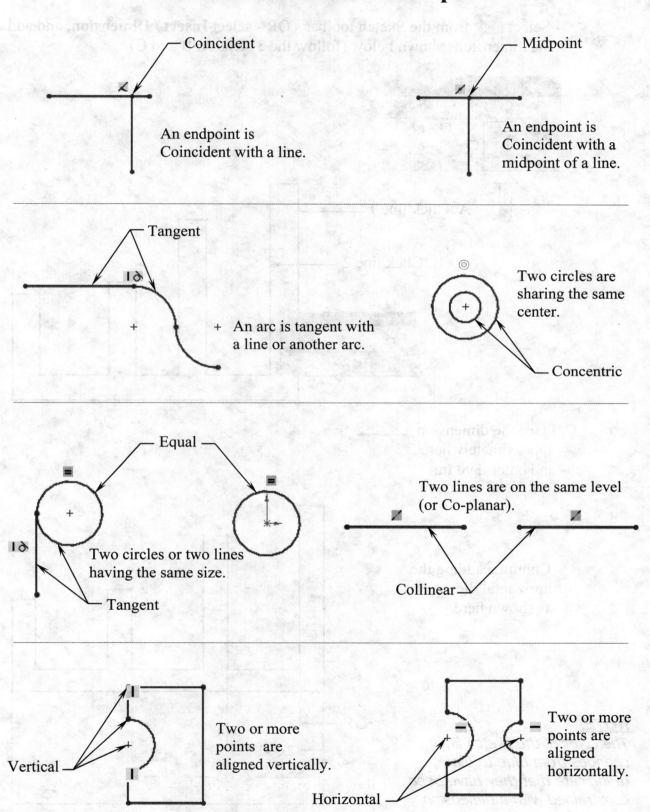

Coincident — An endpoint is Coincident with a line.

Midpoint — An endpoint is Coincident with a midpoint of a line.

Tangent — An arc is tangent with a line or another arc.

Two circles are sharing the same center. — Concentric

Equal — Two circles or two lines having the same size.

Tangent

Two lines are on the same level (or Co-planar). — Collinear

Vertical — Two or more points are aligned vertically.

Two or more points are aligned horizontally. — Horizontal

7. Adding the horizontal dimensions:

- Select 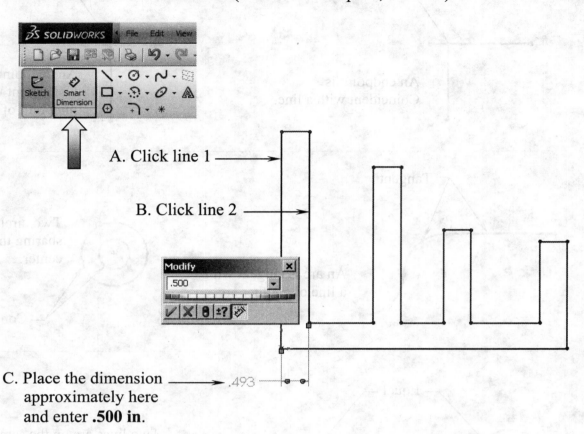 from the Sketch toolbar - OR - select **Insert / Dimension**, and add the dimensions shown below (follow the 3 steps A, B and C).

A. Click line 1

B. Click line 2

C. Place the dimension
   approximately here
   and enter **.500 in**.

- Continue adding the
  horizontal dimensions
  as shown here.

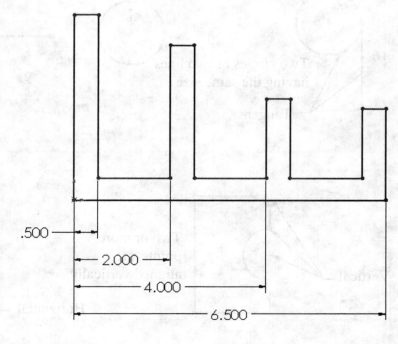

NOTE:
*The color of the sketch lines
changes from Blue to Black,
to indicate that they have been
constrained with a dimension.*

8. Adding the Vertical dimensions:

- With the Smart-
Dimension tool
still selected, click
on line 1 and line 2;
place the dimension
approximately as
shown, and change
the value to **.500 in**.

- Continue adding
other dimensions
until the entire
sketch turns into
the Black color.

The Status of a Sketch:

The current status of a sketch is displayed in the lower right corner of the screen.

Fully Defined	=	**Black**	Fully Defined
Under Defined	=	**Blue**	Under Defined
Over Defined	=	**Red**	Over Defined

Sketch Relation Symbols

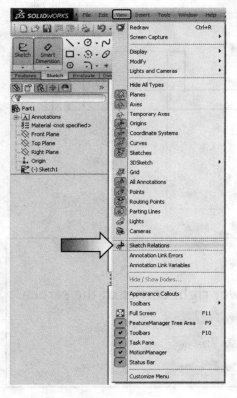

9. Hiding the Sketch Relation Symbols:

- The Sketch Relation Symbols indicates which geometric relation a sketch entity has, but they get quite busy as shown.

- To hide or show the Sketch Relation Symbols, go to the **View** menu and Click off the **Sketch Relations** option.

Sketch Relation Symbols at a Glance

▬ Horizontal relation		▮ Vertical relation
▬ Equal relation		✕ Coincident relation
◈ Tangent relation		▨ Collinear relation

10. Extruding the Base:

- The **Extrude Boss/Base** command is used to define the characteristic of a 3D linear feature.

- Click from the Features toolbar - OR- select **Insert / Boss Base / Extrude**.

- Set the following:

- Direction: **Blind**.

- Depth: **6.00 in**.

- Enabled **Reverse** direction.

- Click **OK** ✓.

11. Sketching on a Planar Face:

- Select the face as indicated.

- Click or select **Insert/Sketch**.

- Click ⊕ from the Sketch Tools toolbar
Or select **Tools / Sketch Entity / Circle**.

(From the View toolbar above the CommandManager, click the Isometric icon
or press the shortcut keys **Ctrl+7**).

Select the Sketch Face

Planar Surfaces

- A planar surface of the
model can also be used as
a Sketch Plane.

- The Sketch will then be
extruded normal to the
selected surface.

- Position the mouse cursor near
the center of the selected face,
click and drag outward to draw
a circle.

- While sketching the circle,
the system displays the radius
value next to the mouse cursor.

- Dimensions are added after the
profile is created.

- Select the **Smart Dimension**

command and add a
diameter dimension to the
circle.

(Click on the circle and move
the mouse cursor outward, at
approximately 45 degrees and
place it).

- To add the location dimensions
click the edge of the circle and
the edge of the model, place
the dimension, then correct
the value.

- Continue adding the
location dimensions
as shown, to fully
define the sketch.

- Select the Line command
and sketch the 3 lines as shown
below. Snap to the hidden edge
of the model when it lights up.

- The color of the sketch should
change to black at this point (Fully
Defined).

Snap to
quadrant
point

Auto-Snap to
hidden edge

12. Using the Trim Entities command:

- Select the **Trim Entities** command from the Sketch toolbar (arrow).

- Click the **Trim to Closest** option (arrow). When the pointer is hovered over the entities, this trim command highlights the entities prior to trimming to the next intersection.

Trim Entities

Use this command to trim, extend or delete a sketch entity.

- Position the pointer over the lower portion of the circle, the portion that is going to be trimmed-off lights up. Click the mouse to trim.

- The bottom portion of the circle is trimmed, leaving the sketch as one-continuous-closed-profile, suitable to extrude into a feature.

- Next, we are going to look at some of the extrude options available in SolidWorks.

13. Extruding a Boss:

- Switch to the Feature toolbar and click or select:
Insert / Boss-Base / Extrude.

┌───┐
| 🔆 **Extrude Options...** |
| |
| Explore each extrude option to |
| see the different results. |
| Press Undo to go back to the |
| original state after each one. |
└───┘

(A) **Using the Blind option:**

- When extruding with the
  Blind option, the
  following conditions
  are required:

  * Direction

  * Depth dimension

- Drag the direction arrow on the preview graphics
  to define the direction, then enter a dimension
  for the depth.

Direction & Depth

Blind
Condition

(B) **Using the Through All
option:**

- When the Through All
  option is selected, the
  system automatically
  extrudes the sketch to the
  length of the part, normal
  to the sketch plane.

Through All
Condition

(C) Using the Up To Next option:

- With the Up To Next option selected, the system extrudes the sketch to the very next set of surface(s), and blends it to match.

Up To Next
Condition

(D) Using the Up To Vertex option:

- This option extrudes the sketch from its plane to a vertex, specified by the user, to define its depth.

Select a Vertex

Up To Vertex
Condition

(E) Using the Up To Surface option:

- This option extrudes the sketch from its plane to a single surface, to define its depth.

Select a Surface

Up To Surface
Condition

F Using the Offset From Surface option:

- This option extrudes
the sketch from its plane
to a selected face, then
offsets at a specified
distance.

Select a surface
to offset from &
enter a distance.

Offset From Surface
Condition

G Using the Up To Body option:

- This option extrudes the sketch from its sketch plane to a specified body.

Select a Solid Body
to extrude to.
(optional)

Up To Body
Condition

- The Up To Body option can also be used in assemblies or multi-body parts.

- The Up To Body option works with either a solid body or a surface body.
It is also useful when making extrusions in an assembly to extend a sketch to
an uneven surface.

(H) Using the Mid Plane option:

- This option extrudes the sketch from its plane equally in both directions.

- Enter the Total Depth dimension when using the Mid-Plane option.

Mid Plane
Condition

- After you are done exploring all the extrude options, change the final condition
  to: **Through All**

- Click OK ✅.

- The system extrudes the circle to the outer most surface as the result
  of the Through All end condition.

- The extra material between the first and the second extruded features is removed automatically.

- Unless the Merge Result checkbox is cleared, all interferences will be detected and removed.

Extrude summary:

* The Extrude Boss/Base command is used to add thickness to a sketch and to define the characteristic of a 3D feature.

* A sketch can be extruded in both directions at the same time, from its sketch plane.

* A sketch can also be extruded as a solid or a thin feature.

14. Adding the model fillets by Lasso*:

- Fillet/Round creates a rounded internal or external face on the part. You can fillet all edges of a face, select sets of faces, edges, or edge loops.

Fillet
Creates a rounded internal or external face along one or more edges in solid or surface feature.

- The **radius** value stays in effect until you change it. Therefore, you can select any number of edges or faces in the same operation.

- Click or select **Insert / Features / Fillet/Round**.

Start here

Stop here

- Enter **.125 in**. for radius value.

- Click-Hold the mouse approximately at the "Start here" position and drag the pointer around the entire model to select all of its edges.

- Click **OK** ✅.

* To set the Lasso Selection as the default, go to:
Tools / Options / Display Selection / Default Bulk Selection Method / Lasso (arrow).

* *In the Training Files folder, in the <u>Built Parts folder</u> you will also find copies of the parts, assemblies, and drawings that were created for cross referencing or reviewing purposes.*

Fillet
(adds material)

Round
(removes material)

* ***Fillets and Rounds:***

Using the same Fillet command, SolidWorks "knows" whether to add material (Fillet) or remove material (Round) to the faces adjacent to the selected edge.

15. Saving your work:

- Select **File / Save As**.

- Change the file type to **Part** file (.sldprt).

- Enter **Extrude Options** for the name of the file.

- Click **Save**.

Questions for Review

Basic Solid Modeling

1. To open a new sketch, first you must select a plane from the FeatureManager tree.
    a. True
    b. False

2. Geometric relations can be used only in the assembly environments.
    a. True
    b. False

3. The current status of a sketch is displayed in the lower right area of the screen as: Under defined, Fully defined, or Over defined.
    a. True
    b. False

4. Once a feature is extruded, its extrude direction cannot be changed.
    a. True
    b. False

5. A planar face can also be used as a sketch plane.
    a. True
    b. False

6. The Equal relation only works for Lines, not Circles or Arcs.
    a. True
    b. False

7. After a dimension is created, its value cannot be changed.
    a. True
    b. False

8. When the UP TO SURFACE option is selected, you have to choose a surface as an end-condition to extrude up to.
    a. True
    b. False

9. UP TO VERTEX is not a valid Extrude option.
    a. True
    b. False

1. TRUE	2. FALSE
3. TRUE	4. FALSE
5. TRUE	6. FALSE
7. FALSE	8. TRUE
	9. FALSE

Exercise: Extrude Boss & Extrude Cut

NOTE: *In an exercise, there will be less step-by-step instruction than those in the lessons, which will give you a chance to apply what you have learned in the previous lesson to build the model on your own).*

1. Dimensions are in inches, 3 decimal places.
2. Use Mid-Plane end condition for the Base feature.
3. The part is symmetrical about the Front plane.
4. Use the instructions on the following pages if needed.

1. Starting with the base sketch:

- Select the <u>Front</u> plane and open a new sketch.

- Starting at the top left corner, using the line command, sketch the profile below.

Origin

Parallel

45.00°

- Add the dimensions shown.

- Add the Parallel relation to fully define the sketch.

- Extrude Boss/Base with **Mid Plane** and **3.000"** in depth.

2. Adding the through holes:

- Select the <u>face</u> as indicated and click the Normal-To button.

- This command rotates the part normal to the screen.

- The hot-key for this command is **Ctrl + 8**.

Select this face and click the Normal-To button

3.000

- Open a new sketch and draw a centerline that starts from the origin point.

- Sketch 2 circles on either side of the centerline.

- Add the diameter and location dimensions shown. Push Escape when done.

Both circles are Symmetric about the Centerline

Ø.500

.707

1.500

- Hold the Control key and select both circles <u>and</u> the centerline, then click the Symmetric relation on the properties tree.

- Create an extruded cut using the **Through-All** condition.

3. Adding the upper cut:

- Select the <u>upper face</u> and click the Sketch pencil to open a new sketch.

- Sketch a centerline that starts at the Origin.

Both lines are Symmetric about the Centerline

- Sketch a rectangle as shown.

- Add the dimensions and relations as indicated.

- Create an extruded cut using the **Up-To-Vertex** condition (up-to-surface also works).

- Select the Vertex indicated.

Select Vertex

- Click **OK**.

4. Adding the lower cut:

- Select the <u>lower face</u> of the part and open a new sketch.

- Sketch a rectangle on this face.

- Add a Collinear <u>and</u> an Equal relations to the lines and the edges as noted.

The line is Collinear <u>and</u> Equal with the edge on both sides.

- Extrude a cut using the Through All condition.

5. Adding a chamfer:

- Click **Chamfer** under the Fillet button.

- Enter **.060** for depth.

- Select the 4 circular edges of the 2 holes.

- Click **OK**.

Select 4 edges

6. Saving your work:

- Click **File / Save As**.

- Enter **Extrudes_Exe1** for the file name.

- Select a location to save the file.

- Click **Save**.

CHAPTER 4

Basic Solid Modeling

Basic Solid Modeling
Extrude & Revolve

- Upon successful completion of this lesson, you will be able to:

* Perform basic modeling techniques.

* Sketch on planar surfaces .

* Add dimensions .

* Add geometric relations or constraints .

* Use extrude with Boss / Base .

* Use Extruded Cut .

* Create revolved features .

* Create Fillets and Chamfers .

- The components created in this lesson will be used again later in an assembly chapter to demonstrate how they can be copied several times and constrained to form a new assembly, check for interferences, and dynamic motion of an assembly.

- Be sure to review self-test questionnaires at the end of the lesson, prior to going to the next chapter. They will help to see if you have gained enough knowledge required in the following chapters.

Link Components
Basic Solid Modeling

View Orientation Hot Keys:

Ctrl + 1 = Front View
Ctrl + 2 = Back View
Ctrl + 3 = Left View
Ctrl + 4 = Right View
Ctrl + 5 = Top View
Ctrl + 6 = Bottom View
Ctrl + 7 = Isometric View
Ctrl + 8 = Normal To
          Selection

Dimensioning Standards: **ANSI**

Units: **INCHES** – 3 Decimals

Tools Needed:

Insert Sketch	Line	Centerline
Circle	Mirror	Dimension
Add Geometric Relations	Fillet	Chamfer
Extruded Boss/Base	Extruded Cut	Boss/Base Revolve

1. Sketching the first profile:

- Select the <u>Front</u> plane from the FeatureManager tree.

- Click (Insert Sketch) and select the **Straight Slot** command .

- First start at the origin, sketch a straight line and then move downward (or upward) to complete the slot (arrows).

- Add 2 circles on the same centers of the arcs.

- Add Dimensions and Relations as shown.

Origin

R.500

Ø.325

1.250

2. Extruding the first solid:

- Click on the Features toolbar or select **Insert / Boss-Base / Extrude**.

- End condition: **Mid Plane**

- Extrude depth: **.750 in**.

- Click **OK** .

R.500

Ø.325

1.250

3. Creating the Bore holes:

- Select the front <u>face</u> as indicated and click (Insert / Sketch).

Sketch Face

> ### 💡 Planar Surfaces
>
> The planar surfaces of the model can also be used as sketch planes; sketch geometry can be drawn directly on these surfaces.

(The Blue origin is the Part's origin and the Red origin is the Sketch's origin).

- Sketch a **circle** ⊕ starting at the center of the existing hole.

- Add **Ø.500** dimension ✎ as shown.

Ø.500

Place cursor here to wake up the center point

Quadrant Points

Center Points

> ### 💡 Wake-Up Entities*
>
> To find the center (or the quadrant points) of a hole or a circle:
>
> * In the Sketch mode, select one of the sketch tools (Circle, in this case), then hover the mouse cursor over the circular edge to "wake-up" the center point & its quadrant points.

- Sketch the 2ⁿᵈ **Circle** ⊕ and add an **Equal** relation between the 2 circles.

- Click off the Circle command. Hold the **Control** key, select the 2 Circles and click the **Equal** relation (arrow).

Equal Relation

∅.500

4. Cutting the Bore holes:

- Click **Extruded Cut** or select **Insert / Cut / Extrude**.

- End Condition: **Blind**

- Extrude Depth: **.150 in**.

- Click **OK** .

∅.500

5. Mirroring the Bore holes:

- Select the <u>Front</u> plane from the FeatureManager Tree as the Mirror Plane.

- Click **Mirror** or select **Insert / Patent Mirror / Mirror**.

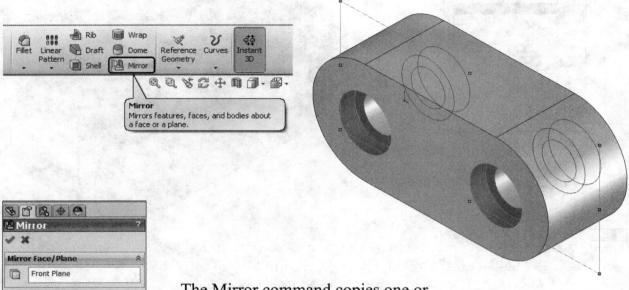

- The Mirror command copies one or more features about a plane or a planar face.

- Select the **Cut-Extrude1** from the FeatureManager Tree, or click one of the Bore holes from the graphics area.

- Click **OK** .

Sketch face

6. Adding more Cuts:

- Select the <u>face</u> as indicated and open a new sketch .

- We will learn to use sketch mirror in this next step.

- Sketch 2 Centerlines 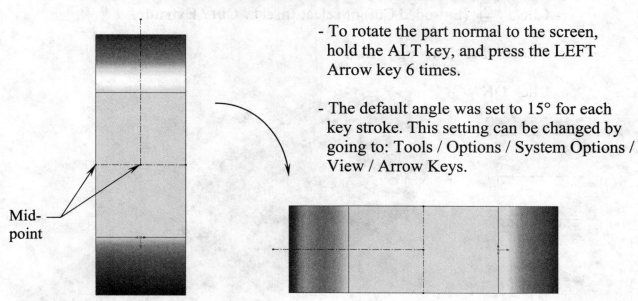 one vertical and one horizontal as shown.

- To rotate the part normal to the screen, hold the ALT key, and press the LEFT Arrow key 6 times.

- The default angle was set to 15° for each key stroke. This setting can be changed by going to: Tools / Options / System Options / View / Arrow Keys.

Mid-point

- Select the vertical centerline and click the **Dynamic Mirror** command or click: **Tools, Sketch Tools, Dynamic Mirror**.

- Sketch a Rectangle on one side of the centerline; it will get mirrored to the other side automatically.

- Click off the Dynamic mirror button. Add a Symmetric relation to the 3 lines as noted .

- Add dimensions to fully define the sketch.

- Click **OK**.

.230

Mid-Point

.300

Coincident

Symmetric

7. Extruding a Through All cut:

- Click (Extruded Cut) or select **Insert / Cut / Extrude**.

- Direction 1: **Through All**

- Click **OK** ✅.

8. Adding the .032" fillets:

- Click **Fillet** 🔵 or select **Insert / Features / Fillet/Round**.

- Enter **.032 in.** for Radius ↗.

- Select the edges as indicated below 🔲 .

- Click **OK** ✅.

Select ALL edges (except for the holes)

9. Adding the .032" chamfers:

- Click **Chamfer** or select **Insert / Features / Chamfer.**

- Enter **.032 in.** for the depth of the chamfer and select the <u>edges</u> of the 4 holes.

- Click **OK** ✅.

Select edges
to add chamfer

10. Saving your work:

- Select **File / Save As / Double Link / Save.**

11. Creating the Sub-Components:

- The 1st sub-component is the **Alignment Pin**.

- Select the <u>Right</u> plane from the FeatureManager Tree.

- Click or select **Insert / Sketch**.

- Sketch the profile below using the Line tool .

- Add dimensions as shown to fully define the sketch.

.600

.150

59.00°

.250

.115 .158

Center of Revolve

Origin

.425

12. Revolving the base feature:

- Click or select **Insert / Boss-Base / Revolve**.

- Revolve Type: **Blind** .

- Revolve Angle: **360 deg**. (default) .

- Click **OK** .

💡 Center of Revolve

A centerline is used when revolving a sketch profile.

A model edge, an axis, or a sketch line can also be used as the center of the revolve.

13. Adding chamfers:

- Click **Chamfer** or select **Insert / Features / Chamfer**.

- Enter **.0325** for Distance .

- Enter **45 deg**. for Angle .

- Select the 2 Edges as indicated.

- Click **OK** .

Select 2 edges

14. Saving your work:

- Select **File / Save As / Alignment Pin / Save**.

15. The 2nd Sub-Components:

- The 2nd sub-component is the **Pin Head**:

- Select the <u>Front</u> plane from the FeatureManager Tree.

- Click or select **Insert / Sketch**.

- Sketch the profile below using the Centerline and the Line tools .

- Add dimensions as shown to fully define the sketch.

Center of revolve

.590

.150

.110

.250

Origin

16. Revolving the base feature:

- Click or select **Insert / Boss-Base / Revolve**.

- Revolve Type: **Blind** .

- Revolve Angle: **360 deg**. (default) .

- Click **OK** .

Revolve1

Axis of Revolution

Line1

Direction1

Blind

360.00deg

.590

.110

.150

.250

17. Adding chamfer:

- Click **Chamfer** or select **Insert / Features / Chamfer**.

- Enter **.025** for Distance .

- Enter **45 deg**. for Angle .

- Select the <u>Edge</u> as indicated.

- Click **OK** .

Select 2 Edges

18. Saving your work:

- Select **File / Save As / Pin Head / Save**.

19. Creating the 3rd Sub-Components:

- The 3rd sub-component is the **Single Link**:

- Select <u>Front</u> plane from FeatureManager Tree.

- Click Insert Sketch and select the **Straight Slot** command.

- Enable the **Add Dimensions** checkbox (arrow below).

- This command requires 3 clicks. Start at the origin for point 1, move the cursor horizontally and click the point 2, then downward to make the point 3.

- Click OK to exit the Straight Slot command and modify the dimensions values to fully define the sketch.

20. Extruding the base:

- Click **Extruded Boss-Base** or select **Insert / Boss-Base / Extrude**.

- End condition: **Mid Plane**

- Extrude depth: **.750 in**.

- Click **OK** ✅.

21. Sketching the Recess Profiles:

- Select the <u>face</u> indicated and open a new sketch .

Sketch Face ——

- Sketch 2 Circles ⊕ at the centers of the circular edges. (with the Circle command already selected, hover over the circular edge to see its center)

- Add a **Ø1.020 in.** dimension 🔷 to one of the circles. (The circles are slightly larger than the part).

Ø1.020

- Add an Equal relation ┴ between the 2 circles.

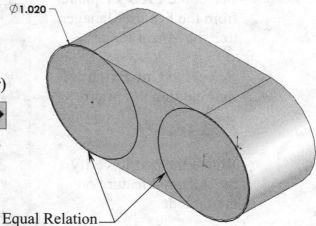

Equal Relation ——

22. Extruding a blind cut:

- Click **Extruded Cut** or select **Insert / Cut / Extrude**.

- End condition: **Blind**

- Extrude Depth: **.235 in.**

- Click **OK** ✓.

23. Mirroring the cut:

- Click 📖 or select **Insert / Pattern- Mirror / Mirror**.

- Select the **FRONT** plane from the FeatureManager tree for Mirror Plane.

- Select the **Cut-Extrude1** for Features-to-Pattern.

- Click **OK** ✓.

- Rotate the part to verify the mirrored feature on the far side.

24. Adding the Holes:

Sketch Face

- Select the Skech
  <u>face</u> as shown and
  open a new sketch .

- Sketch 2 Circles ⊕ on the
  centers of the existing cuts.

- Add dimension ✎ and relations ⊥
  needed to fully define the sketch.

Equal
Relation

∅.325

25. Cutting the holes:

- Click **Extruded Cut** ▣ or select **Insert / Cut / Extrude**.

- End condition: **Through All**

- Click **OK** ✔.

∅.325

Extrude   ?

From
Sketch Plane ▾

Direction 1
⬈ Through All ▾

☐ Flip side to cut

☐ Draft outward

26. Adding the .100" fillets:

- Click **Fillet** or select **Insert / Features / Fillet/Round**.

- Enter **.100 in.** for Radius.

- Select the 8 edges as indicated below.

- Click **OK**.

Select 8 edges
(top & bottom)

Fillet
Creates a rounded internal or external face along one or more edges in solid or surface feature.

27. Adding the .032" fillets:

- Click **Fillet** or select **Insert / Features / Fillet/Round**.

- Enter **.0325 in.** for Radius.

- Select the edges as shown.

- Click **OK**.

No fillet
(4 places)

NOTE:

There are no fillets on the 4 edges as indicated.

28. Saving your work:

- Click **File / Save As / Single Link / Save.**

Questions for Review

Basic Solid Modeling

1. Tangent relations only work with the same type of entities such as an arc to another arc, not between a line and an arc.
    a. True
    b. False

2. The first feature in a part is the parent feature, not a child.
    a. True
    b. False

3. The dimension arrows can be toggled to flip inwards or outwards when clicking on its handle points.

    a. True
    b. False

4. The Shaded with edges option cannot be used in the part mode, only in the drawing mode.
    a. True
    b. False

5. The Concentric relations make the diameter of the circles equal.
    a. True
    b. False

6. More than one model edges can be selected and filleted at the same time.
    a. True
    b. False

7. To revolve a sketch profile, a centerline should be selected as the center of the revolve.
    a. True
    b. False

8. After a sketch is revolved, its revolved angle cannot be changed.
    a. True
    b. False

7. TRUE   8. FALSE
5. FALSE   6. TRUE
3. TRUE   4. FALSE
1. FALSE   2. TRUE

Exercise: Extrude Boss & Extrude Cut

1. Create the solid model using the drawing provided below.
2. Dimensions are in Inches, 3 decimal places.
3. Tangent relations between the transitions of the Arcs should be used.
4. The Ø.472 holes are Concentric with R.710 Arcs.
5. Use the instructions on the following pages, if needed.

1. Creating the Base sketch:

- There are many ways to create this part but let try this basic method first.

- Select the <u>Top</u> plane and open a new sketch.

- Create the construction circles (toggle the **For Construction** checkbox), then create the Sketch Geometry over them.

Construction geometry

Sketch geometry

- Either re-create the rest of the geometry or mirror them as noted.

- To mirror the sketch geometry, hold the Control key and select the entities that you want to mirror <u>AND</u> the centerline as noted, then click the Mirror-Entities command.

⊛ Add a Tangent Arc to the left side of the profile.

Re-create or mirror these entities

- Add the geometric relations as indicated. Remember to add the Equal relations to the circles and the arcs.

- Add the Smart-Dimensions to fully define the sketch.

Tangent relation
(all around)

Vertical relation

2.000

.630

.315

1.000

2.000

R.710

R2.000

R.600

Ø.472

Equal Relation

2. Extruding the Base:

- Click **Extruded Boss-Base**.

- Use the **Blind** type for Diretion1.

- Enter **.394"** for extrude Depth.

- Click **OK**.

2.000

1.000

2.000

R.710

R2.000

R.600

Ø.472

3. Creating the Tail-End sketch:

- Select the <u>Front</u> reference plane from the Feature tree and open another sketch.

- Sketch the construction circles and add the sketch geometry right over them.

- Add the Tangent relation as noted.

- Add the Smart Dimensions to fully define the sketch.

Tangent

Tangent

R4.500

R.875

Ø.785

4.325

4. Extruding the Tail-End:

- Click **Extruded Boss-Base**.

- Use the **Mid Plane** type for Diretion1.

- Enter **.630"** for extrude Depth.

- Click **OK**.

5. Saving your work:

- Click **File / Save As**.

- Enter **Extrudes_Exe2**.

- Click **Save**.

CHAPTER 5

Revolved Parts

Revolved Parts
Ball Joint Arm

- The Revolve command rotates one or more sketch profiles around a centerline, up to 360° to create a <u>thin</u> or a <u>solid</u> feature.

Open profile
= Thin Feature

Closed profile
= Solid Feature

- The revolved sketch should have a continuous closed contour and it can either be a polygon, a circle, an ellipse, or a closed spline.

Valid profile —
1 continuous,
closed contour.

Invalid profile
Multiple closed
contours.

- If there is more than one centerline in the same sketch, the center of rotation must be specified when creating the revolve.

- In the newer releases of SolidWorks, the center of the revolve (centerline) can be replaced with a line, an axis, or a linear model edge.

- The revolve feature can be a cut feature (which removes material) or a revolve boss feature (which adds material).

- This chapter will guide you through the basics of creating the revolved parts.

Ball Joint Arm
Revolved Parts

View Orientation Hot Keys:

Ctrl + 1 = Front View
Ctrl + 2 = Back View
Ctrl + 3 = Left View
Ctrl + 4 = Right View
Ctrl + 5 = Top View
Ctrl + 6 = Bottom View
Ctrl + 7 = Isometric View
Ctrl + 8 = Normal To
       Selection

Dimensioning Standards: **ANSI**

Units: **INCHES** – 3 Decimals

Tools Needed:

Insert Sketch	Line	Circle
Rectangle	Sketch Fillet	Trim
Add Geometric Relations	Dimension	Centerline
Base/Boss Revolve	Fillet/Round	Mirror Features

1. Creating the Base Profile:

- Select the <u>Front</u> plane from the FeatureManager tree.

- Click or select **Insert / Sketch**.

- Sketch the profile using the Line and Circle commands.

- Trim the circles as shown.

- Add Dimensions and Relations needed to fully define the sketch. (It is easier to add the R.050" fillets after the sketch is fully defined).

R.368 R.050

.275

.125

.475

2.518

R.375

Origin

Add Centerline to revolve...

Arc center is **Coincident** with Centerline

2. Revolving the Base Feature:

- Click **Revolve** or select **Insert / Boss-Base / Revolve**.

- Revolve Type: **Blind** .

- Revolve Angle: **360 deg.** .

- Click **OK** .

3. Sketching the Opened-End Profile:

- Select the <u>Top</u> plane from the FeatureManager tree.

- Click or select **Insert / Sketch**.

- Switch to Hidden Lines Visible mode: click on the VIEW toolbar.

- Sketch 2 circles as shown.

- Add a **Coradial** relation between the small circle and the hidden edge.

Coradial

- Add a line along the bottom
  edge and a 3-Point Arc.
  The Arc is tangent with
  both circles.

Add a Line &
a 3-Point Arc

- Trim the line and the 2 circles.

- Add a Collinear relation between the line and the bottom edge of the part.

Collinear relation

.250

R.425

- Add the dimensions shown to fully define the sketch.

4. Revolving the Opened-End Feature:

- Click **Revolve** or select **Insert / Boss-Base / Revolve**.

- Revolve Type: **Mid Plane** .

- Revolve Angle: **75 deg.** .

- Click **OK** .

Ø.850

.312

5. Mirroring the Revolved feature:

- Click **Mirror** or select **Insert / Pattern Mirror / Mirror**.

- Select the <u>Front</u> plane from the FeatureManager tree as mirror plane 🔲.

- Select the Revolve2 feature either from the graphics area or from the Feature-Manager tree, as Features to Mirror ⬚.

- Click **OK** ✓.

6. Adding the .080" Fillets:

- Click **Fillet** 🔲 or select **Insert / Features / Fillet / Round**.

- Enter **.080** in. as the Radius 📐.

- Select the <u>two edges</u> as shown for Items to Fillet 🔲.

- Click **OK** ✓.

Fillet 2 edges

7. Adding the .015" Fillets:

- Click **Fillet** or select **Insert / Features / Fillet / Round**.

- Enter **.015** in. as the Radius .

- Select the <u>edges</u> of the 2 revolved features as shown.

- Click **OK** .

Fillet all edges

8. Saving Your Work:

- Select **File / Save As / Ball-Joint-Arm / Save**.

Questions for Review

Revolved Parts

1. A proper profile for use in a revolved feature is a single closed contour, created on one side of the revolved centerline.
   - a. True
   - b. False

2. If there is more than one centerline in the same sketch, one centerline should be selected prior to revolving the sketch.
   - a. True
   - b. False

3. A revolve feature should *always* be revolved a complete 360°.
   - a. True
   - b. False

4. The Sketch Fillet command can also be used on solid features.
   - a. True
   - b. False

5. To mirror a 3D feature, a plane, or a planar surface should be used as a mirror plane.
   - a. True
   - b. False

6. To mirror a series of features, a centerline can be used as a mirror plane.
   - a. True
   - b. False

7. After a fillet feature is created, its parameters (selected faces, edges, fillet values, etc.) cannot be modified.
   - a. True
   - b. False

8. Either an axis, a model edge, or a sketch line can be used as the center of the revolve. (Newer releases of SolidWorks only).
   - a. True
   - b. False

7. FALSE   8. TRUE
5. TRUE   6. FALSE
3. FALSE   4. FALSE
1. TRUE   2. TRUE

Exercise: Flat Head Screw Driver

1. Create the part using the drawing provided below.
2. Dimensions are in inches, 3 decimal places.
3. The part is symmetrical about the Top plane.
4. Unspecified radii to be R.050 max.
5. Use the instructions on the following pages, if needed.

DETAIL B
SCALE 4 : 1

6. Save your work as: **Flat Head Screw Driver**.

1. Creating the base sketch:

- Select the Front plane and open a new sketch.

- Sketch the profile shown and add the dimensions noted.

2. Revolving the base:

- Click **Revolve / Boss-Base**.

- For Direction 1: Use **Blind**.

- Angle = **360°**

- Click **OK**.

3. Creating the flat head:

- Select the Front plane and open another sketch.

- Sketch the lines as shown and add the dimensions to fully define the sketch.

- Create an **extruded cut** using **Through-All** for both directions.

- Since the sketch was open, Through All is the only extrude option in this case.

4. Creating the flat handle:

- Select the <u>flat surface</u> on the right end of the handle and open a new sketch.

- Sketch a rectangle and mirror it using the vertical and horizontal centerline (the sketch can be left under defined for this example).

Sketch face

- Create an extruded cut using the opposite end of the handle as the end condition for the Up-To-Surface option. (Through-All can also be used to achieve the same result).

Up to Surface

5. Adding the .050" fillets:

- Apply a **.050"** fillet to the 2 faces as indicated.

Select 2 faces

6. Saving your work:

- Save your work as **Flat Head Screw Driver**.

Revolved Parts (cont.)

Derived Sketches

Derived Sketches
Center Ball Joint

- The derived sketch option creates a copy of the original sketch and places it on the same or different plane, within the same part document.

  * The derived sketch is the child feature of the original.

  * The derived sketch (copy) cannot be edited. Its size and shape are dependent on the parent sketch.

  * Derived sketches can be moved and related to different planes or faces with respect to the same model.

  * Changes made to the parent sketch are automatically reflected in the derived sketches.

- To break the link between the parent sketch and the derived copies, right click on the derived sketch and select **Underived**.

- After the link is broken, the derived sketches can be modified independently and will not update when the parent sketch is changed.

- One major difference between the traditional copy / paste option and the derived sketch is:

  * The copy/paste creates an Independent copy. There is no link between the parent sketch and the derived sketch.

  * The derived sketch creates a dependent copy. The parent sketch and the derived sketch are fully linked.

Center Ball Joint
Derived Sketches

Dimensioning Standards: **ANSI**

Units: **INCHES** – 3 Decimals

Tools Needed:

Insert Sketch	Line	Center Line
Circle	Sketch Fillet	Trim
Add Geometric Relations	Dimension	Plane
Derived Sketch	Fillet/Round	Base/Boss Revolve

1. Creating the Base Profile:

- Select the <u>Front</u> plane from the Feature Manager tree.

- Click or select **Insert / Sketch**.

- Sketch the profile using Lines ![line], Circles ![circle], Sketch Fillets ![fillet] and

the Trim Entities ![trim] tools (use step 1 on page 5-3 for reference).

- Add the Dimensions ![dim] and Relations ![rel] needed to fully define the sketch.

R.368

R.050

1.250

.275

.125

.475

Origin

Mirror Centerline

Revolve Centerline

2. Revolving the Base Feature:

- Click **Revolve** ![revolve] or select **Insert / Boss-Base / Revolve**.

- Revolve Type: **Blind** ![blind].

- Revolve Angle: **360 deg**. ![angle].

- Click **OK** ![ok].

Revolve1

Axis of Revolution

Line1

Direction1

Blind

360.00deg

3. Creating a new work plane*:

- Click **Plane** or select **Insert / Reference Geometry / Plane**.

- Select the <u>Right</u> plane from the FeatureManager tree.

- Choose the **Offset Distance** option.

- Enter **1.250** in. (place the new plane on the right side).

- Click **OK**.

TIPS: Control + Drag the right plane will also make a copy of it.

4. Creating a Derived Sketch:

- Hold the **Control** key, select the new plane (**Plane1**) and the **Sketch1** (under Base-Revolved1) from the FeatureManager tree.

- Select **Derived Sketch** under the **Insert** menu.

Hold the Control key & select the Plane1 & the Sketch1.

- A copy of Sketch1 is created and placed on Plane1, and is automatically activated for positioning.

5. Positioning the Derived Sketch:

- Add a **Collinear** relation between the Top plane and the Line as indicated.

- Add a **Collinear** relation between the Front plane and the Centerline as shown.

- Click **OK** .

Collinear with
Top plane

Collinear with
Front plane

6. Revolving the Derived Sketch:

- Click **Revolve** or select **Insert / Boss-Base / Revolve**.

- Revolve Type: **Blind** .

- Revolve Angle: **360 deg**. .

- Click **OK** .

7. Adding Fillets:

- Click **Fillet** ⬡ or select **Insert / Features / Fillet / Round**.

- Enter **.100 in.** for Radius size ◹ .

- Select the <u>edges</u> shown as the Edges-To-Fillet ⬚ .

- Click **OK** ✓ .

Fillet
2 edges

8. Saving Your Work:

- Select **File / Save As / Center Ball Joint / Save**.

Questions for Review

Derived Sketches

1. The first feature in a part is the parent feature.
   - a. True
   - b. False

2. More than one centerline can be selected at the same time to revolve a sketch profile.
   - a. True
   - b. False

3. A parallel plane can be created from another plane or a planar surface.
   - a. True
   - b. False

4. A derived sketch can be copied and placed on a different plane / surface.
   - a. True
   - b. False

5. A derived sketch can be edited just like any other sketch.
   - a. True
   - b. False

6. A derived sketch is an independent sketch. There is no link between the derived sketch and the parent sketch.
   - a. True
   - b. False

7. A derived sketch can only be positioned and related to other sketches / features.
   - a. True
   - b. False

8. When the parent sketch is changed, the derived sketches will be updated automatically.
   - a. True
   - b. False

7. TRUE	8. TRUE
5. FALSE	6. FALSE
3. TRUE	4. TRUE
1. TRUE	2. FALSE

Exercise: Revolved Parts - Wheel

1. Create the 3D model using the drawing provided below.
2. Dimensions are in inches, 3 decimal places.
3. The part is Symmetrical about the horizontal axis.
4. The 5 mounting holes should be created as a Circular Pattern.
5. Use the instructions on the following pages if needed.

.750

2X .250

.425
(Hold the SHIFT key
when adding this dim.)

.250

2.256

4X 15.00°

R.100
TYP

Ø1.250
THRU

1.500

2.500

Ø6.900

Ø7.750

3.000

Ø3.500
Bolt Circle

5X Ø.300
THRU

6. Save your work as: **Wheel_Exe**.

1. Start with the Front plane.

- Sketch 2 centerlines and use the vertical centerline for Dynamic Mirror.

- Sketch the profile as shown.

- Add a tangent arc to close off the upper portion of the sketch.

- Add the dimensions and relations as indicated.

A = 180° R = 0.101

.250

.750

.425 (Hold the Shift key when adding this dimension)

Collinear

2.256

15.00°

3.450

Parallel (2X)

.250

1.250

1.500

2. Revolve the profile.

3. Add the 5 holes.

4. Save your work as Wheel_Exe.sldprt.

Exercise: Revolved Parts - Bottle
Extrude / Revolve / Sweep and Circular Pattern

1. Copying the document:

<u>Go to:</u>
Training Files folder, browse to the file named:
Basic Solid Modeling_Bottle

Make a Copy of this file and **Open the copy**.

(To review how this part was made, open the sample part from the Training Files folder, in the Built-Parts folder).

1.550
.575
.750
.525
.080
6.625
5.750
4.000
3.875
3.625
1.550
.850
R2.375
R.250
4 PLCS
R1.250
R.600
R.500
1.625

2. Revolving the Base feature:

- Click **Revolve** or select **Insert / Boss-Base / Revolve**

- Select the **Vertical Centerline** as the Center of the rotation.

- Direction: **Blind** (Default).

- Revolve Angle: **360 deg**.

- Click **OK** .

Revolve line

Revolve1

Axis of Revolution
Line1

Direction1
Blind
360.00deg

Direction2

Selected Contours

6.625
5.750
4.000
3.875
3.625
1.550
.850
1.550
.575
.750
.525
.080
R2.375
R.250
R1.250
R.600
R.500
1.625

3. Creating the Upper Sketch:

- Select the <u>Front</u> plane and open a new sketch.

- Sketch the profile as shown **and** add dimensions and/or relations needed to fully define the sketch.

4. Revolving the Upper Cut:

- Click **Revolved Cut** or select **Insert / Cut / Revolve**.

- Select the **Angular Centerline (40°)** as Center of the rotation.

- Revolve **One-Direction** (Default).

- Revolve Angle: **360 deg**.

- Click **OK**.

5. Creating the Bottom Cut:

- Select the <u>Front</u> plane and open a new sketch.

- Sketch the profile as shown, use **Convert-Entities** where needed.

- Add Dimensions and Relations to fully define the sketch.

- Click **Revolve Cut**.

- Revolve Direction: **Mid-Plane**

- Revolve Angle: **45 Deg**.

- Click **OK**.

Line Tangent with Edge of bottle

Perpendicular

Convert Entities

6. Adding .075" Fillets:

- Click **Fillet** 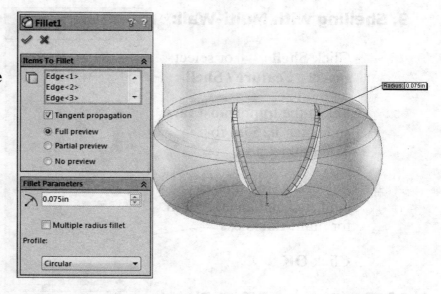 or
select: **Insert / Feature
/ Fillet-Round**

- Enter **.075 in**. for
Radius.

- Select the **2 inner
edges**.

- Click **OK** ✅.

7. Adding .125" Fillets:

- Click Fillet or
select: **Insert / Feature
/ Fillet-Round**

- Enter **.125 in**. for
Radius.

- Select the **2 outer edges**.

- Click **OK** ✅.

8. Circular Pattern the Cutouts:

- Click **Circular Pattern** or
select **Insert / Pattern-Mirror
/Circular Pattern**.

- Select the **Center Axis** for use
as the Pattern-Axis.

- Pattern Angle: **360deg**.

- **Equal Spacing** enabled.

- Number of Copies: **5**

- Select the **Upper Cut,** the **Lower
Cut,** the **Fillet 1,** and **Fillet 2**.

- Click **OK** ✅.

9. Shelling with Multi-Wall:

- Click **Shell** or select: **Insert / Feature / Shell.**

- Select the **uppermost face** and enter **.025 in**. for default thickness

- Select the **side face** as indicated and enter **.050 in**. for multi-thickness

- Click **OK** ✓.

.025" wall

.050" wall

10. Creating an Offset Plane:

- Click **Plane** ◇ or select **Insert / Reference Geometry / Plane.**

- Select the **upper face** as noted.

- Enter **.450 in**. for offset Distance.

- Click **OK** ✓.

Offset from top surface

.450

Plane1

11. Creating the Helix ⊗ (Sweep Path):

- Select the <u>new plane</u> and open a new sketch.

- **Convert** the uppermost circular edge into a circle.

- Select: **Insert / Curve / Helix-Spiral.**

- Pitch: **.115 in**.

- Revolution: **3.5**

- Start Angle: **0.00deg**.

- Enable Counterclockwise.

- Click **OK** ✓.

12. Sketching the Thread Profile:

- Select the <u>Right</u> plane and open a new sketch.

- Sketch the profile (Triangle), add the dimensions and relations needed to fully define the sketch.

- Use Dynamic Mirror to keep all sketch entities symmetrical.

- Add a **Pierce** relation (between the the endpoint of the centerline and the helix) to properly snap the sweep profile on the Helix.

- **Exit** the Sketch .

13. Adding the Threads:

- Click **Swept Boss Base** or select: **Insert / Boss-Base / Sweep**.

- Select the Sketch Profile (the triangle) for use as the Sweep Profile.

- Select the Helix for use as the Sweep Path.

- Click **OK**.

14. Rounding the ends:

- Select the end-face of the Swept feature and open a new sketch.

- Click **Convert-Entities** to covert the selected face into a new sketch profile.

- Add a **Vertical Centerline** as shown.

- Click **Revolve** or select: **Insert / Boss-Base / Revolve**.

- Revolve **Blind** (Default), click Reverse if needed.

- Revolve Angle: **100 deg**.

- Click **OK** .

- *Repeat Step 14 to round off the other end of the threads.*

Sketch face

Convert Entities

15. Saving your work:

- Click **File / Save As / Basic Solid Modeling_Bottle**.

- Click **Save**.

CHAPTER 6

Rib & Shell Features

The Rib and Shell Features
Formed Tray

- A **Rib** is a special type of extruded feature created from open or closed sketched contours. It adds material of a specified thickness in a specified direction between the contour and an existing part. A rib can be created using single or multiple sketches.

- Rib features can have draft angles applied to them either inward, or outward.

- The **Detailed Preview** Property Manager can be used with multi-body parts to enhance detail and select entities to display.

- The **Shell** tool hollows out a part, leaves selected faces open, and creates thin walled features on the remaining faces. If nothing (no face) is selected on the model, a solid part can be shelled, creating a closed hollow model.

- Multiple thicknesses are also supported when shelling a solid model.

- In most cases, the model fillets should be applied before shelling a part.

- One of the most common problems when the shell fails is when the wall thickness of the shell is smaller than one of the fillets in the model.

- If errors appear when shelling a model, you can run the **Error Diagnostics**. The shell feature displays error messages and includes tools to help you identify why the shell feature failed. The diagnostic tool **Error Diagnostics** is available in the **Shell** Property Manager.

Formed Tray
Rib & Shell Features

Dimensioning Standards: **ANSI**

Units: **INCHES** – 3 Decimals

Tools Needed:

Insert Sketch	Line	Circle
Add Geometric Relations	Dimension	Fillet
Boss/Base Extrude	Rib	Shell

1. Sketching the Base Profile:

- Select the <u>Top</u> plane from the FeatureManager tree.

- Click Sketch or select **Insert / Sketch**.

- Sketch the profile as shown; the center the rectangle on the Origin.

- Add sketch fillets and dimensions as shown to fully define the sketch.

2. Extruding the Base feature:

- Click **Extruded Boss-Base** or select **Insert / Boss-Base / Extrude**.

- End condition: **Blind**

- Extrude depth: **2.00 in**.

- Draft angle: **5.00 deg.**

- Click OK

3. Adding the Side Cutouts:

- Select the <u>Front</u> plane from the FeatureManager tree.

- Click Sketch or select **Insert / Sketch.**

- Sketch the profile as shown and add Dimensions / Relations necessary to fully define the sketch.

45.00°

5.000

.500

Symmetric

- Click **Extruded Cut** .

- Select **Through All** for both directions.

- Click **OK** .

Extrude2

From

Sketch Plane

Direction 1

Through All - Both

Flip side to cut

Draft outward

Direction 2

Through All

Selected Contours

45.00°

5.000

500

45.00°

5.000

500

4. Removing more material:

- Select the top surface and open a new sketch.

- Select the outer edges and create an **offset** of **.250"** as indicated.

Sketch face

Offset from
outer edges

- Repeat for the opposite side.

- Drag the endpoint of the lines
to merge the 2 ends into one
continuous profile.

- Extrude a **cut** with **5°** draft using the
bottom surface to offset the cut.

Drag the endpoints of the
2 lines to merge them

Offset from
the bottom
surface

- Click **OK** ✅.

5. Creating the Rib Profiles:

- Select the <u>face</u> as indicated and open a new sketch .

- Sketch the profile and add dimensions / relations needed to fully define the sketch.

— Sketch face

- Click **Rib** or select **Insert / Features / Rib**.

- Enter **.250 in.** for Thickness.

- Select the **Normal To Sketch** option .

- Click the **Draft** option and enter **5.00** deg.

- Enable **Draft Outward** checkbox.

- Click **OK** .

6. Adding the .500" Fillets:

- Click **Fillet** or select **Insert / Features / Fillet-Round**.

- Enter **.500 in.** as the Radius and select the 8 Edges as shown.

- Click **OK** ✅.

Select 8 Edges
(Both Sides)

7. Adding the .125" Fillets:

- Click **Fillet** or select **Insert / Features / Fillet-Round**.

- Enter **.125 in.** for radius size and select all edges **except** for the bottom edges.

- Click **OK** ✅.

Box select

Select All-Edges except for the bottom

- Right click in the graphics area and select: **Box Selection** to change from the Lasso mode.

8. Shelling the lower portion:

- Click **Shell** or select **Insert / Features / Shell**.

- Select the <u>bottom face</u> and enter **.080** in. for Thickness.

- Click **OK** ✓.

Select face to Shell

9. Saving Your Work:

- Click **File / Save As / Rib and Shell / Save**.

Questions for Review

Rib & Shell Features

1. A fully defined sketch can be re-positioned after its relations/dimensions to the origin have been removed.
   - a. True
   - b. False

2. The Mid-Plane extrude option extrudes the profile in both directions and at equal depths.
   - a. True
   - b. False

3. Draft Outward is the only option available; the Draft Inward option is not available.
   - a. True
   - b. False

4. The Shell feature hollows out the part starting with the selected face.
   - a. True
   - b. False

5. If nothing (no face) is selected, a solid model cannot be shelled.
   - a. True
   - b. False

6. A Rib is a special type of extruded feature; no drafts may be added to it.
   - a. True
   - b. False

7. A Rib can only be created with a closed-sketch profile; opened-sketch profiles may not be used.
   - a. True
   - b. False

8. The Rib features can be fully edited, just like any other feature in SolidWorks.
   - a. True
   - b. False

7. FALSE   8. TRUE
5. FALSE   6. FALSE
3. FALSE   4. TRUE
1. TRUE   2. TRUE

CHAPTER 6 (cont.)

Using Shell & Mirror

Using Shell & Mirror
Styrofoam Box

- In most cases, creating a model as a solid and then shell it out towards the end of the process would probably be easier than creating the model as a thin walled from the beginning.

- Although the model can be made as a thin walled part in the newer releases of SolidWorks, but this lesson will guide us through the process of creating the solid model, and the shell feature is added in the end.

- The shell command hollows out a model, it deletes the faces that you select and creates thin walled feature on the remaining faces. But if you do not select any faces of the model, it will still gets shelled, and the model will become a closed hollow part. Multi-thickness can be create at the same time.

- Mirror on the other hand, offers a quick way to make a copy of one or more features, where a plane or a planar surface is used to mirror about.

- The options that are available for mirror are:

    * Mirror Features: is used to mirror solid features such as Extruded Boss, Cuts, Fillets and Chamfers.

    * Mirror Faces: is used when the model, or an imported part, has faces that make up the features, but not the solid features themselves.

    * Mirror Bodies: is used to mirror solid bodies, surface bodies, or multibodies.

- If Mirror bodies option is selected, the Merge Solids and the Knit Surfaces options appear, requiring you to select the appropriate checkboxes, prior to completing the mirror function.

Using Shell & Mirror
Styrofoam Box

Dimensioning Standards: **ANSI**

Units: **INCHES** – 3 Decimals

Tools Needed:

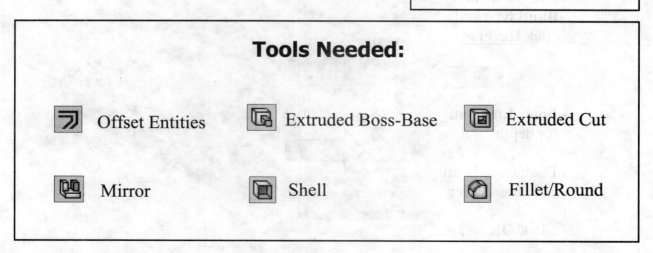

Offset Entities   Extruded Boss-Base   Extruded Cut

Mirror   Shell   Fillet/Round

1. Starting a new part:

- Click **File / New / Part**. Set the Units to Inches and number of Decimal to 3.

- Select the <u>Top</u> plane and open a new sketch ✎.

- Sketch a **rectangle** a little to the right of the Origin as shown below.

- Add a reference centerline from the origin and connect it to the mid point of the line on the left.

- Add the dimensions as as pictured to fully define this sketch.

Top Plane

6.000

.400

Origin

Mid Point

6.300

2. Extruding the base:

- Click **Extruded Boss-Base** 🔲.

- Use the default **Blind** type and click **Reverse**.

- Enter **1.000"**in. for depth.

- Enable the Draft and enter **10deg**.

- Click **OK** ✅.

Extrude1

From

Sketch Plane

Direction 1

Blind

1.000in

10.00deg

Draft outward

Direction 2

Selected Contours

.400

6.000

6.300

3. Adding the .750" fillets:

- Click the **Fillet** command from the Features toolbar.

- Enter **.750in** for radius.

- Select the **4 edges** as noted.

- Click **OK** ✓.

Select 4 edges

4. Adding the .250" fillets:

- Press **Enter** to <u>repeat</u> the previous command or click the Fillet command again.

- Enter **.250in** for radius.

- Select one of the edges at the bottom of the part. The fillet should propagate automatically because the Tangent Propagation checkbox was enabled by default.

- Click **OK** ✓.

5. Creating an offset sketch:

- Open a new sketch on the <u>bottom face</u> as indicated.

- Right click on one of the edges as noted and pick: **Select Tangency**.

- Click the **Offset Entities** command on the Sketch toolbar.

- Enter **.400in** for offset dimension and click the **Reverse** checkbox to place the new profile on the <u>inside</u>.

R/C Select Tangency

Sketch face

6. Creating a recess:

- Click **Extruded Cut** .

- Use the default **Blind** type.

- Enter **.200in** for extrude depth.

- Enable the Draft button and enter **10.00deg**. for angle.

- Click **OK** .

7. Adding the .200" fillets:

- From the Features toolbar, click the **Fillet** command .

- Enter **.200in** for radius value.

- Select one of the <u>upper</u> edges of the recess. The fillet propagates around the recess feature once again.

- Click **OK** ✅.

Select 1 edge

8. Adding the .125" fillets:

- Press **Enter** to repeat the last command (or click the Fillet command again).

- Enter **.125in** for radius value.

- This time select the rectangular <u>face</u> of the recess instead. The fillet propagates along all edges of the selected face.

Select face

- Click **OK** ✅.

9. Creating the rim:

- Select the <u>upper face</u> of the part and open a new sketch .

- Hold the Control key and select the <u>5 edges</u> as noted.

- Click the **Offset Entities** command on the Sketch toolbar.

- Enter **.600in** for offset dimension.

- Be sure to place the new entities on the <u>outside</u>.

- Click **OK** ✓.

- Add a vertical line to the left of the Origin.

- Extend the line to close off both ends of the profile.

- Add the **.600"** spacing dimension to fully define the sketch.

- Click **Extruded Cut**.

- Use the **Blind** type.

- Enter **.400in** for extrude depth.

- Enter **10deg** for draft. Enable Draft Outward.

- Click **OK** ✓.

Sketch face

Select 5 edges

Trim / Extend to close off both ends

10. Adding another .125" fillet:

- Click the **Fillet** command from the Feature toolbar.

- Enter **.125in** for radius.

- Rotate the part and select one of the edges of the last extruded boss.

- The fillet propagates around the boss automatically.

Select 1 edge

- Click **OK** ✓.

11. Creating the fold feature:

- Select the <u>Front</u> plane and open a new sketch . Press **Ctrl + 8** to rotate the view normal to the sketch.

- Sketch a triangle using the line tool. Add the dimensions shown.

Front Plane

Coincident to origin

45.00°

.118

- Click **Extruded Boss-Base**.

- For **Direction 1**, select the **Up-To-Surface** option from the list and click the face on the right side of the part.

- For Direction 2, also select the **Up-To-Surface** option, and click the face on the left side.

- This way the width of the fold feature is linked to the width of the part, allowing them to change at the same time.

- Click **OK** ✅.

Direction 1: Up-To-Surface

Direction 2: Up-To-Surface

12. Mirroring the solid body:

- Select the <u>Right</u> plane from the Feature tree and click the **Mirror** button.

- Expand the **Bodies to Mirror** section and click the part in the graphics area.

- Enable the **Merge Solid** checkbox

- Click **OK** ✅.

- To mirror one or more features of a part, use the Features-To-Mirror option.

- To mirror the entire part, use the Bodies-to-Mirror option.

13. Creating the lock feature:

Sketch face

- Rotate the part, select the <u>bottom face</u> of the rim and open a new sketch .

- Sketch a centerline from the origin and use it as the mirror line.

- Sketch a small rectangle above the centerline.

- Use one of the mirror options to mirror the rectangle below the centerline.

- Add the dimensions shown to fully define the sketch.

- Click **Extruded Cut** .

- Use the default **Blind** type.

- Enter **.150in** for depth.

- Enable the Draft checkbox and enter **3deg** for taper angle.

- Click **OK** ✓.

14. Creating the lock cavity:

- Select the <u>bottom face</u> of the rim & open a new sketch .

- Similar to the last step, sketch a center-line from the origin and create a small rectangle above it.

- Mirror the rectangle to the other side of the centerline.

- Add the dimensions shown to fully define the sketch (notice the rectangles are slightly smaller than the last ones).

- Click **Extruded Boss-Base** .

- Use the default **Blind** type.

- Enter **.140in** for depth.

- Enable the Draft checkbox and enter 3deg for taper angle.

- Click **OK** ✓.

15. Adding the .032" fillets:

- Click the **Fillet** command from the Features toolbar.

- Enter **.032in** for radius.

- Expand the FeatureManager tree (push the + symbol) and select the last 2 features, the **Cut-Extrude2** and the **Extrude4**.

- This method is a little bit quicker than selecting the edges individually.

Select 2 features

- All edges of the selected features are filleted using the same radius value. Create the fillets separately if you want the features to have different radiuses.

- Rotate and zoom a little closer to verify the fillets on both features.

16. Shelling the part:

- The shell command hollows a solid model, deletes the faces you select, and creates thin walled features on the remaining faces.

- During the shell mode, if you do not select any face of the model, the part will still shelled, creating a closed hollow model.

- The first selection box is used to specify the faces of the model to remove, and the second selection box is used to specify different wall thicknesses.

Select 9 faces

- Click the **Shell** command . from the Features toolbar.

- Enter **.025in** for wall thickness.

- Select the <u>upper face</u> of the model and the <u>8 faces</u> of the rim to remove.

- Click **OK** ✓.

- Compare your model with the image shown below. Edit the shell to correct it if needed.

17. Adding the .050" fillets:

- Zoom in on the fold section in the middle of the part.

- Click **Fillet**

- Enter **.050in** for radius.

- Select the <u>3 edges</u> as noted, (2 on the top and 1 on the bottom).

- Click **OK**.

Select 3 edges

- Verify the resulting fillets.

- We could have used the Multiple Radius option to create both fillets, the .050" and the .032" (in the next step), but the screen will get very busy, hard to see which edge is which to apply the correct fillets.

- Instead, we are going to create the two fillets separately, that will also give you a chance to practice using the fillet command once again.

18. Adding the .032" fillets:

- Click the **Fillet** command again.

- Enter .032" for radius size.

- Select the 3 edges as indicated (one edge on the top and two edges on the bottom).

- Click **OK**.

19. Saving your work:

- Save your work as **Using Shell_ Mirror**.

Questions for Review

Using Shell & Mirror

1. It is easier to create a thin walled part by making it out of solid and then shell it out in the end.
    a. True
    b. False

2. The shell commands hollows out a solid model and removes the faces that you select.
    a. True
    b. False

3. If you do not select any faces of the model the part will still be shelled into a closed volume.
    a. True
    b. False

4. Only one wall thickness can be created with the shell command.
    a. True
    b. False

5. To mirror a feature, you must use a centerline to mirror about.
    a. True
    b. False

6. To mirror one or more features, a planar face or a plane is used as the center of the mirror.
    a. True
    b. False

7. To mirror the entire part you must use mirror-features and select all features from the tree.
    a. True
    b. False

8. To mirror the entire part you must use mirror-body and select the part from the graphics area.
    a. True
    b. False

7. FALSE   8. TRUE
5. FALSE   6. TRUE
3. TRUE   4. FALSE
1. TRUE   2. TRUE

CHAPTER 6 (cont.)

Using the Intersect Feature

Using the Intersect Feature
Water Warrior Submarine

The Intersect command creates new geometry by intersecting the existing solids, surfaces, or planes.

For example, a solid can be used to add open surface geometry, remove material, or create geometry from an enclosed volume. With the Intersect tool solids bodies can also be merged, or cap some surfaces to define closed volumes.

Surface, Body, or Plane to Intersect

Regions to Exclude from Solution

A solid can be made from a cavity by merging coincident surface or solid bodies in a model, and the geometry is removed by defining the bodies that enclose the cavity.

Water Warrior Submarine
Using the Intersect Feature

Dimensioning Standards: **ANSI**
Units: **INCHES** – 3 Decimals

Tools Needed:

 Section View   Intersect   Move/Copy Bodies

1. Opening the 1st part of the document:

- Click **File / Open**.

- Browse to the Training Files folder, locate and open the document named:
  Water Warrior Submarine Body.

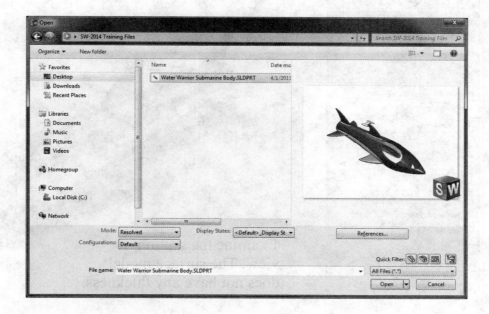

- This model is a surface-model, it does not have any thickness to it.

- A second surface model will get inserted into this same document, located over the cockpit area, as pictured below.

- After placed into position, the 2 surface bodies will be used to create a solid enclose volume with the intersect tool.

2. Viewing the inside details:

- Click the **Section View** command from the View Heads-Up toolbar.

- Use the **Front** reference plane and create a section at **0.00"** distance (Default).

- Examine the section view. The surface model does not have any thickness.

- **Exit** out of the Section View command.

3. Inserting the 2nd surface body:

- Select **Insert / Part** (arrow).

- Browse to the Training Files folder, locate and open the document named: **Water Warrior Submarine Cockpit**.

- In the **Insert Part** dialog, enable the Solid Bodies and the Surface Bodies checkboxes, clear all others (arrow).

Click OK to place the surface body on the origin

- Click **OK** to place the surface body on the origin (arrow).

4. Creating a section view:

- Click the **Section View** command from the View Heads-Up toolbar once again.

- Use the **Front** reference plane and create a section at **0.00"** distance (Default), similar to the last one.

- Zoom in and examine the section view. Both surface bodies have no thickness to them at this point, but they will become a single solid body after the intersect feature is performed.

5. Creating an Intersect feature:

- The Intersect command is similar to the options Combine-Add, Combine-Subtract, and Combine-Common where you can to perform complex tasks to quickly combine solid bodies, planes, or surfaces without the need for cut, trim or fill features. The preview options allows you to see the final shape that you can pick and choose while selecting the different areas to exclude.

Select 2 surface bodies

- Select **Insert / Features / Intersect**.

- Select the **2 surface bodies** either from the Feature tree or directly from the graphics area (arrow).

- Click the **Intersect** button (arrow). Do not select anything inside the Regions to Exclude section.

- Enable the **Merge Result** checkbox

- Click **OK**.

- The resulting solid body.

6. Creating another section view:

- Click the **Section View** command once again.

- Use the same settings as the last one and create a section through the center of the model.

- The Intersect operation has converted the 2 surface bodies into a single solid.

- **Exit** the Section View command.

7. Hiding the surfaces:

- Expand the **Surface Bodies** folder on the Feature tree.

- Click the **2 surface bodies** inside this folder and select **Hide** (arrow).

8. Saving your work

- Select **File / Save As**.

- Enter **Water Warrior Submarine Completed** for the name of the file.

- Click **Save**.

9. Rendering Options:

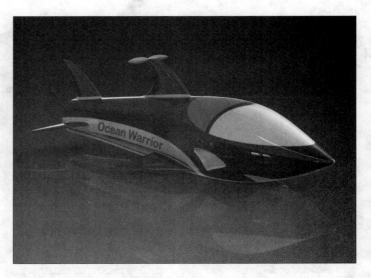

- Open the model named:
  Ocean Warrior (for Rendering).
- Program: **PhotoView 360**
- Appearance: **Black High Gloss Plastic**
- Scene: **Reflective Floor Black**.
- Output Image Size:
  1280 X 1024
- Save image as **TIF** format.

<u>Exercise:</u> Using the Intersect Feature

Similar to the options in the Combine command, the Intersect command enables you to perform complex tasks to quickly combine solid bodies, planes, or surfaces without the need for cut, trim or fill features. The preview options allows you to see the final shape that you can pick and choose while selecting the different areas to exclude.

This exercise discusses another use of the Intersect command where 2 cavity models are used to create a solid model as pictured.

1. Opening a SolidWorks document:

    - Click **File / Open**.

    - Browse to the Training Files folder, locate and open the document named:
      Intersect_Cavity.

    - This document has 2 solid bodies and their feature histories are omitted to
      help focus on the Intersect feature.

2. Rolling back:

- Drag the Roll-back line up 1 step to temporarily suppress the Body-Move feature.

- Make sure the 2 solid bodies are in the collapsed position before moving to the next step.

3. Creating an Intersect feature:

- Select **Insert / Features / Intersect** (arrow).

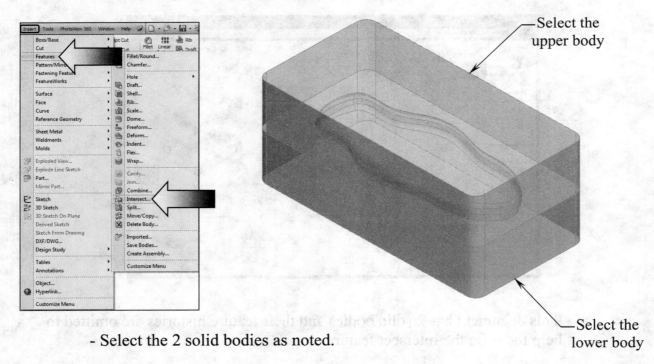

Select the upper body

Select the lower body

- Select the 2 solid bodies as noted.

- Click the **Intersect** button after selecting the 2 solid bodies (arrow).

- Explore the options in the Regions to Exclude section by checking the checkboxes for each of the solid body.

- The Preview shows the different results when the checkboxes are enabled or disabled.

- Select the **Region1** and the **Region3** checkboxes to exclude the 2 solid bodies from this operation.

- Enable the **Merge Result** checkbox.

- Click **OK** to complete the Intersect operation.

- A solid model is created from the cavities of the 2 solid bodies.

4. Saving your work:

- Select **File / Save As**.

- Enter **Intersect Using Cavity** for the name of the file.

- Click **Save**.

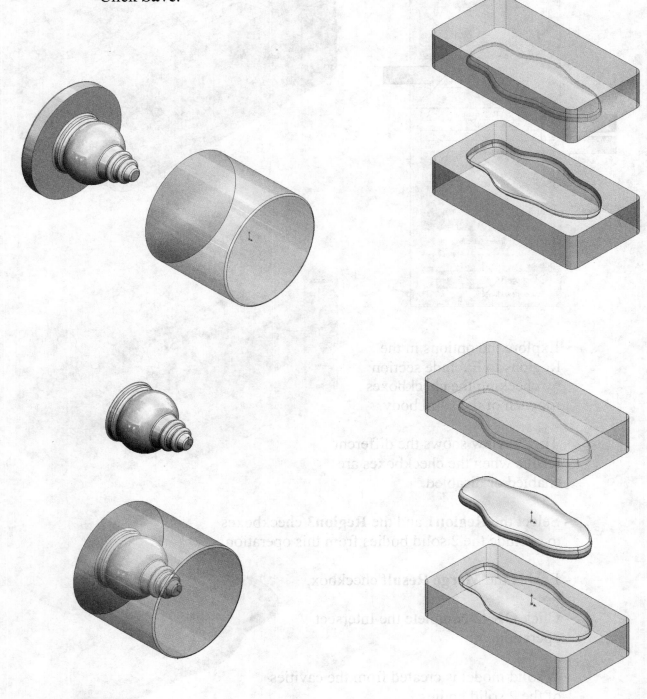

CHAPTER 7

Linear Patterns

Linear Patterns
Test Tray

- The Linear Pattern is used to arrange multiple instances of selected features along one or two linear paths.

- The following 4 elements are needed to create a linear pattern:

    * Direction of the pattern (linear edge of the model or an axis) .

    * Distance between the pattern instances .

    * Number of pattern instances in each direction .

    * Feature(s) to the pattern .

- When the features used to create the pattern are changed, all instances within the pattern will be updated automatically.

- The options available in Linear Patterns:

    * Pattern instances to skip. This option is used to hide / skip some of the instances in a pattern.

    * Pattern only the seed feature. This option is used when only the original feature gets repeated, not its instances.

- This chapter will guide you through the use of the pattern commands such as: Linear, Circular, and Curve Driven Patterns.

Test Tray
Linear Patterns

Dimensioning Standards: **ANSI**

Units: **INCHES** – 3 Decimals

Tools Needed:

Insert Sketch	Rectangle	Circle
Dimension	Add Geometric Relations	Base/Boss Extrude
Shell	Linear Pattern	Fillet/Round

1. Sketching the Base Profile:

- Select the <u>Top</u> plane from the FeatureManager tree.

- Click or select **Insert /Sketch**.

- Sketch a **Corner Rectangle** ▢ starting at the Origin.

- Add the dimensions ◇ shown.

2. Extruding the Base Feature:

- Click ▣ or select **Insert / Boss-Base / Extrude**.

- End Condition: **Blind.**

- Extrude Depth: **.500 in**.

- Click **OK** ✓.

3. Sketching the seed feature:

- Select the <u>face</u> indicated as the sketch plane.

- Click or select **Insert / Sketch**.

- Sketch a **circle** and add dimensions as shown.

Sketch Face

Ø1.000

1.000

1.000

4. Extruding a seed feature:

- Click or select **Insert / Boss-Base / Extrude**.

- End Condition: **Blind.**

- Extrude Depth: **2.00 in**.

- Draft On/Off: **Enabled.**

- Draft Angle: **7 deg**.

- Click **OK**.

Extrude2

From
Sketch Plane

Direction 1
Blind

2.000in

☑ Merge result

7.00deg

☐ Draft outward

☐ Direction 2

Selected Contours

5. Creating a Linear Pattern:

- Click or select **Insert / Pattern Mirror / Linear Pattern**.

For **Direction 1**:

- Select the bottom **horizontal edge** as Pattern Direction1 .

- Enter **1.500** in. as the Spacing .

- Enter **6** as the Number Of Instances .

For **Direction 2**:

- Select the **vertical edge** as Pattern Direction2 .

- Enter **1.500** in. as the Spacing .

- Enter **3** as the Number of Instances .

- Click Extrude2 as the Features to Pattern .

- Click **OK** .

> ### Linear Patterns
>
> The Linear Pattern option creates multiple instances of one or more features uniformly along one or two directions.

6. Shelling the Base feature:

- Select the upper face as shown.

- Click or select **Insert / Features / Shell**.

- Type **.100** in. for the Thickness.

- Click **OK** ✓.

Select face

- The shelled part.

7. Adding Fillets:

- Click **Fillet** or select **Insert / Features / Fillet / Round.**

- Enter **.050** in. for Radius size .

- Select the <u>all edges</u> except for the top area (To use Box-Select method right click in the graphics area and select: Box-Selection).

- Click **OK** .

No fillet
on top

> ### Fillets
>
> A combination of faces and edges can be selected within the same fillet operation.
> (Box-select the entire part to select all edges).

8. Saving your work:

- Select **File / Save As / Test Tray / Save.**

Questions for Review

Linear Patterns

1. SolidWorks only allows you to pattern one feature at a time. Patterning multiple features is not supported.
    a. True
    b. False

2. Only the spacing and number of copies are required to create a linear pattern.
    a. True
    b. False

3. SolidWorks does not require you to specify the 2nd direction when using both directions option.
    a. True
    b. False

4. The Shell feature hollows out the part using a wall thickness specified by the user.
    a. True
    b. False

5. After the Shell feature is created, its wall thickness cannot be changed.
    a. True
    b. False

6. A combination of faces and edges of a model can be selected in the same fillet operation.
    a. True
    b. False

7. The value of the fillet can be changed at anytime.
    a. True
    b. False

8. "Pattern a pattern" is not supported in SolidWorks.
    a. True
    b. False

7. TRUE   8. FALSE
5. FALSE   6. TRUE
3. FALSE   4. TRUE
1. FALSE   2. FALSE

CHAPTER 7 (cont.)

Circular Patterns

Circular Patterns
Spur Gear

- One or more instances can be copied in a circular fashion or around an Axis.

- The center of the pattern can be defined by a circular edge, an axis, a temporary axis, or an angular dimension.

- In the newer releases of SolidWorks, a circular edge can be used as the center of the pattern, instead of an axis.

- The information required to create a circular pattern are:

  * Center of rotation.

  * Spacing between the instances.

  * Number of copies.

  * Feature(s) to copy.

- Only the original feature can be edited; changes made to the original are automatically updated within the pattern.

- The features to the pattern can be selected directly from the graphics area or from the Feature Manager tree.

- The instances in a pattern can be skipped. The skipped instances can be edited during or after the pattern is made.

Spur-Gear
Circular Patterns

Dimensioning Standards: **ANSI**

Units: **INCHES** – 3 Decimals

Tools Needed:

	Insert Sketch		Line		Center Line
	Dynamic Mirror		Add Geometric Relations		Dimension
	Convert Entities		Trim Entities		Base/Boss Revolve
	Circular Pattern		Base/Boss Extrude		Extruded Cut

1. Sketching the Body profile:

    - Select the <u>Front</u> plane from the FeatureManager Tree.

    - Click or select **Insert / Sketch**.

    - Sketch a **Centerline** ⋮ starting at the Origin.

    - Select the **Mirror** tool and click the centerline to active the Dynamic-Mirror mode (or select: **Tools / Sketch Tools / Dynamic Mirror**).

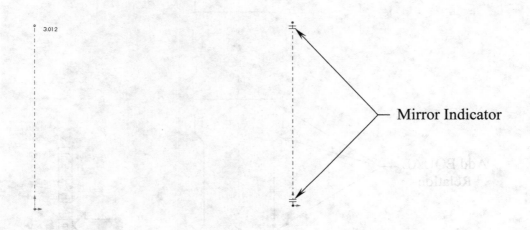

Mirror Indicator

    - Sketch the profile below using the Line tool .

To cancel Auto-Relations (dotted inference lines), either hold down the Control key while sketching the lines – OR – just simply avoid sketching over the dotted lines.

Using the Dynamic Mirror:

- Sketch on one side of the centerline only.

- The sketch should not cross the centerline.

- The system creates **Symmetric** relations between all mirrored sketch entities.

- Add the following Geometric Relations to the entities indicated below:

Add COLLINEAR
Relation

Add EQUAL
Relation

- Sketch a horizontal Centerline ⁝ starting at the Origin.

Delete the Parallel
relations if needed

Add Centerline
to revolve…

💡 **Auto-Relations**

To cancel Auto Relation
from snapping to other
entity, hold down the
CONTROL key while
Sketching.

- Add the **dimensions** as shown below:

NOTE: If this dimension causes the sketch to be over defined, then select this other line to see if it has a Parallel relation and delete it.

The Parallel relation was added automatically when the line was sketched over the inference lines. (see step 1, page 7-11)

Revolve Centerline.

2. Revolving the Base Body:

- Select the horizontal centerline as indicated above.

- Click or select **Insert / Boss-Base / Revolve**.

- Revolve direction: **One Direction**

- Revolve Angle: **360°**

- Click **OK** .

3. Sketching the Thread Profile:

- Select the <u>face</u> as indicated and click or select **Insert / Sketch**.

Sketch Face

- Click **Normal To** from the Standard View Toolbar.

- Sketch a vertical **Centerline** starting at the origin.

- Select the **Mirror** tool and click the centerline to active the Dynamic-Mirror mode.

- Sketch the profile using the Line and the 3-Point-Arc tools.

3 Point Arc

Line

4. Converting the entities:

- Select the **outer edge** of the part and click **Convert Entities** from the Sketch toolbar.

Select edge

Convert into circle

- The selected edge is converted into a circle.

5. Trimming the Sketch Entities:

- Select the **Trim** tool from the Sketch toolbar; select the **Trim-to-Closest**

option ⊞ , and click on the **lower right edge** of the circle to trim.

Click here to trim

6. Adding Dimensions:

- Select the **Dimension** Tool from the Sketch-Tools toolbar and add the dimensions shown.

.225

.515

R.750

2.625

- Switch to the Isometric View or press **Ctrl + 7**.

7. Cutting the First Tooth:

- Click **Extruded Cut** from the Features toolbar.

- End Condition: **Through All**.

- Click **OK** ✓.

8. Circular Patterning the Tooth:

- Select **Temporary Axis** from the **View** pull-down menu. An axis in the center of the hole is created automatically; this axis will be used as the center of the pattern.

For pattern direction
select the Axis
– or –
the Circular Edge

- Click **Circular Pattern** ⊞ from the Features toolbar.

- Click on the center **axis** as Direction 1 🔃 .

- Click the **Equal Spacing** check box.

- Set the Total Angle to **360°** 📐 .

- Set the Number of Instances to **24** 🔢 .

- Click inside the Features to Pattern box 🔵 and select one of the faces of
  the cut feature (or select the previous **Extruded-Cut** feature from the tree).

- Click **OK** ✅ .

- The resulting circular Pattern.

9. Adding the Keyway:

- Select the <u>face</u> as indicated and click or select **Insert / Sketch**.

Sketch Face

- Click **Normal To** ⬆ from the Standard Views toolbar (Ctrl + 8).

- Sketch a vertical **Centerline** ⋮ starting at the Origin.

- Select the **Mirror** tool ⬢ and click the centerline to activate the Dynamic-Mirror mode.

> 💡 **Sketch Mirror**
>
> Use the Mirror option in a sketch to make a symmetrical profile.
>
> When a sketch entity is changed, the mirrored image will also change.

- Sketch the profile of the keyway and add dimension as shown:

10. Extruding a Cut:

- Click on **Extruded Cut** 📇 from the Features toolbar.

- End Condition: **Through All**

- Click **OK** ✅ .

11. Saving Your Work:

- Select **File / Save As**.

- Enter **Spur Gear** for the file name.

- Click **Save**.

Questions for Review

Circular Patterns

1. The Revolve sketch entities should not cross the Revolve centerline.
   - a. True
   - b. False

2. The system creates **symmetric** relations to all mirrored sketch entities.
   - a. True
   - b. False

3. An Equal relation makes the entities equal in size.
   - a. True
   - b. False

4. The system creates an On-Edge relation to all converted entities.
   - a. True
   - b. False

5. The Trim tool is used to trim 2D sketch entities.
   - a. True
   - b. False

6. The center of the circular pattern can be defined by an axis, a linear edge, or an angular dimension.
   - a. True
   - b. False

7. The center of rotation, spacing, number of copies, and features to copy are required when creating a circular pattern.
   - a. True
   - b. False

8. When the original feature is changed, all instances in the pattern will also change.
   - a. True
   - b. False

1. TRUE
2. TRUE
3. TRUE
4. TRUE
5. TRUE
6. TRUE
7. TRUE
8. TRUE

CHAPTER 7 (cont.)

Circular Patterns

Circular Patterns
Circular Base Mount

- As mentioned in the 1st half of this chapter, the Circular Pattern command creates an array of feature(s) around an axis.

- The elements required to create circular patterns are:

  * Center axis (Temporary Axis, Axis, an Edge, etc.)

  * Spacing between each instance

  * Number of instances in the pattern

  * Feature(s) to the pattern

- Only the original feature may be edited and changes made to the original feature will automatically be passed onto the instances within the pattern.

- The features to the pattern can be selected directly from the graphics area or from the Feature Manager tree.

- Instances in a pattern can be skipped. The skipped instances can be edited during or after the pattern is complete.

- The Temporary axis can be toggled on or off (View/Temporary Axis).

- This 2nd half of the chapter will guide you through the use of the Circular Pattern command, as well as the Curve Driven Pattern command.

Circular Base Mount
Circular Patterns

Dimensioning Standards: **ANSI**

Units: **INCHES** – 3 Decimals

Tools Needed:

Insert Sketch	Line	Mirror Dynamic
Add Geometric Relations	Dimension	Base/Boss Revolve
Revolve Cut	Circular Pattern	Fillet/Round

1. Creating the Base Sketch:

- From the <u>Front</u> plane, start a new Sketch .

- Sketch the profile on the right side of the revolve centerline as shown.

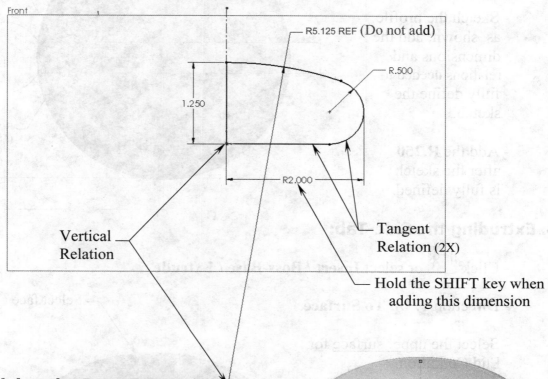

R5.125 REF (Do not add)

R.500

1.250

R2.000

Vertical Relation

Tangent Relation (2X)

Hold the SHIFT key when adding this dimension

2. Revolving the Base Feature:

- Click or select: **Insert / Boss Base / Revolve**.

- Revolve Direction: **Blind**.

- Revolve Angle: **360 deg**.

- Click **OK** .

3. Creating the first Side-Tab sketch:

- Select the <u>Top</u> plane and open a new Sketch

- Sketch the profile as shown; add the dimensions and relations needed to fully define the sketch.

- Add the **R.250** after the sketch is fully defined.

Top

R.250

R.575

.500

R 1.500
(Arc's Center is Coincident with Origin).

2.500

4. Extruding the Side-Tab:

- Click or select **Insert / Boss-Base / Extrude**.

- Direction 1: **Up To Surface**.

- Select the <u>upper surface</u> for End Condition.

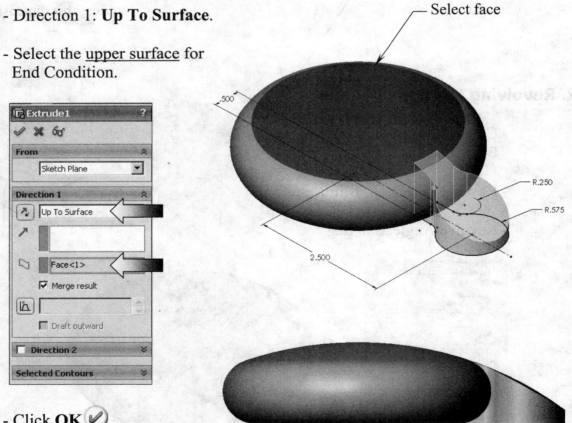

Select face

Extrude1

From

Sketch Plane

Direction 1

Up To Surface

Face<1>

☑ Merge result

☐ Draft outward

☐ Direction 2

Selected Contours

.500

R.250

R.575

2.500

- Click **OK** ✓ .

5. Adding a CounterBore Hole:

- Using the "traditional method" sketch the profile of the Counter-Bore on the <u>Front</u> plane.

(To create the "Virtual Diameter" dimensions 1st click the centerline then any other entity and place the dimension on the other side of the centerline).

Virtual Diameter: Add dimension from the center-line to the end point of the line on the left of the profile.

- Add the 2 Diameter and the 2 Depth dimensions .

- Add the relations needed to fully define the sketch.

Mid-Point Relation

6. Cutting the C'Bore:

- Click or select: **Insert /Cut / Revolve**.

- Revolve Direction: **Blind**.

- Revolve Angle **360 deg**.

- Click **OK** .

7. Creating the circular pattern:

- Click 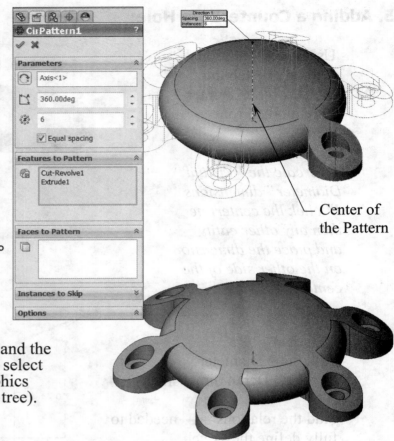 Circular Pattern (below Linear).

- From the **View** menu, select the **Temporary-Axis** option.

- Select the **Axis** in the middle of the part as noted.

- Set Pattern Angle to **360°**

- Enter **6** for the Number of Instances.

- For Features to Pattern, select both the **Side Tab** and the CounterBore hole (either select the C'Bore from the graphics area or from the Feature tree).

- Click **OK** ✓.

Center of the Pattern

8. Creating a new Plane:

- Click or select: **Insert / Reference Geometry / Plane**.

- Select **Offset Distance** option.

- Enter **1.300 in.** as the distance.

- Select the **TOP** reference plane from the Feature Manger tree to offset from.

- Click **OK** ✓.

9. Creating the Pockets Sketch:

- Select the <u>new plane</u> (Plane1) and open a new sketch.

- Use the **Dynamic Mirror** and sketch the profile as shown.

- Add the dimensions and relations as needed to fully define the sketch.

- Use **Circular Sketch Pattern** to make a total of 6 instances of the pocket.

10. Cutting the Pockets:

- Click or select: **Insert / Cut / Extrude**.

- For direction 1: use **Offset From Surface**.

- Select the **bottom surface** to offset from.

- Enter **.125 in**. for Depth.

- Click **OK** .

11. Adding the .0625" Fillets:

- Click **Fillet** or select: **Insert / Features / Fillet-Round**.

- Enter **.0625 in**. for Radius size.

- Select all upper and lower <u>edges of the 6 tabs</u>.

Top & bottom 12 edges

- Click **OK** ✅.

12. Adding the .125" Fillets:

- Click **Fillet** or select: **Insert / Features / Fillet-Round.**

- Enter **.125 in**. for Radius size.

- Select all edges on <u>the side of the 6 tabs</u> or select the 6 faces as noted.

Either select 12 Edges, or select 6 Faces

- Click **OK** ✅.

13. Adding the .015" Fillets:

- Click **Fillet** or select **Insert / Features / Fillet-Round**.

- Enter **.015 in**. for radius size.

- Select <u>all edges</u> of the 6 Pockets and the 6 Counterbores.

- Click **OK** ✓.

14. Saving your work:

- Click **File / Save As**.

- Enter **Circular Base Mount** for file name.

- Click **Save**.

Questions for Review

Circular Patterns

1. The Circular Patterns command can also be selected from Insert / Pattern Mirror / Circular Pattern.
    a. True
    b. False

2. A Temporary Axis can be used as the center of the pattern.
    a. True
    b. False

3. A linear edge can also be used as the center of the circular pattern.
    a. True
    b. False

4. The Temporary Axis can be toggled ON / OFF under View / Temporary Axis.
    a. True
    b. False

5. The instances in the circular pattern can be skipped during and after the pattern is created.

    a. True
    b. False

6. If an *instance* of the patterned feature is deleted, the whole pattern will also be deleted.
    a. True
    b. False

7. If the *original* patterned feature is deleted, the whole pattern will also be deleted.
    a. True
    b. False

8. When the Equal spacing check box is enabled, the total angle (360°) must be used.
    a. True
    b. False

7. TRUE	8. FALSE
5. TRUE	6. FALSE
3. TRUE	4. TRUE
1. TRUE	2. TRUE

CHAPTER 7 (cont.)

Curve Driven Patterns

Curve Driven Patterns
Universal Bracket

- The **Curve Drive Pattern** PropertyManager appears when you create
  a new curve driven pattern feature or when you edit an existing curve driven pattern feature.

- The PropertyManager controls the following properties:

Pattern Direction: Select a curve, edge, sketch entity, or select a sketch from the FeatureManager to use as the path for the pattern. If necessary, click Reverse Direction to change the direction of the pattern.

Number of Instances: Set a value for the number of instances of the seed feature in the pattern.

Equal spacing: Sets equal spacing between each pattern instance. The separation between instances depends on the curve selected for Pattern Direction and on the Curve method.

Spacing: (Available if you do not select Equal spacing) Set a value for the distance between pattern instances along the curve. The distance between the curve and the Features to Pattern is measured normal to the curve.

Curve method: Defines the direction of the pattern by transforming how you use the curve selected for Pattern Direction. Select one of the following:

* **Transform curve**. The delta X and delta Y distances from the origin of the selected curve to the seed feature are maintained for each instance.

* **Offset curve**: The normal distance from the origin of the selected curve to the seed feature is maintained for each instance.

Alignment method: Select one of the following:

* **Tangent to curve**: Aligns each instance tangent to the curve selected for Pattern direction

* **Align to seed**: Aligns each instance to match the original alignment of the seed feature of **Curve method** and **Alignment method** selections.

* **Face normal:** (For 3D curves only) Select the face on which the 3D curve lies to create the curve driven pattern.

Curve Driven Pattern and Hole Wizard
Universal Bracket

Dimensioning Standards: **ANSI**

Units: **INCHES** – 3 Decimals

Tools Needed:

 Insert Sketch

 Convert Entities

 Offset Entities

 Boss Base Extrude

 Hole Wizard

 Curve Driven Pattern

1. Opening the existing file:

- Go to: The Training Files folder
   Open a copy of the file named:
   Curve Driven Pattern.sldprt

- **Edit** the **Sketch1.**

- Make sure the sketch1 is fully define before extruding.

2. Extruding the Base:

- Click or select:
**Insert / Features /
Boss Base Extrude**.

- Use **Mid Plane**
for Direction1.

- Enter **2.00 in**. for
Depth.

- Click **OK** ✅.

3. Creating the sketch of the 1st hole:

- Select the <u>face</u> as indicated and open a new sketch.

- Sketch a Centerline at the
Mid-Point of the two arcs.

- Add a Circle on the Mid-
Point of the centerline.

- Add a Ø**.250 in**. dimension.

Sketch face

Ø.250

Mid Point
with edges

4. Cutting the hole:

- Click or select:
Insert / Cut / Extrude.

- Select **Through All**
for Direction1.

- Click **OK** ✅ .

5. Constructing the Curve-Sketch to drive the Pattern:

- Select the <u>face</u> as noted* and open a new sketch .

- Select all Outer-Edges of the part (Right mouse click on an edge & Select-Tangency).

- Click or select **Tools / Sketch Entities / Offset Entities**.

- Enter **.563 in**. for Offset Distance.

- Click Reverse if necessary to place the new profile on the **INSIDE**.

- **Exit** the sketch mode and change the name of the sketch to **CURVE1**.

Select all Outer Edges to offset.

Sketch Face*

6. Creating the Curve-Driven Pattern:

- Click 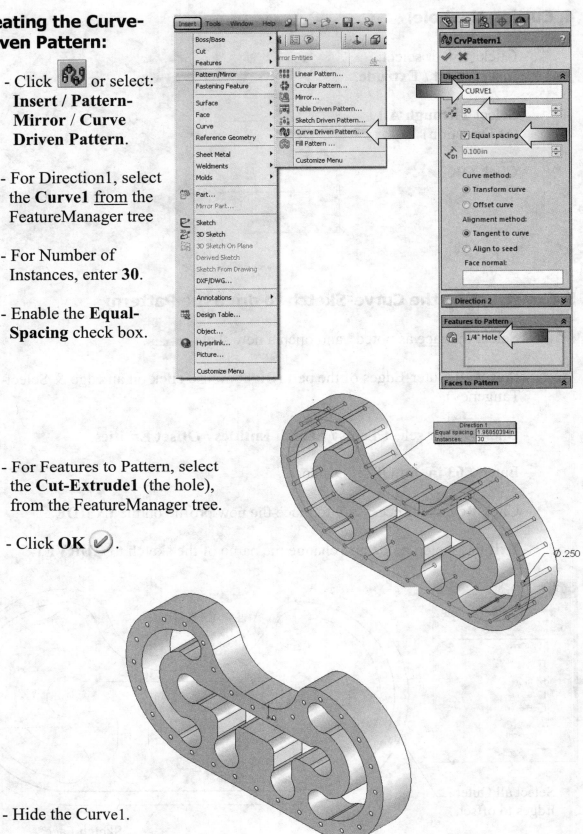 or select: **Insert / Pattern-Mirror / Curve Driven Pattern**.

- For Direction1, select the **Curve1** <u>from</u> the FeatureManager tree

- For Number of Instances, enter **30**.

- Enable the **Equal-Spacing** check box.

- For Features to Pattern, select the **Cut-Extrude1** (the hole), from the FeatureManager tree.

- Click **OK** ✅.

- Hide the Curve1.

7. Constructing the 2nd Curve:

- Select the <u>Front</u> plane and open a new sketch.

- Select all **Outer-Edges** of the part and click or select: **Tools / Sketch Entities / Convert Entities**.

- **Exit the Sketch** and change the sketch name to: **CURVE2**.

Front Plane

Right click & pick Select Tangency

8. Adding the Hole Wizard:

- Click or select **Insert / Features / Hole Wizard**.

- Select the Counter-Sink button and set the following:

* Standard: **Ansi Inch**
* Type: **Flat Head Screw** (100)
* Size: **1/4**
* Fit: **Normal**
* End Condition: **Blind**
* Depth: **1.250 in**.

- Select the **Position** tab (arrow) and click the **3D Sketch** button `3D Sketch`
  This option allows the holes to be placed on non-planar surfaces as well.

1st: Place the center of hole approx. here, on the flat surface...

- Click **OK** ✔.

2nd: Add a Mid-Point relation between the center point and the line.

9. Creating the Curve Driven Pattern:

- Click or select:
**Insert / Pattern-Mirror
Curve Driven Pattern**.

- For Direction1, select
the **Curve2** from the
FeatureManager tree.

- For Number of Instances,
enter **30**.

- Enable **Equal Spacing** option.

- Enable **Tangent To Curve** option.

Direction 1	
Equal spacing:	1.96850394in
Instances:	30

- For Features to Pattern, select the
CSK-Hole from the FeatureManager tree.

- Click **OK** ✅.

10. Saving a copy your work:

- Click **File / Save As**.

- Enter **Curve Driven Pattern** for file name.

- Click **Save**.

CHAPTER 8

Part Configurations

Part Configurations
Machined Block

- This chapter reviews most of the commands that were covered in the previous chapters. Upon successful completion of this lesson, you will have a better understanding of how and when to:

  * Sketch on planes and planar surfaces.

  * Sketch fillets and model fillets.

  * Dimensions and Geometric Relations.

  * Extruded Cuts and Bosses.

  * Linear Patterns.

  * Using the Hole-Wizard option.

  * Create new Planes.

  * Mirror features.

  * Create new Part Configurations; an option that allows the user to develop and manage families of parts and assemblies.

- Configuration options are available in Part and Assembly environments.

- After the model is completed, it will be used again in a drawing chapter to further discuss the details of creating an Engineering drawing.

Machined Block
Part Configurations

View Orientation Hot Keys:

Ctrl + 1 = Front View
Ctrl + 2 = Back View
Ctrl + 3 = Left View
Ctrl + 4 = Right View
Ctrl + 5 = Top View
Ctrl + 6 = Bottom View
Ctrl + 7 = Isometric View
Ctrl + 8 = Normal To
        Selection

Dimensioning Standards: **ANSI**
Units: **INCHES** – 3 Decimals

Tools Needed:

	Insert Sketch		Line		Rectangle
	Circle		Sketch Fillet		Dimension
	Add Geometric Relations		Extruded Boss/Base		Extruded Cut
	Hole Wizard		Fillet		Linear Pattern

1. Sketching the base profile:

- Select the <u>Front</u> plane from the FeatureManager tree.

- Click or select **Insert / Sketch**.

- Sketch the profile below using the Line tool ⟍ .

- Add the dimensions ⬦ shown.

Zero is at the Origin

2. Extruding the base feature:

- Click 🗇 or select **Insert / Boss-Base / Extrude**.

- End Condition: **Blind** ⬈ .

- Extrude Depth: **6.00 in**. 🗠 .

- Click **OK** ✅ .

Reverse Direction →

3. Creating the pocket profiles:

- Select the <u>face</u> as indicated below for sketch plane.

- Click or select **Insert / Sketch**.

- Sketch the profile below using Rectangle ☐ and Sketch Fillet ⌐ tools.

- Add dimensions* ◇ or Relations ⊥ needed to fully define the sketch.

.625   .500   .500

1.250   1.250   1.250

R.080

1.000

2.000

Sketch Face

* To eliminate some of the redundant dimensions, use the Linear Pattern options to array the rectangle. (Tools/Sketch Tools/Linear Pattern).

▦ Linear Pattern...

* When using the Sketch Pattern options, a spacing dimension and a relation such as Collinear should be added, in order to fully define the sketch.

4. Cutting the pockets:

- Click ▣ or select **Insert / Cut / Extrude**.

- End Condition: **Blind**.

- Extrude Depth: **.500 in**.

- Click **OK** ✓.

Cut-Extrude1

From
Sketch Plane

Direction 1
Blind

0.500in

☐ Flip side to cut

☐ Draft outward

.500
1.250
.500
1.250
1.250
.625
R.080
1.000

5. Adding a CounterBore from the Hole Wizard:

- Select the face* as shown for sketch plane.

- Click or select **Insert / Features / Hole / Wizard**.

- Click the **Counterbore** button (Circled).

  - Use CBORE for ¼ Binding Head Machine Screw.

- Set the following: - Hole ∅: **.625**

        - C'bore ∅: **.875**

        - C'bore Depth: **.250**

  - **Uncheck** the Near Side Countersink check box.

Sketch Face*

- Select the **Positions Tab** (arrow). (Note: the 3D Sketch button is only available if none of the faces were selected prior to clicking the Hole Wizard).

- Add Dimensions as shown to position the C'bore.

- Click **OK** ✓.

6. Patterning the Counterforce:

- Click or select **Insert / Pattern Mirror / Linear Pattern**.

- Select the **bottom edge** as direction .

- Enter **2.00 in**. for Spacing .

- Type **3** for Number of Instances .

- Select the C'bore feature as Features to Pattern .

- Click **OK** .

7. Creating the Mirror-Plane:

- Click or select **Insert / Reference Geometry / Plane.**

- Select the <u>Right</u> plane as Reference Entities .

- Click Offset Distance and enter **2.00 in**. .

- Use the Flip option if needed to place
  the new plane on the **right side**.

- Click **OK** .

8. Mirroring the C'bores:

- Click or select **Mirror** under **Insert / Pattern Mirror menu**.

- Select the <u>new plane</u> (Plane1) as Mirror Face/Plane .

- Choose the C'bore and its Pattern as Features to Pattern .

- Click **OK** .

- Rotate the model around to verify the results of the mirror.

9. Creating the blind holes on the top surface:

- Select the <u>top face</u>* as the new sketch plane.

- Click or select **Insert / Sketch**.

- Sketch 4 Circles as shown.

- Add Dimensions and Relations needed to fully define the sketch.

Ø.275

Sketch Face*

5.000

.500

.500   1.000

10. Cutting the 4 holes:

- Click or select **Insert / Cut / Extrude**.

- End Condition: **Blind.**

- Extrude Depth: **1.00 in.**

- Click **OK** .

11. Creating a Cutaway section: (in a separate configuration).

Default Configuration   **New Cutaway Configuration**

- At the top of the FeatureManager tree, select the Configuration tab.

- Right click on the name of the part and select **Add Configuration**.

- Under Configuration Name, enter: **Cutaway View.**

- Click **OK**

Optional: enter a comment to reference the changes in this configuration.

> ### 💡 Configurations
>
> The Configuration option allows you to create multiple variations of a part or assembly and save all changes within the same document.

12. Sketching a profile for the cut:

- Select the face indicated as the new sketch plane.

- Click or select **Insert / Sketch**.

- Sketch the profile as shown using the Corner Rectangle 🔲 tool.

- Add the dimensions or relations needed to fully define the sketch.

Sketch face

3.250

.250

1.500   2.750

13. Making the section cut:

- Click or select **Insert / Cut / Extrude**.

- End Condition: **Through All.**

- Click **OK** ✅ .

- The Cutaway section view.

14. Switching between the Configurations:

- Double-click on Default configuration to see the original part.

- Double-click on Cutaway View configuration to see the cut feature.

Double-click to toggle
between Configurations*

* The **Yellow** icon next to the name of the configuration means it is **active**.

* The **Grey** icon next to the name of the configuration means it is **inactive**.

Default Configuration

Cutaway Configuration

- The Cutaway configuration will be used again in one of the drawing chapters.

- There is no limit on how many configurations can be created and saved in a part document.

- If a part has many configurations, it is might be better to use a design table to help manage them (refer to chapter 20 in this textbook for more infomation on how to create multiple configurations using the Design Table option).

15. Splitting the FeatureManager pane:

- Locate the Split Handle on top of the FeatureManager tree and drag it down about half way.

Drag the
Split Handle

- Click the ConfigurationManager tab (arrow) to change the lower half to ConfigurationManager.

- Double click on the **Default** configuration to activate it.

16. Creating a new configuration:

- Right click the name of the part (arrow) and select: **Add Configuration** (arrow).

- For the name of the new configuration, enter: **Machine Features Suppressed**.

- Click **OK** to close the config. dialog (see next page)

- Hold the Control key and select the following cut features from the tree: **Cut-Extrude1, C'Bore for 1/4 Binding Head, LPattern1, Mirror1,** and **Cut-Extrude2**.

- Release the Control key and click the **Suppress** button from the popup window.

- The machine features are now suppressed and their feature icons are diplayed in grey color on the feature tree.

The machine features are now suppressed

- Double click on each configurations to see the changes between each one.

17. Saving your work:

- Select **File / Save As / Machined Block / Save**.

Questions for Review

Part Configurations

1. The five basic steps to create an extruded feature are:
   - Select a sketch Plane OR a planar surface
   - Activate Sketch Pencil (Insert / Sketch)
   - Sketch the profile
   - Define the profile (Dimensions / Relations)
   - Extrude the profile
     a. True
     b. False

2. When the extrude type is set to Blind, a depth dimension has to be specified as the End-Condition.
   a. True
   b. False

3. More than one closed sketch profiles on the same surface can be extruded at the same time to the same depth.
   a. True
   b. False

4. In the Hole Wizard definition, the Counter bore's parameters such as bore diameter, hole depth, etc. cannot be changed.
   a. True
   b. False

5. Holes created using the Hole Wizard cannot be patterned.
   a. True
   b. False

6. Configurations in a part can be toggled ON / OFF by double clicking on their icons.
   a. True
   b. False

7. Every part document can only have *one* configuration in it.
   a. True
   b. False

7. FALSE

5. FALSE   6. TRUE

3. TRUE   4. FALSE

1. TRUE   2. TRUE

Exercise: Using Vary-Sketch.

1. The Vary Sketch allows the pattern instances to change dimensions as they repeat.
2. Create the part as shown, focusing on the Linear Pattern & Vary-Sketch option.

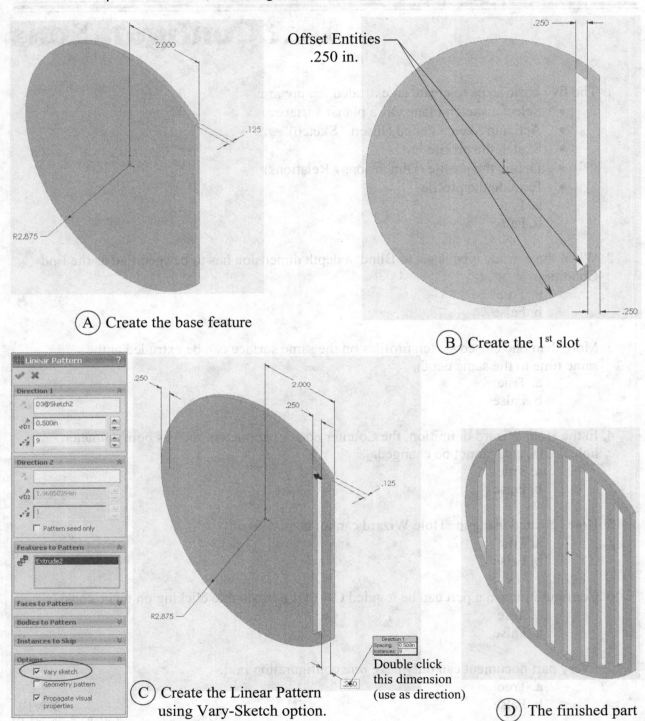

Ⓐ Create the base feature

Offset Entities
.250 in.

Ⓑ Create the 1st slot

Ⓒ Create the Linear Pattern
using Vary-Sketch option.

Double click
this dimension
(use as direction)

Ⓓ The finished part

3. Save your work as: **Vary Sketch_Exe.**

CHAPTER 8 (cont.)

Using Contour Selection

Contour Selection
Fixture

- The **Contour Selection** tool allows the SolidWorks user to select one or more closed contours in a sketch for use in a feature.

- Any sketches created in SolidWorks or imported from another CAD program, can be <u>reused</u> by using the Contour Select tool. This useful command allows the user to use a partial sketch to create features.

- The examples below show many possible contours available for extruding solid features within a single sketch.

- This chapter and its exercise will guide you through the use of the Contour-Selection tool to convert 2D sketches into 3D models.

Fixture
Using Contour Selection

Dimensioning Standards: **ANSI**
Units: **INCHES** – 3 Decimals

Tools Needed:

 Insert Sketch   Line   Centerline

 Circle   Mirror   Dimension

 Add Geometric Relations   Fillet   Chamfer

 Extruded Boss/Base   Extruded Cut   Contour Select Tool

1. Opening the main sketch:

- From the Training Files folder, open the SolidWorks document named:
    Contour Selection.sldprt

- **Edit** the sketch. Verify that the sketch is fully defined.

2. Extruding the Base:

- Click or select **Insert / Boss-Base / Extrude**.

- End Condition: **Blind**.

- Extrude Depth: **1.00 in**.   - Reverse Direction **Enabled**

- Click **OK**.

3. Showing the Sketch:

- From the FeatureManager tree, click the + symbol next to **Extrude1** to expand it.

- Right click on **Sketch1** and select **Show**.

- The sketch1 is now visible in gray color.

4. Using the Contour Selection Tool:

- Right click on the line as indicated and select **Contour Selection Tool** .

Right click on
one of the lines...

Select Other
Select Chain
Contour Select Tool
View   ▶
Edit Sketch
Edit Sketch Plane
Hide Sketch
Parent/Child...
Go To Feature (in Tree)
Feature Properties
Rollback
       ⌄

💡 **Contour Selection**

* When **reusing a sketch**, you can select only on the original face that has the original sketch on it. If, for example, part of the face has been extruded, the Contour Select tool does not recognize the new face.

- Hold down the CONTROL key and select the areas as indicated.

Hold down the
CONTROL key
and select 2 faces.

💡 **Color indicators**

* As you move the pointer over the circles, the color of the contours changes to Brown and then Purple when you select them.

5. Extruding the selected contours as cut features:

- Click or select **Insert / Cut / Extrude**.

- End Condition: **Though All**

- Click **OK** ✓.

- The slots are created from a sketch containing multiple contours.

6. Re-using the same sketch:

- Right click on the line indicated and select **Contour Selection Tool** .

Right click on
one of the lines...

- Hold down the *CONTROL* key and select inside the faces as indicated.

Hold down the
Control key and
select 2 faces...

7. Cutting the selected contours:

- Click or select **Insert / Cut / Extrude**.

- End Condition: **Blind.**

- Extrude Depth: **.250 in**.

- Click **OK** ✅.

- The Recesses are
  created from
  the same sketch.

8. Continuing with other contours:

- Right click on the circle indicated and select: **Contour Selection Tool** .

Right click on
one of the circles...

Select Other
Select Chain
Contour Select Tool
View
Show Curvature
Edit Sketch
Edit Sketch Plane
Hide Sketch
Parent/Child...
Go To Feature (in Tree)
Feature Properties

- Hold down the CONTROL key and select the faces as shown below.

Hold down the
CONTROL key
and select 4 faces.

9. Extruding the selected contours:

- Click or select **Insert / Boss-Base / Extrude**.

- End Condition: **Blind.**

- Extrude Depth: **1.00 in**.

- Click **OK** ✓.

- The 4 alignment pins are created from the same sketch.

10. Selecting the center contours:

- Right click on the circle indicated and select: **Contour Selection Tool** .

Right click
on this circle...

Select Other
Select Chain
Contour Select Tool
View
Show Curvature
Edit Sketch
Edit Sketch Plane
Hide Sketch
Parent/Child...
Go To Feature (in Tree)
Feature Properties

- Hover the mouse cursor over the circle in the center, select the contour when the color changes to Brown.

Select this face when
it turns Brown...

11. Extruding the selected contours as cut features:

- Click or select **Insert / Cut / Extrude**.

- End Condition: **Though All.**

- Click **OK** ✓.

- The center hole
  is created from
  the main sketch.

12. Selecting the next contour:

- Right click on the circle indicated and select: **Contour Selection Tool** .

Right click on
the outer circle...

Select Other
Select Chain
Contour Select Tool
View
Show Curvature
Edit Sketch
Edit Sketch Plane
Hide Sketch
Parent/Child...
Go To Feature (in Tree)
Feature Properties

- Select the face as indicated when its color changes to Brown.

Select this face when
it turns Brown...

13. Cutting the center hole:

- Click or select **Insert / Cut / Extrude**.

- End Condition: **Blind.**

- Extrude Depth: **.500 in**.

- Click **OK** ✅.

- The center hole is created from the main sketch.

☀ Hide Sketch

* When the Contour Select Tool is being used, the sketch remains visible (Yellow Icon) so that it can be reused in other features.

* When finished, right-click on the sketch and select **Hide**.

14. Save your work as: Contour Selection.

Questions for Review

Using Contour Selection

1. The Contour Select Tool allows you to select one or more closed contours in a sketch to convert into a feature.
    a. True
    b. False

2. When extruding several contours at the same time, they can have different depths.
    a. True
    b. False

3. Opened contours can be selected and extruded.
    a. True
    b. False

4. If several contours are selected, they will have to be extruded to the same depth.
    a. True
    b. False

5. As you drag the pointer over the contours, their colors change from Brown to Purple when selected.
    a. True
    b. False

6. The sketches cannot be reused; a new sketch has to be made each time.
    a. True
    b. False

7. The selected contours can be edited at anytime.
    a. True
    b. False

8. To select multiple contours, hold down the key:
    a. Shift
    b. Control
    c. Alt

1. True   2. False
3. False   4. True
5. True   6. False
7. True   8. B

Exercise: Contour Selection

1. From the Training Files folder, open the document named: **Contour Selection_Exe**.
2. Use the Contour Selection tool to extrude all features.
3. The 4 holes are thru holes.
4. The upper boss is centered of the thickness.
5. Use the instructions on the next page, if needed.

6. Save a copy of your work as: **Contour Selection_Exe**.

1. Activating the Contour Select tool:

- Right click on one of the lines and pick: **Contour-Select Tool**.

- Hove the mouse in the area as noted and select it when the color changes to magenta.

Select in this area

2. Extruding the base:

- Create an **Extruded Boss-Base** using **Mid Plane** at **1.500"** thick.

3. Selecting another contour:

- Expand the Boss-Extrude1 feature and **show** the **Sketch1**.

Select this contour

- Right click on one of the lines and pick: **Contour Select Tool**.

- Select the upper contour when the color changes to magenta.

4. Extruding the upper boss:

- Extrude the selected contour using **Mid Plane** at **.750"** thick.

5. Adding fillets:

- Add a **.500"** fillet to the 4 Edges as indicated.

Fillet 4 edges

6. Saving your work:

- Save a copy of your work as: **Contour_Selection_Exe**.

CHAPTER 8 cont.

Repairing Part Errors

Understanding and Repairing Part Errors

When an error occurs, SolidWorks will try and solve it based on the settings below:

To pre-set the rebuild action:

A. Click **Options** (Standard toolbar) or **Tools**, **Options**.

B. Select **Stop**, **Continue**, or **Prompt** for **When rebuild error occurs**, then click **OK**. With **Stop** or **Prompt**, the rebuild action stops for each error so you can fix feature failures one at a time.

Error Symbols and Description

Indicates an error with the model. This icon appears on the document name at the top of the FeatureManager design tree, and on the feature that contains the error. The text of the part or feature is in red.

Indicates an error with a feature. This icon appears on the feature name in the FeatureManager design tree. The text of the feature is in red.

Indicates a warning underneath the node indicated. This icon appears on the document name at the top of the Feature-Manager design tree and on the parent feature in the FeatureManager design tree whose child feature issued the error. The text of the feature is in Olive Green.

Indicates a warning with a **feature** or **sketch**. This icon appears on the specific feature in the FeatureManager design tree that issued the warning. The text of the feature or sketch is in Olive Green.

1. Opening a part document:

- Insert the Training File folder, browse to the Repair Errors folder, and open the part named: **Repair Errors**.

- When opening a document that contains errors, the What's Wrong dialog box will appear and display where the errors are located and suggest some solutions in solving them.

- **Expand** each feature on the FeatureManager tree and hover the pointer over the **Sketch3**.

- An explanation about the error or the warning is displayed in the tooltip. This is the same as right clicking on the error and selecting What's Wrong.

- Another way to see the explanation about the error is to right click on the error and select: What's Wrong.

- The What's Wrong dialog box pops up displaying the same explanation about the selected error. Enable the **Show Warnings** checkbox (arrow) to see the warnings after each rebuild.

- From the Sketch toolbar click the **Display / Delete-Relations** button.

- The relations or dimensions that contain errors will appeared in different colors, Olive Green in this case.

Display/Delete Relations
Displays and deletes geometric relations.

Tangent8 is missing an entity

- **Select** the relation **Tangent8** from the relation dialog box. An arc and the missing entity are highlighted. The missing entity appears in **Red** along with an **Olive Green** tangent symbol above.

- **Delete** the **Tangent8** relation.

- A message on the bottom right of the screen appears, indicating that: **The sketch can now find a valid solution**.

- To see the status for the rest of the relations and dimensions, change from **Over Defining / Not Solved** to **All In This Sketch**.

- Select the **Coincident3**. An endpoint of the line is coincident to a missing edge. **Delete** this Coincident3.

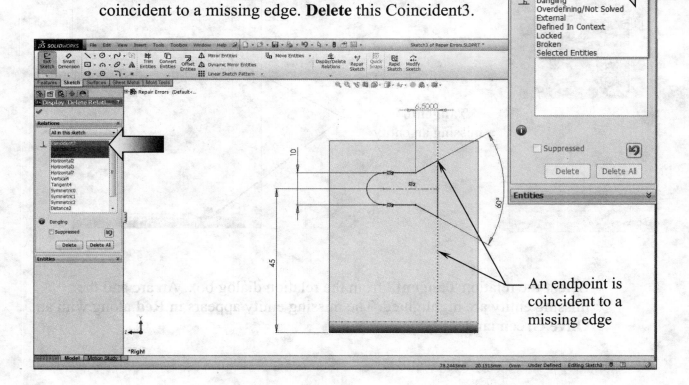

An endpoint is coincident to a missing edge

- **Delete** also the **Coincident5**. It's missing the same edge as the previous relation.

- The dimension **6.500** is dangling. It was also measured to a missing entity, **delete it**.

- **Add** 3 new dimensions as indicated to fully define this sketch. **Exit** the sketch when completed.

Delete this
Dangling dimension —

Add 3 new →
dimensions

- After exiting the sketch, SolidWorks continues to report other errors still remained in the part. The **Sketch4** and **Sketch11** still need to be repaired.

- **Close** the What's Wrong dialog box.

3. Repairing the 2nd error:

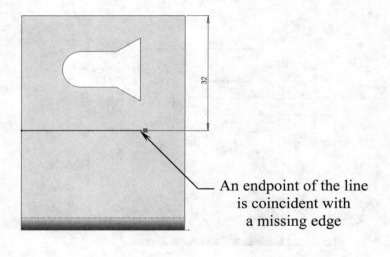

- Right click the **Sketch4** (under the Sketched Bend1 feature) and select **Edit Sketch**.

- Click the **Display / Delete Relations** button once again.

- Change the display relations option to **Dangling** (arrow).

- The **Coincident1** is dangled and has the Olive Green color. **Delete it**.

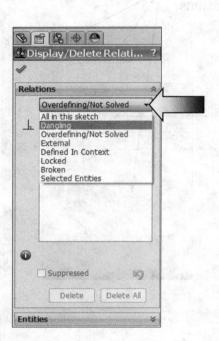

An endpoint of the line is coincident with a missing edge

- The endpoint of the line turns to Blue color. This indicates the sketch is under defined.

- **Drag and drop** the endpoint of the line until it touches the vertical right edge of the part. A coincident relation should be created automatically.

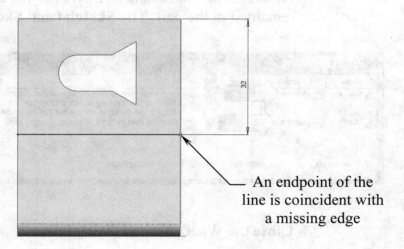

An endpoint of the line is coincident with a missing edge

- **Exit** the sketch or press **Control + Q**.

- SolidWorks continues to report the last error in the model. Click the **Continue (Ignore Error)** button to continue.

4. Repairing the 3rd error:

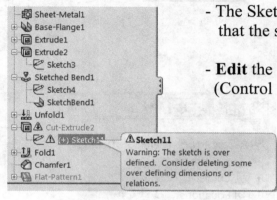

- The Sketch11 has a plus sign next to its name, this indicates that the sketch is Over Defined.

- **Edit** the **Sketch11**. Change to the Top orientation (Control + 5).

- Click the **Display / Delete Relations** button.

- Set the display relations option to: **Over Defining / Not Solved**.

- Select the **Collinear1** from the list. This relation shows a **Magenta** color next to its Collinear symbol.

- Delete the **Collinear1** from the list.

- This last step should bring the sketch back to its Fully Define status.

- **Exit** the sketch or press **Control + Q**.

5. Saving your work:

- Click **File / Save As**.

- Enter **Repair Errors (Completed)** for the name of the file.

- Click **Save**.

- All errors have been repaired. The Feature-Manager tree is now free of errors.

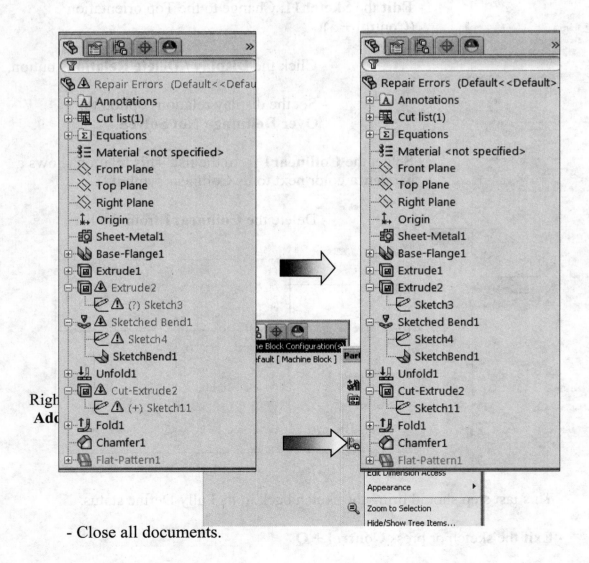

- Close all documents.

CHAPTER 9

Modeling Threads

Modeling Threads (external)
Threaded Insert

- Most of the time threads are not modeled in the part, instead they are represented with dashed lines and callouts in the drawings. But for non-standard threads they should be modeled in the part for use in some applications such as Stereo Lithography, Finite Element Analysis, etc.

- Two sketches are involved in making the threads:

  * A sweep path (a helix that controls the pitch, revolutions, starting angle, and left or right hand threads).

  * A sweep profile (shape and size of the threads).

- The sweep profile should be related to the sweep path with a **pierce** relation, which will move the sketch profile to the end of the path.

- The profile is swept along the path with the command swept cut and the interfered material is removed as the result of the cut.

- Most of the time the sweep cut command is used when creating threads but in some cases, the sweep boss command can also be used to add material to the sweep path when making the external threads.

- This chapter and its exercises will guide you through some special techniques on how internal and external threads can be modeled in SolidWorks.

Modeling Threads – External
Threaded Insert

View Orientation Hot Keys:

Ctrl + 1 = Front View
Ctrl + 2 = Back View
Ctrl + 3 = Left View
Ctrl + 4 = Right View
Ctrl + 5 = Top View
Ctrl + 6 = Bottom View
Ctrl + 7 = Isometric View
Ctrl + 8 = Normal To
        Selection

Dimensioning Standards: **ANSI**

Units: **INCHES** – 3 Decimals

Tools Needed:

 Insert Sketch   Line   Convert Entities

 Dimension   Add Geometric   Helix/Spiral
                                            Relations

 Extruded   Cut Sweep   Mirror
        Base / Revolve

1. Sketching the base profile:

- Select the <u>Front</u> plane from the FeatureManager Tree.

- Click Sketch or select: **Insert / Sketch**.

- Sketch the profile as shown below using the Line tool .

- Add dimensions to fully define the sketch.

(The Ordinate dimension options are under the Smart Dimension command).

2. Revolving the base feature:

- Click **Revolve** or select **Insert / Base / Revolve**.

- Revolve Direction: **Blind**.

- Revolve Angle: **360°**

- Click **OK** .

3. Creating the Sweep path:

- Select the <u>face</u> indicated as sketch face.

- Click Sketch or select: **Insert / Sketch**.

- Select the **circular edge** as indicated.

- Click **Convert Entities** , the select edge is converted to a circle and brought to the sketch face.

Select edge to convert

Sketch face

4. Creating the Helix:

- Switch to the Features tool tab and select the helix command under the Curves button or select:
Insert / Curve / Helix Spiral.

- Defined by: **Pitch and Revolution.**

    * Pitch: **.125 in**.

    * Revolution: **11.00**

    * Start Angle: **0.00°**

    * Reverse direction: **Enabled.**

- Click **OK** .

- The resulting Helix (the sweep path).

5. Sketching the Sweep profile:

- Select the <u>Top</u> plane from the FeatureManager Tree.

- Click or **Insert / Sketch**.

- Sketch a Triangle and dimension as shown.

- Add a Pierce relation between the upper endpoint of the centerline and the Helix.

(Either use the Mirror option to create this sketch, or add a Symmetric relation between the two angled lines and the centerline).

Virtual Sharp

R.010

.100

60.00°

R.010

.100

60.00°

Pierce relation between the Helix & Endpoint (Click on the helix, near the end of the last revolution and the end-point of the centerline).

- The sketch should be fully defined at this point.

- **Exit** the Sketch or click .

6. Sweeping the profile along the path.

- From the Features tool tab click 🖻 or Select **Insert / Cut / Sweep**.

- Select the triangular profile as sweep profile ⌒⁰ .

- Select the helix as sweep path ⌒ .

- Click **OK** ✅ .

- The 1st half of the threads, clockwise direction (right hand).

7. Using the Mirror Bodies option:

- Select **Mirror** from the Features tool tab or click: **Insert / Pattern-Mirror/Mirror**.

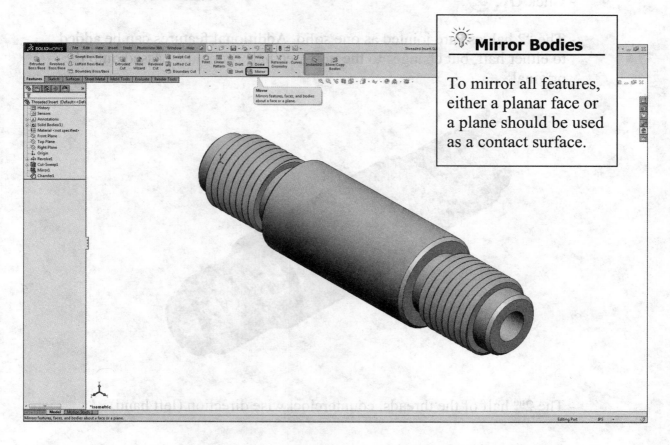

> **Mirror Bodies**
>
> To mirror all features, either a planar face or a plane should be used as a contact surface.

- Select the mirror face as indicated.

- Expand the Bodies-To-Mirror section and select the part from the graphics area as noted.

Body to Mirror

Select face

- Click **OK** ✅.

- The "2 halves" are jointed as one solid. Additional features can be added to either half, but changes to the mirrored half cannot be passed onto the original.

- The 2nd half of the threads, counterclockwise direction (left hand).

8. Adding chamfers:

- Click **Chamfer** or **Insert / Features / Chamfers**.

- Select the **4 edges** as indicated.

- Enter **.050 in**. for Depth .

- Enter **45°** for Angle .

- Click **OK** .

Select 4 edges

9. Saving the finished part.

- Select **File / Save as / Threaded Insert / Save**.

Questions for Review

Modeling Threads

1. It is proper to select the sketch plane first before activating the sketch pencil.
   - a. True
   - b. False

2. To create a sweep feature, the sweep path should be created first and the sweep profile created later.
   - a. True
   - b. False

3. The Helix / Spiral command can be selected from Insert / Curve / Helix-Spiral menus.
   - a. True
   - b. False

4. Taper Helix option is not supported in SolidWorks.
   - a. True
   - b. False

5. A Helix can be defined by pitch and revolution.
   - a. True
   - b. False

6. The Sweep profile should not have any relations with the sweep path.
   - a. True
   - b. False

7. Either a planar surface or a plane can be used to perform a Mirror-Bodies (All) feature.
   - a. True
   - b. False

8. Several model edges can be chamfered at the same time if their values are the same.
   - a. True
   - b. False

9. The mirrored half is a dependent feature; it cannot be used to change the original half.
   - a. True
   - b. False

9. TRUE
7. TRUE
5. TRUE
3. TRUE
1. TRUE

8. TRUE
6. FALSE
4. FALSE
2. TRUE

Exercise: Modeling Threads - Internal

1. Dimensions provided are for solid modeling practice purposes.
2. Dimensions are in Inches, 3 decimal places.
3. Use the instructions on the following pages, if needed.
4. Save your work as **Nut – Internal Threads**.

DETAIL B

SECTION A-A

1. Starting with the base sketch:

- Select the <u>Front</u> plane and open a new sketch.

- Sketch a 6 sided Polygon and add the dimensions and relation shown.

Ø.650

1.125

Horizontal

2. Extruding the base:

- Extrude the sketch using **Mid Plane** and **.525"** thick.

3. Removing the Sharp edges:

- Select the <u>Top</u> plane and open another sketch.

- Sketch the profile shown.
  * (See the note on page 9-15 on Virtual Diameter dim).

(*) 1.034

.060

- Add the dimensions and the Tangent relation as noted.

- Mirror the profile using the horizontal centerline.

Tangent

1.034

.060

- Revolve Cut with **Blind** and **360°** angle.

- Click **OK**.

4. Creating a new plane:

- Select the <u>front face</u> of the part and click **Insert / Reference Geometry / Plane**.

- The **Offset Distance** should be selected automatically; enter **.105"** for distance.

- Click **OK**.

5. Creating the sweep path:

- Select the <u>new plane</u> and open a new sketch. (Starting from this offset location will prevent an undercut from happening where the thread starts).

Convert this edge

- Select the circular edge as indicated and click: **Convert Entities**.

- The selected edge turns into a sketch circle.

- Click the **Helix** command or select: **Insert / Curve / Helix-Spiral**.

- Enter the following:
  * Pitch = **.105"**
  * Reverse Direction: **Enabled**.
  * Revolutions: **7**
  * Start Angle: **0.00 deg**.
  * **Clockwise**

- Click **OK**.

6. Creating the sweep profile:

- Select the <u>Top</u> plane, open a new sketch and sketch the profile using Dynamic Mirror.

- Add the dimensions as shown to fully define the sketch.

- Add a **.010"** sketch fillet to the tip.

R.010

45.00°

.094

- Add a **Pierce** relation between the midpoint of the vertical line and the 1st revolution of the helix.

- **Exit** the sketch.

Pierce

7. Creating the swept cut:

- Change to the **Features** toolbar.

- Click **Swept Cut**.

- Select the triangular sketch for Profile.

- Select the Helix for Path.

- The Profile is Swept along the Path.

- Click **OK**.

8. Verifying the cut:

- Select the <u>Right</u> plane and click **Section View**.

- Verify the cut. Look at the section view from different orientations.

- Change the dimension **.094"** in the profile sketch to **.100"**. Click **Rebuild** to update the change.

9. Saving your work:

- Save your work as **Nut – Internal Threads**.

Change from .094 to .100

Exercise: Internal & External Thread

A. Internal Threads:

1. Creating the Revolve Sketch:

- Select the <u>Front</u> plane and open a new sketch plane as shown.

- Sketch the profile and add relations & dimensions as shown.

Front Plane

4.090

20.00°

Ø.500

Ø.280

Ø.940

Diameter Dimension*

* To create the Virtual Diameter dimension:
- Select the centerline and the line above it as shown, move the mouse cursor below the centerline until the preview of the diameter-dimension pops up, click to place it.

2. Revolving the Body:

- Revolve the sketch a full 360 deg. and click **OK** ✅.

Revolve1

Axis of Revolution

Line1

Direction1

Blind

360.00deg

4.090

Ø.500

20.00°

Ø.280

Ø.94

3. Creating the cutout features:

- From the <u>Front</u> plane, sketch the profiles of the cutouts.

- Use the Mirror function where applicable. Add Relations & Dimensions to fully
  define the sketch.

4. Extruding the Cutouts:

- Click **Extruded Cut** and select **Through All** for **Both-Directions**.

- Click **OK** ✅.

5. Sketching the Slot Profile:

- From the <u>Top</u> plane, sketch the profile of the slot (use the Straight Slot options).

- Add Relations & Dimensions to fully define the sketch.

6. Cutting the Slot:

- Click **Extruded Cut** and select **Through All** for Both-Directions.

- Click **OK** .

7. Adding Chamfers:

- Add a **chamfer** to both ends of the holes.

- Chamfer Depth = **.050 in**. - Chamfer Angle = **45 deg**.

- Click **OK** .

Select 2 edges

8. Adding Fillets:

- Add **fillets** to the **4 edges** as noted.

- Radius = **.250 in**.

- Click **OK** .

Select 4 edges

9. Filleting all edges:

- Box-Select the entire part and add a fillet of **.03125 in**. to all edges. (If Lasso-Selection was the default, right click in the graphics area and choose: **Box Selection**).

- Click **OK** ✓.

10. Creating an Offset-Distance Plane:

- Click **Plane** or select **Insert / Reference Geometry / Plane**.

- Click **Offset-Distance** option and enter **2.062 in**.

- Select the <u>Right</u> plane to copy from; place the new plane on the right hand side.

- Click **OK** ✓.

11. Creating the Helix (the sweep path):

- Select the <u>new plane</u> and open a new sketch.

(Using an offset of "1-pitch" can help prevent the under-cut from happening where the thread starts).

- Convert the **Inner Circular Edg**e into a Circle.

Convert Entity

- Click **Helix** or select **Insert / Curve / Helix-Spiral**.

- Pitch: **.055 in**.

- Revolutions: **11**

- Start Angle: **0 deg**.

- Clockwise   - Click **OK** ✅.

12. Sketching the Thread Profile:

- Select the <u>Top</u> reference plane and open a new sketch.

- Sketch the thread profile as shown. Add the relation and dimensions needed to define the profile.

- **Exit** the Sketch.

R.005
.047

R.005
.0475
60°
Pierce
to Helix

13. Sweeping the Cut:

- Click **Cut-Sweep** or select **Insert / Cut / Sweep**.

- Select the triangular sketch as Profile and select the helix as Sweep Path.

- Click **OK** .

Profile(Sketch5)

Path(Helix/Spiral1)

14. Mirroring the Threads:

- Click **Mirror** or select **Insert / Pattern Mirror / Mirror**.

- Select the **Right** plane as the Mirror Plane.

- For Features to Mirror select the **Cut-Sweep1** feature.

- Click **OK** .

15. Creating the Cross-Section to view the Threads:

- Select the <u>Front</u> plane from the FeatureManager tree.

- Click **Section View** or select **View / Display / Section**.

- Zoom in on the threaded areas and examine the thread details.

- Click **Cancel** when you are done viewing.

- Save the part as **Internal Threads**.

B. External Threads:

1. Sketching the Sweep Path:

- Select the <u>Front</u> plane and open a new sketch.

- Sketch the profile shown; add Relations & Dimensions needed to fully define.

Front Plane

R.375

Ø1.250

15.00°

3.730

2. Creating a plane Perpendicular to the line:

Plane1

Message
Fully defined

First Reference

Line1@Sketch1

⊥ Perpendicular

☑ Set origin on curve

Coincident

Project

Second Reference

Point6@Sketch1

Coincident

Project

- Click **Plane** or select **Insert / Reference Geometry/ Plane**.

- Select the Horizontal line and the Endpoint on the left side.

- A new plane is created normal to the line

- Click **OK** ✅.

Select this Line and its Endpoint

3. Sketching the Sweep Profile:

- Select the <u>new plane</u> and open a new sketch.

- Sketch a **Circle** as shown and add
  a diameter dimension.

4. Creating the Sweep feature:

- Click **Swept Boss-Base** or select **Insert / Features / Sweep**.

- Select the **Circle** as Sweep Profile and select the **Sketch1** as Sweep Path.

- Click **OK** ✅.

5. Adding Chamfers:

- Click **Chamfer** or select **Insert / Features / Chamfer**.

- Select the **2 Circular Edges** at the 2 ends.

- Enter **.050 in**. for Depth.

- Enter **45 deg**. for Angle.

- Click **OK** .

Sketch face

Convert Entity

6. Creating the Helix:

- Select the <u>face</u> as indicated and open a new sketch.

- Select the **circular edge** at the end as shown and click Convert Entities or select: **Tools/Sketch Tools/Convert Entities**.

- Click **Helix** or select **Insert/Curve/Helix-Spiral**.

- Enter **.055** in. for Pitch.

- Enter **39** for Revolutions.

- Enter **0 deg**. for Start Angle.

- Click **OK** .

7. Creating the Thread Profile:

- Either copy the previous thread profile or recreate it.

- Add a **Pierce** relation to position the thread profile at the end of the helix.

- Click **OK** .

NOTE:
There should be a clearance between the 2 threaded parts so that they can be moved back and forth easily.

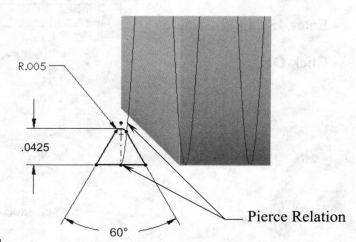

Pierce Relation

8. Sweeping Cut the Threads:

- Click **Swept Cut** or select **Insert / Cut / Sweep.**

- Select the **triangular sketch** as the Sweep Profile.

- Select the **Helix** as the Sweep path.

- Click **OK** .

Sketch Face

Converted Sketch

9. Removing the Undercut:

- Select the <u>face</u> as noted and open a new sketch.

- **Convert** the selected **face** into a new triangular sketch.

- Click Extruded-Cut or select **Insert / Cut / Extrude**.

- Select **Through All** for End Condition.

- Click **OK** ✅.

10. Saving your work:

- Save a copy of your work as **External Threads**.

11. Optional:

(This step can also be done after completing the Bottom Up Assembly chapter).

- Start a New Assembly document and assemble the 2 components.

- Create an Assembly Exploded View as shown below.

- Save the assembly as: **TurnBuckle.sldasm**

CHAPTER 10

Bottom Up Assembly

Bottom Up Assembly
Ball Joint Assembly

- When your design involves multiple parts, SolidWorks offers 4 different assembly methods to help you work faster and more efficient. The first method is called Bottom-Up-Assembly, the second method is called Layout-Assembly, the third Top-Down-Assembly, and the fourth, Master-Modeling.

- We will explore the first two methods, the Bottom-Up and the Lay-Out Assemblies in this Part-1 textbook.

- When individual components get inserted into an assembly document and mated (constrained) together, is called Bottom Up Assembly.

- The first component inserted into the assembly will be fixed by the system automatically. If it is placed on the Origin, then the Front, Top, and the Right planes of the first component will automatically be aligned with the assembly's planes.

- Only the first part will be fixed by default, all other components are free to move or be re-oriented.

- Each component has a total of 6 degrees of freedom; depending on the mate type, once a mate is assigned to a component one or more of its degrees of freedom are removed, causing the component to move or rotate only in the desired directions.

- All Mates (constraints) are stored in the FeatureManager tree under the Mates group. They can be edited, suppressed, or deleted.

Ball Joint Assembly
Bottom-Up Assembly

6 Degrees of Freedom

View Orientation Hot Keys:

Ctrl + 1 = Front View
Ctrl + 2 = Back View
Ctrl + 3 = Left View
Ctrl + 4 = Right View
Ctrl + 5 = Top View
Ctrl + 6 = Bottom View
Ctrl + 7 = Isometric View
Ctrl + 8 = Normal To
         Selection

Dimensioning Standards: **ANSI**

Units: **INCHES** – 3 Decimals

Tools Needed:

 Mates   Move Component   Rotate Component

 Concentric Mate   Inference Origins   Placing New Component

1. Starting a new Assembly template:

- Select **File / New / Assembly / OK**.

- In the Insert Component dialog, click Browse Browse... .

- Select the **Center Ball Joint** document from the Training folder and click **Open**.

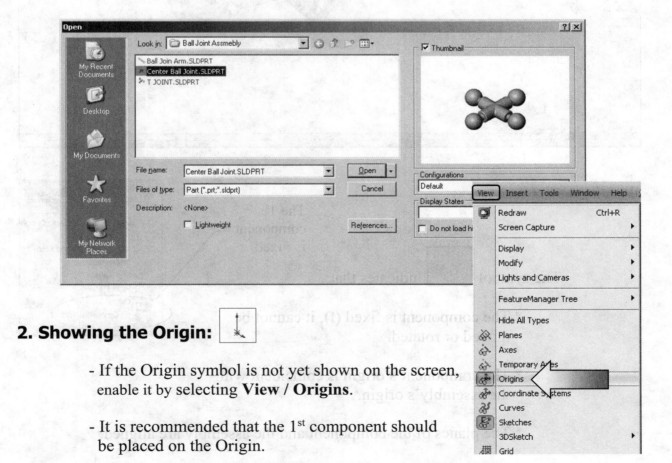

2. Showing the Origin:

- If the Origin symbol is not yet shown on the screen, enable it by selecting **View / Origins**.

- It is recommended that the 1st component should be placed on the Origin.

3. Inserting the 1st component (the Parent) on the Origin:

- Position the mouse cursor on the origin, an Origin-Inference symbol appears to confirm the location of the 1st component.

- Click the Origin point to place the component.

- The symbol indicates that:

The 1st component is Fixed.

* The component is fixed (**f**), it cannot be moved or rotated.

* The component's origin is coincident with the assembly's origin.

* The planes of the component and the assembly are aligned.

4. Inserting the second component (a child) into the assembly:

- Click or Select **Insert / Component / Existing Part/Assembly**.

- Click **Browse** [Browse...] .

- Select **Ball Joint Arm.sldprt** from the Training Files folder and click **Open**.

- The preview graphic of the component is attached to the mouse cursor.

- Place the new Child component above the Parent component as shown below.

5. Mating the components:

- Click or select **Insert / Mate**.

- Assembly mate options appear on the FeatureManager tree.

- Select the **two (2) faces** as indicated below.

- The **Concentric** mate option is selected automatically and the system displays the preview graphics of the two (2) mated components.

- Review the options on the Mate Pop-up toolbar.

- Click **OK** ✅.

- The **two faces** are constrained.

- The second component is still free to rotate around the spherical surface.

6. Moving the component:

- Click **Move Component**.

- Click and drag the **face** as noted.

- Move the component to the approximate shown position.

- Click **OK** ✅.

Drag here

7. Inserting another instance into the assembly:

- Click **Insert Compon...** Select **Insert / Component / Existing Part/ Assembly**.

- Click **Browse...**.

NOTE: Not all assemblies are fully constrained. In an assembly with moving parts, leave at least one degree of freedom open so that the component can still be moved or rotated.

- Select **Ball Joint Arm.sldprt** (the same component) and click **Open**.

- Place the new component next to the first one as shown.

Copy Components

A quick way to create a copy of a component is to click and drag on the component while holding down the *Control* key.

8. Constraining the components:

- Click or select **Insert / Mate**.

- Select the **two faces** as shown.

- The **Concentric** mate option is selected automatically and the system displays the preview graphics of the two mated components.

- Click **OK** ✓.

Select Faces

- The two selected faces are mated together with a Concentric mate.

9. Repeating the step 5:

- Insert (or copy) two more instances of the **Ball Joint Arm** and add the mates to assemble them as shown.

<u>**Optional**</u>:

- Insert the T-Join component (from the Training Files folder) as pictured below and mate it to the assembly.

T-Joint —

- Check the assembly motion by dragging the T-Joint back and forth.

- Each component has only one mate applied, they are still free to move or rotate around their constrained geometry.

10. Saving your work:

- Select **File / Save As**.

- Enter **Ball-Joint-Assembly** for the name of the file.

- Click **Save**.

(Open the pre-built assembly in the Training Files folder, to check your work against it, if needed).

Questions for Review

Bottom Up Assembly

1. The 1st component should be fixed on the Origin.
   - a. True
   - b. False

2. The symbol (f) next to a file name means:
   - a. Fully defined
   - b. Failed
   - c. Fixed

3. After the first component is inserted into an assembly, it is still free to be moved or re-oriented.
   - a. True
   - b. False

4. Beside the first component, if other components are not yet constrained they cannot be moved or rotated.
   - a. True
   - b. False

5. You cannot copy multiple components in an assembly document.
   - a. True
   - b. False

6. To make a copy of a component, click and drag that component while holding the key:
   - a. Shift
   - b. Control
   - c. Alt
   - d. Tab

7. Once a mate is created, its definitions (mate alignment, mate type, etc.) cannot be edited.
   - a. True
   - b. False

8. Mates can be suppressed, deleted, or changed.
   - a. True
   - b. False

7. FALSE   8. TRUE
5. FALSE   6. B
3. FALSE   4. FALSE
1. TRUE   2. C

CHAPTER 10 (cont.)

Bottom Up Assembly

Bottom Up Assembly
Links Assembly

- After the parts are inserted into an assembly document, they are now called components. These components will get re-positioned and mated together. This method is called Bottom Up Assembly.

- The first component inserted into the assembly will be fixed by the system automatically. If it is placed on the Origin, then the Front, Top, and Right planes of the first component will also be aligned with the assembly's planes.

- Only the first part will be fixed by default, all other components are free to be moved or re-oriented. Depending on the mate type, once a mate is assigned to a component, one or more of its degrees of freedom are removed, causing the component to move or rotate only in the desired directions.

- Standard mates are created one by one to constraint components.

- Multi-Mates can be used to constrain more than one component, where a common entity is used to mate with several other entities.

- This second half of the chapter will guide you through the use of the Bottom Up assembly method once again. Some of the components are exactly identical. We will learn how to create several copies of them and then add 2 mates to each one, leaving one degree of freedom open, so that they can be moved or rotated when dragged. There will be an instance number <1> <2> <3> etc., placed next to the name of each copy, to indicate how many times the components are used in an assembly.

Links Assembly
Bottom-Up Assembly

6 Degrees of Freedom

Dimensioning Standards: **ANSI**

Units: **INCHES** – 3 Decimals

Tools Needed:

Mates

Insert New Component

Rotate Component

Move Component

Inference Origins

Place/Position Component

Align & Anti-Align

Concentric Mate

Coincident Mate

1. Starting a new Assembly Template:

- Select **File / New / Assembly / OK**.

- A new assembly document is opened.

- Select **Insert Component** command from the Assembly tool tab.

- Click the **Browse** button (arrow).

2. Inserting the 1st Component:

- Go to: The Training Files folder and open the part **Double Link.sldprt**.

- Place the part Double Link on the assembly Origin.

The mouse cursor changes into this pointer. Click on the origin to fix the component.

☀ "Fixing" the 1st component

- The first component inserted into the assembly will be fixed automatically by the system, the symbol (f) next to the document's name means the part cannot be moved or rotated.

- Other components can be added and mated to the first one using one of the three options:

      1. Drag & Drop from an opened window
      2. Use the Windows Explorer to drag the component into the assembly.
      3. Use the Insert Component command.

3. Adding other components:

- Select **Insert / Component / Existing Part/Assembly** (or click) and add five (**5**) more copies of the first component into the Assembly document.

- Place the new components around the Fixed one, approximately as shown.

- The Feature Manager tree shows the same name for each component but with an indicator that shows the number of times used <**2**>, <**3**>, <**4**>, etc...

- The (**-**) signs in front of each file name indicate that the components are under defined, still able to move or rotate freely.

Hold the CONTROL key, click and drag the part to make a copy.

Fixed part

4. Changing colors:

- For Clarity, change the color of the 1st component to a different color, this way we can differentiate the parent component from the copies.

- Click the 1st component and select the **Appearances** button (the beach ball) and click the **Edit Part Color** option (arrow).

Change the color of the Fixed component to a different color than the others.

- Move the copies away from one another, approximately as shown.

- Click **OK** ✓.

5. Inserting the Single Link into the assembly:

- Click **Insert Component** on the Assembly toolbar and select the part **Single Link**, from the previous folder.

- Place the Single Link approximately as shown.

6. Using the Selection Filters:

- The Selection Filters help select the right type of geometry to add the mates such as filter Faces, Edges, Axis or Vertices, etc...

- Click **Selection Filter** icon, or press the **F5** function key.

- Select **Filter Faces** option .

Filter Faces

7. Adding Mates:

- Click **Mate** on the Assembly toolbar or select **Insert / Mate**.

- Select the faces of the **two holes** as indicated.

Select 2 Faces

- The **Concentric** mate option is selected automatically and the system displays the preview graphics for the two mated components.

- Click **OK** to accept the concentric mate.

Click OK

The 2 holes are concentric

8. Adding a Width mate:

- The Width mate centers the 2 parts (width of part 1 and groove/tab of part 2).

- Click **Mate** [icon] on the Assembly toolbar or select **Insert / Mate**.

- Expand the **Advanced Mates** section and click the **Width** option.

- Select **2 faces** for **each part** as indicated. A total of 4 faces must be selected.

2 faces of Single Link

2 faces of Double Link

Select 2 faces for Width Selection (front & back)

- The two components are centered by the **Width** mate.

- Click **OK** [icon].

Select 2 faces for Tab Selection (front & back)

9. Making copies of the component:

- Select the part Single-Link and click **Edit / Copy**, then click anywhere in the graphics area and select **Edit / Paste** – OR – Hold down the CONTROL key, click/hold and drag the part Single Link to make a copy.

Hold down the CONTROL key, Click/hold and drag the Single Link to make a copy.

10. Repeating: make a total of 4 instances.

Fixed part

Notes:

- *The correct mates are displayed in Black color* *on the FeatureManager tree.*

- *The Incorrect mates are displayed with a red X* ✎ ⊗ (+) *or a yellow*

exclamation mark ✎ ⚠ (+) *next to them.*

Continue with adding the Concentric and the Width mates to the other components.

- Expand the Mate group ⊟ 🔗 Mates (Click on the **+** sign).

- Verify that there are no "Red Flags" under the Mate Group.

- If a mate error occurs, do the following:

⊟ 🔗 Mates
  ✎ Concentric1 (Single Link<1>,Single Link<2>)
  ✎ ⊗ (+) Perpendicular1 (Single Link<1>,Single Link<4>)
  ✎ ⚠ (+) Coincident3 (Single Link<1>,Single Link<4>)
  ✎ Concentric3 (Single Link<2>,Single Link<3>)
  ✎ Coincident4 (Single Link<2>,Single Link<3>)
  ✎ ⚠ (+) Concentric4 (Single Link<3>,Single Link<4>)
  ✎ Concentric5 (Single Link<3>,Single Link<5>)
  ✎ Coincident5 (Single Link<3>,Single Link<5>)
  ✎ Coincident6 (Single Link<4>,Single Link<6>)
  ✎ Concentric6 (Single Link<4>,Single Link<6>)

** **Right click** over the incorrect mate, select Edit-Feature, and correct the selections for that particular mate - **OR** -

** Simply delete the incorrect mates and re-create the new ones.

11. Inserting other components into the Assembly:

- Click or select **Insert / Component / Existing Part/Assembly.**

- Click **Browse**, select **Alignment Pin** and click **Open.**

- Place the component on the left side of the assembly as shown.

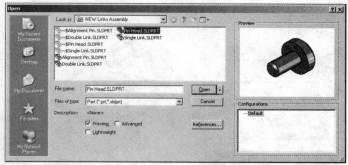

- Insert the **Pin Head** and place it on the right side.

12. Rotating the Pin Head:

- Select the Rotate Component command and rotate the Pin-Head to the correct orientation.

Make 5 more copies of both, the Pin-Head and the Alignment Pin.

13. Constraining the Alignment Pin:

- Click **Mate** on the Assembly toolbar.

- Select the **body** of the Alignment Pin and the **hole** in the Double Link..

- A Concentric Mate is automatically added to the two (2) selected faces.

- Click **OK** ✓.

Select 2 Faces to add a **Concentric** mate

Select the Bottom face of the Bore…

… and select the end face of the Head to add a **Coincident** Mate.

14. Constraining the Pin-Head:

- Align the Pin-Head with its mating hole, using a **Concentric Mate**.

Select the cylindrical
body of the Pin-Head...

... and select the inside
surface of the hole to
add a **Concentric** Mate.

- Click **OK** ✓.

- Click **Mate** again, if you have already closed out of it from the last step.

- Select the **two faces** as indicated to add a Coincident Mate.

…and select the end
face of the Pin-Head to
add a Coincident Mate

Select the bottom
face of the Bore…

- The system adds a **Coincident** mate
between the 2 entities.

- Click **OK** .

15. Using the Align & Anti-Align Options:

- When the Mate command is active, the options **Align** and **Anti-Align** are also available in the Mate dialog box.

- Use the alignment options to flip the mating component 180º .

- The last two (2) pins will be used to demonstrate the use of Align and Anti-Align (see step 16).

16. Using Align and Anti-Align:

- When mating the components using the **Concentric** option, the **TAB** key can be used to flip the component 180° or from Align into Anti-Align.

Align

Anti-Align
press **TAB**

17. Viewing the assembly motion:

- Drag one of the links to see how the components move relative to each other.

18. Saving your work:

- Select **File / Save As.**

- Enter **Links Assembly** for the name of the file.

- Click **Save**.

(Open the pre-built assembly in the Training Files folder, to compare your work).

Questions for Review

Bottom Up Assembly

1. Parts inserted into an assembly document are called documents.
    a. True
    b. False

2. Each component in an assembly document has six degrees of freedom.
    a. True
    b. False

3. Once a mate is applied to a component, depends on the mate type, one or more of its degrees of freedom is removed.
    a. True
    b. False

4. Standard mates are created one by one to constraint the components.
    a. True
    b. False

5. A combination of a Face and an Edge can be used to constraint with a Coincident mate.
    a. True
    b. False

6. Align and Anti-Align while in the Mating mode can toggle by pressing:
    a. Control
    b. Back space
    c. Tab
    d. Esc.

7. Mates can be deferred so that several mates can be done and solved at the same time.
    a. True
    b. False

8. Mates can be:
    a. Suppressed
    b. Deleted
    c. Edited
    d. All of the above

7. TRUE   8. D
5. TRUE   6. C
3. TRUE   4. TRUE
1. FALSE   2. TRUE

Exercise: Gate Assembly

Go to: The Training Files folder
Gate Assembly Folder.

1. Create an Assembly document from the components provided.
2. Create a Mirror plane at **26.125 in**. offset from the RIGHT plane.

Gate Support

Gate

Arm

Arm Connector

Base Stand
Fixed Part

Connecting Arm

Connector Joint

Double Joint

7.000

1.000

Right Plane

PLANE1

26.125

3. Mirror all components to create the complete Gate Assembly.
4. Save your work as: **Gate Assembly.**

(Use the instructions on the following pages for details).

1. Starting a new assembly:

- Click **File / New / Assembly**.

- From the Assembly tool-bar, select **Insert / Components**.

- Brows to the part **Base Stand** and place it on the assembly's origin.

Place the 1st part on origin

2. Inserting other components:

- Insert all components (total of 8) into the assembly.

- **Rotate** the **Gate** <u>and</u> the **Gate-Support** approximately **180 degrees**.

- Move the Gate and the Gate-Support to the positions shown.

- By rotating and positioning the components before mating them, it helps seeing the mating entities a little easier.

Rotate 180°

3. Adding a Distance mate:

- Click **Mate** on the Assembly toolbar.

- Select the **2 side faces** of the **Base Stand** and the **Gate-Support** as indicated.

- Click the **Distance** button and enter **7.00"**.

- Click **OK**.

Select 2 side faces

4. Adding a Coincident mates:

- Click **Mate** on the Assembly toolbar, if not yet selected.

- Select the **2 front faces** of the **Base Stand** and the **Gate Support** as indicated.

- The **Coincident** option is automatically selected.

- Click **OK**.

Coincident

5. Adding other mates:

- The **Mate** command should still be active, if not, select it.

- Select the **2 bottom faces** of the **Base Stand** and the **Gate Support** as indicated.

- The **Coincident** option is automatically selected.

- Click **OK**.

Coincident

Concentric

- Click the Circular Bosses on the sides of the **Gate** and the **Gate Support**; a **concentric** mate is automatically added.

- Click **OK**.

- Add a **Distance** mate of **1.000"** between the **upper face** of the Gate Support and the **bottom face** of the Gate, as noted.

1.00"distance

- Add a **Concentric** mate between the **circular face** of the Base-Stand and the **center hole** of the Arm-Connector.

- Add a **Width** mate between the **4 faces** of the same components.

Concentric

Select 2 faces for Width

Select 2 faces for Tab

- Add a **Concentric** mate between the side Hole of the Arm Connector and **the hole** in the Arm.

Concentric mate

- Add another **Width** mate between the **4 faces** of these two components.

Width mate

- Add a **Concentric** mate between **the hole** in the Arm and **the hole** in the Connecting Arm.

Concentric mate

- Add a **Width** mate between the **4 faces** of the same components.

Width mate

- Add a **Concentric** mate between **the hole** of the Connecting Arm and **the hole** in the Connector Joint.

Concentric

- Add another **Width** mate between the **4 faces** of these two components.

Width

- Add a Concentric mate between **the hole** in the Connector Joint and **the hole** in the Double Joint.

Concentric

Width

- Add a **Width** mate between the **4 faces** of these two components.

- Click **OK**.

- Move the components to the position shown.

- Since the Double Joint has several components connected to its left side, this time it might be a little easier if we create the Width mate before the Concentric mate.

6. Adding more mates:

- Click the **Mate** command again, if not yet selected.

- Select the **Advanced** tab.

- Click the **Width** option.

- Select the **2 faces** of the **Double Joint** for Width selection.

- Select the other **2 faces** of the tab on the **Gate** for Tab selection.

- Click **OK**.

Move the components to approx. here

Select 2 faces for each part

- Change to the **Standard Mates** tab.

- Select **the hole** in the Double-Joint and **the hole** on the tab of the Gate.

- A **Concentric** mate is added automatically to the selected holes.

- Click **OK** twice to close out of the mate mode.

Concentric mate

7. Creating an Offset Distance plane:

- Select the **Right** plane of the
assembly and click the **Plane**
command, or **select Insert /
Reference Geometry / Plane**.

- The **Offset Distance** button
is selected by default.

- Enter **26.125"** for distance.

- Click **OK**.

8. Mirroring the components:

- Select the **new plane** and click:
Insert / Mirror Components.

Select all components

- Expand the Feature tree and
select all components from
there.

NEXT

- Click the **Next** arrow
on the upper corner
of the Feature tree.

- Select the part **Gate**
from the list and click
the **Create Opposite Hand Version** button.

- Click **OK** and drag one of the gates to test out your assembly.

- **Save** and **Close**.

Gate Closed

Gate Open

CHAPTER 11

Using Advanced Mates

Rack & Pinion Mates

The Rack and Pinion mate option allows linear translation of the Rack to cause circular rotation in the Pinion, and vice versa.

For each full rotation of the Pinion, the Rack translates a distance equal to π multiplied by the Pinion diameter. You can specify either the diameter or the distance by selecting either the Pinion Pitch Diameter or the Rack Travel / Revolution options.

1. Open an assembly document:

- From the Training Files folder, browse to the Rack & Pinion folder and open the assembly named **Rack & Pinion mates**.

- The assembly has two components, the Rack and Gear1. Some of the mates have been created to define the distances between the centers of the two components.

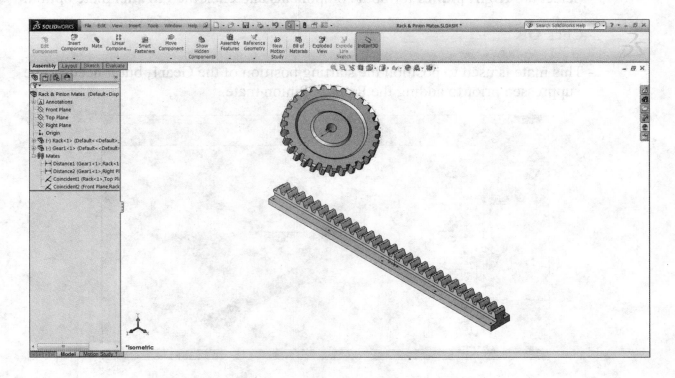

2. Adding standard mates:

- Click the **Mate** command from the assembly toolbar, or select **Insert / Mate**.

- Expand the FeatureManager tree and select the **Front planes** for both components. A coincident mate is automatically created for the two selected planes.

- Click **OK** .

- Click the **Mate** command if not already selected.

- Select the **Right planes** for both components and click the **Parallel** mate option.

- Click **OK** .

- This mate is used to position the starting position of the Gear1, but it needs to be suppressed prior to adding the Rack & Pinion mate.

3. Suppressing a mate:

- Expand the **Mate Group** (click the + sign) at the bottom of the FeatureManager tree.

- Right click the Parallel mate and select the **Suppress** button from the pop-up window (arrow).

- The Parallel mate icon should turn grey to indicate that it is suppressed.

4. Adding a Mechanical mate:

- Move down the Mate properties and expand the **Mechanical Mates** section (arrow).

- Click the **Rack Pinion** button. The option Pinion Pitch Diameter should be selected already. For each full rotation of the pinion, the rack translates a distance equal to π multiplied by the pinion diameter, and the Pinion's diameter appears in the window.

- In the Mate Selections, highlight the Rack section and select the **Bottom-Edge** of one of the teeth on the Rack as indicated.

- Click in the Pinion section and select the **Construction-Circle** on the gear as noted.

Select this circle for Pinion

Select this edge for Rack

- Enable the **Reverse** checkbox.

- Click **OK** to close out of the Mate option.

5. Testing the mates:

- Change to the Isometric orientation (Control + 7).

- Drag either the Rack or the Gear1 back and forth and see how the two components will moved relative to each other.

- Hide the construction circle. Next we will create an animation using a linear motor to drive the motions.

6. Creating a Linear Motion:

- Remain in the Isometric view, click the **Motion Study1** tab on the lower left corner of the screen.

- The screen is split into 2 viewports showing the Animation program on the bottom.

- Click the **Motor** button (arrow) on the Motion Study toolbar.

- Under the **Motor Type**, select the **Linear Motor (Actuator)** option.

- Under the **Motion** section, use the default **Constant Speed** and set the speed to **50mm/s** (50 millimeters per second).

- Click **OK**.

Select this edge for direction

7. Creating a Linear Motion:

- Click the **Playback Mode** arrow and select: **Playback Mode Reciprocate**.

- Click the **Play** button to view the animation.

- By default the Solid-Works-Animator sets the play time to 5 seconds.

- To change the **Playback Time**, drag the diamond key to **10 second** spot (arrow).

- To change the **Playback Speed**, click the drop down arrow and select **5X** (arrow).

- Click the **Play** ▷ button again to re-run the animation.

8. Saving your work:

- Click **File / Save As**.

- Enter **Rack & Pinion Mates** for the name of the file.

- Overwrite the old file when prompted.

- Click **Save**.

CHAPTER 11 (cont.)

Limit & Cam Mates

1. Opening a part file:

- Browse to the Training Files folder and open the part file named: **Limit & Cam Mates**.

Limit mates: Allow components to move within a specified distance or angle. The user specifies a starting distance or angle as well as a maximum and minimum value.

Cam Mate: is a type of coincident or tangent mate. Where a cylinder, a plane, or a point can be mated to a series of tangent extruded faces.

- This assembly document has 2 components. The Part1 has been fixed by the Inplace1 and the Part2 still has 6 degrees of freedom.

- We will explore the use of Limit and Cam mates when positioning the Part2.

2. Adding a Width mate:

- Click the **Mate** command from the Assembly tab.

- Click the **Advanced Mates** tab and select the **Width** option.

- The Width mate aligns the two components so that the Part2 is centered between the faces of the Part1 (Housing). The Part2 can translate along the center plane of the Housing and rotate about the axis that is normal to the center plane. The width mate prevents the Part2 from translating or rotating side to side.

- For the **Width Selection**, select the **2 side faces** of the **Part2** (arrow).

- For the **Tab Selection**, select the **2 side faces** of the **Part1** (Housing).

- It does not matter which component you select first or second, just be sure to select both faces of the same part before selecting the next set.

- Click **OK** .

Select the left and the right faces…

Select the left and the right faces…

3. Adding a Cam mate:

- Click the **Mechanical Mates** tab below the Standard and Advanced tabs (Arrow).

- Select the **Cam** mate button from the list.

- A Cam mate forces a cylinder, a plane, or a point to be coincident or tangent to a series of tangent extruded faces.

- For the **Cam Selection**, right click a face of the slot and pick: **Select Tangency**.

Right click a face of the slot and pick: Select Tangency

- For the **Cam Follower**, select the <u>cylindrical face</u> of one of the pins.

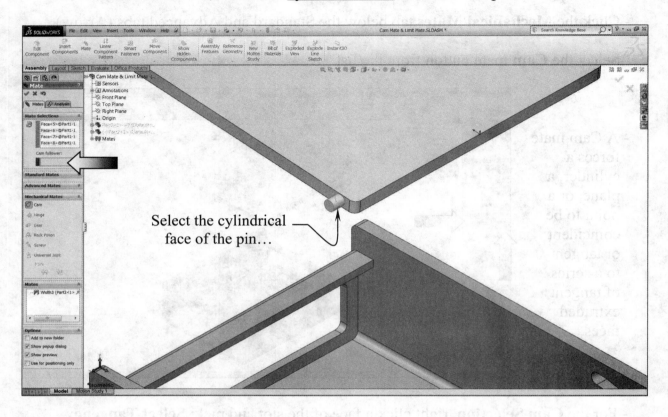

Select the cylindrical
face of the pin…

- Zoom in and check the alignment between the pin and the slot.

- Toggle between
the 2 mate
alignment
buttons (arrow)
to make sure
the two
components
are properly
oriented.

- Click **OK** ✓ .

4. Adding a Parallel mate:

- Click the **Standard Mates** tab (arrow) and select the **Parallel** option from the list.

- Select the **2 faces** as indicated to make parallel.

- Click **OK** ✅ .

Select 2 faces
for Parallel...

- The Parallel mate is used to precisely rotate the Part2 to its vertical position. But we will need to suppress it so that other mates can be added without over defining the assembly.

- Expand the Mate group by clicking the plus sign (+) next to the Mates folder.

- Click the Parallel mate and select the **Suppress** button (arrow).

- Do not move the component, a Limit mate is going to be added next.

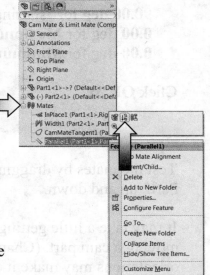

5. Adding a Limit mate:

- Click the **Advanced Mates** tab (arrow) and select the **Angle** option from the list.

- Select the **2 faces** of the 2 components as indicated.

Select 2 faces

- Enter the following:

  9**0.00 deg** for "starting" Angle.
  0.00 deg for **Maximum** value.
  0.00 deg for **Minimum** value.

- Click **OK** ✓

- Test the mates by dragging the Part2 up and down.

- It may take a little getting used to when moving a cam part. (Changing to other orientations may make it easier).

Drag here

- Try pulling the right end of the Part2 downward. It should stop when it reaches the 90 degrees angle.

Drag here

- Let us explore some other options of dragging a cam part.

- Change to the Front orientation (Control + 1).

- Drag the **circular face** of the Pin upward. Start out slowly at first, then move a bit faster when the part starts to follow your mouse pointer.

Drag here

Drag here

- Now try dragging the same part from the side as shown here. Also start out slowly then speed up a little when the part starts to catch on.

6. Saving your work:

- Click **File / Save As**.

- Enter **Limit & Cam Mates** for file name.

- Click **Save**.

- Overwrite the document if prompted.

(In the Training Files folder, locate the Built-Parts folder; open the pre-built assembly to check your work against it).

Exercise: Using Cam Followers*

1. Copying the Cam Followers Assembly folder:

- Go to: The Training Files folder.
- Copy the entire folder named **Cam Followers** to your desktop.

A Cam-Follower mate is a type of tangent or coincident mate. It allows you to mate a cylinder, a plane, or a point to a series of tangent extruded faces, such as you would find on a cam. You can make the profile of the cam from lines, arcs, and splines, as long as they are tangent and form a closed loop.

Crank Handle

CamPart1

CamPart3

CamPart2

CamPart4

CamPart2 (Copy)

Cam Base
Fixed Part

2. Assembling the components using the Standard Mates:

- Create a **Concentric** mate between the **shaft** and the **hole** as shown below.

Select 2 faces
(Concentric)

- Create a **Coincident** mate between the **two faces** as shown below.

Select 2 faces
(Coincident)

- Create a **Coincident** Mate between the **2 upper surfaces** of the 2 components as indicated.

Select 2 faces (Coincident)

- Repeat the Coincident Mates for all other parts (except for the Crank-Handle) to bring them up to the same height.

3. Using Mechanical Mates:

All Upper Faces are Coincident with the Campart1.

- Locate the **Mechanical Mates** section and expand it.

- Select the **Cam** option (arrow).

- **Right click** on the side of the CamPart1 and pick **Select-Tangency** from the menu.

Right Click
Select Tangency

- Click in the **Cam-Follower** section (circled) and select the **left face** of the part CamPart2,

Select this face for Cam-Follower)

NOTES:

- *In order for the components to "behave" properly when they're being rotated, their center-planes should also be constrained.*

- *Create a Coincident Mate between the FRONT plane of the CamPart1 and the FRONT plane of the CamPart3, then repeat the same step for the others.*

4. Viewing the Cam Motions

- Drag the Crank Handle clockwise or counter-clockwise to view the Cam-Motion of your assembly.

Move the Crank Handle to test the Cam Motions

5. Saving your Work:

- Click **File / Save As**.

- Enter **Cam Follower** for the name of the file.

- Click **Save**.

CHAPTER 11 (cont.)

Using Smart-Mates

Fixture Assembly
Using Smart-Mates

- Beside the standard mates such as Concentric, Coincident, Tangent, Angle, etc., which must be done one by one, SolidWorks offers an alternative option that is much more robust called: Smart-Mates.

- There are many advantages for using Smart-mates. It can create several mates at the same time, depends on the type of entity selected. For example: If you drag a circular edge of a hole and drop it on a circular edge of another hole, SolidWorks will automatically creates 2 mates, a concentric mate between the two cylindrical faces of the holes and a coincident mate between the two planar faces.

- Using Smart-mates, you do not have to select the Mate command every time. Simply hold the ALT key and drag an entity of a component to its destination, a smart-mate symbol will appear to confirm the types of mates it is going to adds. At the same time, a mate toolbar will also pop up offering some additional options such as Flip Mate Alignment, change to a different mate type, or simply undo the selection.

- Using the Alt + Drag option, the Tab key is used to flip the mate alignments, this is done by releasing the Alt key and pressing the Tab key, while the mouse button is still pressed. This option works well even if your assembly is set to lightweight.

- In addition to the Alt + Drag, if you hold the Control key and Drag a component, SolidWorks will create an instance of the selected component and apply the smart-mates to it at the same time. Using this option you will have to click the Flip Mate Alignment button on the pop-up toolbar to reverse the direction of the mate, the Tab key does not work.

- This lesson will guide you through the use of the Smart-mate options, and for some of the steps, use the standards mate options as well.

Fixture Assembly
Using Smart-Mates

View Orientation Hot Keys:

Ctrl + 1 = Front View
Ctrl + 2 = Back View
Ctrl + 3 = Left View
Ctrl + 4 = Right View
Ctrl + 5 = Top View
Ctrl + 6 = Bottom View
Ctrl + 7 = Isometric View
Ctrl + 8 = Normal To
　　　　　　Selection

Dimensioning Standards: **ANSI**

Units: **INCHES** – 3 Decimals

Tools Needed:

Concentric &
Coincident

Concentric two
cylindrical faces

Coincident
two edges

Coincident
two planar faces

Coincident
two vertices

Coincident
two origins

1. Opening an existing assembly document:

- Select **File / Open**.

- Browse to the Training Files folder, locate and open the document named: **Fixture Assembly**.

2. Enabling the Selection options:

- Go to **Tools / Options / Display / Selection** and enable the two checkboxes:
* Allow Selection in Wireframe...
* Allow selection in HLR and...

Locate the bottom edge and the upper edge of the 2 holes

3. Exploring the Smart-Mate options:

- Some types of Smart-Mates can be created in an assembly by dragging and dropping one entity to another.

- Depends on the entity that you drag. You will get different mate result. Use either a linear or circular edge of the model, a planar or cylindrical face, or a vertex to drag with Smart-Mates.

	Concentric & Coincident 2 circular edges
	Concentric 2 cylindrical faces
	Coincident 2 linear edges
	Coincident 2 planar faces
	Coincident 2 vertices
	Coincident 2 origins or coordinate systems

Start Here - Hold the **ALT** key, drag the hidden edge of the hole to the upper edge of the mating hole but do not release the mouse. Hover the cursor over the edge of the hole until the Smart-Mate symbol appears, then release the mouse button.

Mates
- Coincident1 (Base<1>,Front Plane)
- Coincident2 (Base<1>,Top Plane)
- Coincident3 (Base<1>,Right Plane)
- Concentric1 (Base<1>,Sub-Assem2<
- Coincident4 (Base<1>,Sub-Assem2<

- Two new mates are added automatically. Expand the Mates folder to see them.

Smart-Mate symbol for Concentric & Coincident

4. Using Smart-Mate Concentric:

- The concentric mate is created when two cylindrical surfaces are dragged and dropped onto one another.

- <u>Hold</u> the **ALT** key, drag the <u>cylindrical face</u> of the 1st hole and drop on the <u>cylindrical face</u> of the 2nd hole. The mouse cursor must be stopped on an entity and must not be moving, in order for the Smart-Mate symbol to appear.

- Release the mousse cursor when the concentric symbol pops up, click the **OK** on the pop-up toolbar to accept the concentric mate.

Drag & drop the cylindrical faces of the 2 holes

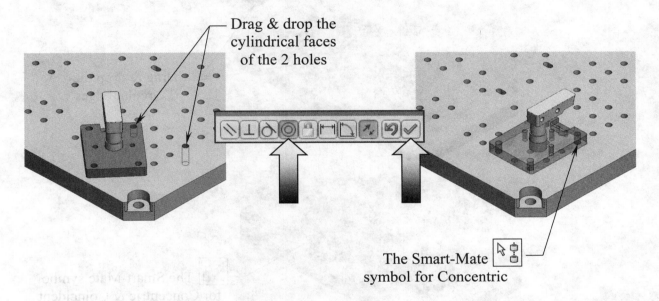

The Smart-Mate symbol for Concentric

- The sub assembly becomes fully defined. There is no minus sign (-) before the name Sub-Assem2.

- The Base component is considered the parent part, it was previously mated to the 3 planes of the assembly, therefore it is also fully defined. It does not have the the minus sign before its name.

- The rest of the components and sub-assemblies are still under defined, they still have 6 degrees of freedom to move or rotate about any direction.

- We going to explore the Smart-Mates some more and assemble the entire assembly using this dynamic mate options.

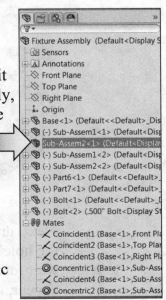

5. Creating a Smart-Mate Concentric & Coincident:

- Zoom in closer between the two components that will get mated next.

- <u>Hold</u> the **ALT** key, drag and drop the <u>hidden edge</u> of the hole1 onto the <u>upper edge</u> of the hole2 as noted.

- Keep the mouse cursor steady until the Smart mates symbol appears, and then release the mouse button.

Drag & drop the 2 circular edges

The Smart-Mate symbol for Concentric & Coincident

Drag & drop the cylindrical faces of the 2 holes

- Next, drag and drop the <u>cylindrical face</u> of the hole1 to the <u>cylindrical face</u> of the hole2, wait for the Smart-Mate Concentric symbol to appear, then click the check mark to accept it.

6. Repeating the previous Mate:

- Move the cylindrical part above the base as shown.

- We are going to use the same mate techniques to assemble this part.

- The Explode Lines are added for clarity only, you do not have to add them.

- <u>Hold</u> the **ALT** key, drag & drop the <u>hidden edge</u> of the hole in the cylindrical part onto the <u>upper edge</u> of the mating hole in the base.

Drag the bottom circular edges of hole1 & drop on the upper circular edge of hole2

- If done properly, there should 2 mates added to the selected entities already. check the Mates group and look for the new Concentric and Coincident mates.

- <u>Repeat</u> the same step and mate one other hole of the same components, to fully define their positions.

7. Mating other components:

- Since the holes in the components were patterned and have the exact same diameters, two mates per component would be enough to fully define them.

- The Explode Lines are added for clarity again, you do not need to add them.

- Use the same techniques and add the Smart-Mates to the other components, use the explode lines for reference locations, and only create two mates for each component.

- Do not mate the bolts just yet, we are going to take a look at the configurations that come with the bolts, and switch them to different sizes and use in them different locations.

Add 2 mates
for each hole

Add 2 mates
for each hole

Add 2 mates
for each hole

8. Checking the status of the components:

- After adding two mates to each component, the FeatureManager updates and shows only the minus signs (-) before the bolts.

Config.
.500" Bolt

Configuration
Default

The minus sign (-) appear before the
parts that still free move or rotate...

9. Switching Configuration:

- The Bolt has 2 configurations, the **Default** and the **.500"**.

- We have been using the Default size for most of the components, we now need 2 of the .500" for the next part.

- Click the part Bolt and select the **Component-Properties** button (arrow).

- Select the **.500"** configuration as noted.

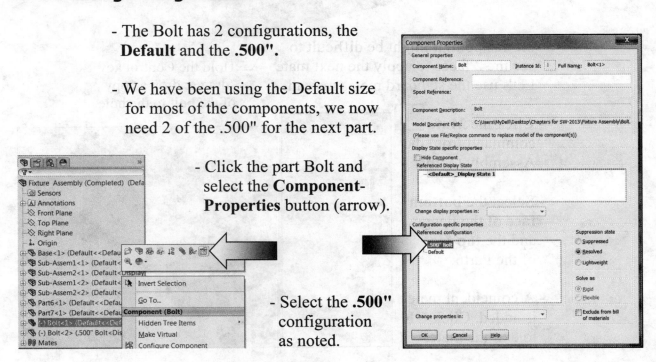

10. Creating an instance of the .500" bolt:

An instance of the bolt is mated to the hole

- When holding the Alt key and dragging a component the smart-mate is activated for mating the 2 components.

- But if you hold the Control key and drag a component, SolidWorks makes a copy of the component and smart-mates it to the other component at the same time.

- <u>Hold</u> the **Control** key, drag and drop (the shaft body) <u>an instance</u> of the bolt to the mating hole as pictured below. Release the mouse button when the smart-mate symbol appears. Click the Flip Alignment button if needed (arrow).

Hold the Control key drag & drop a copy of the bolt to the hole

- At this point it might be difficult to see the 2 faces to apply the next mate. Let's use the standard mates instead.

- Click the **Mate** command from the Assembly toolbar.

- Select the **bottom face** of the flange and the **top face** of the Part6.

- A coincident mate is added. Click **OK** to exit the mate.

11. Creating another instance of the bolt:

- Move the Default-Bolt closer to the Sub-Assembly1 on the right as noted.

- <u>Hold</u> the **Control** key, drag and drop an instance of the (default) bolt to the mating hole as noted. Look for the smart-mate symbol before releasing the mouse button.

- Click the Flip Mate Alignment button if needed (arrow).

Hold the Control key when dragging

- Click **OK** to close the mate toolbar.

- It would be easier to use the standard mates again for the next mate.

- Click the **Mate** command from the assembly toolbar.

- Select the **bottom face** of the flange and the **top face** of the Part2 as noted.

- A **coincident** mate is added automatically.

- Click **OK**.

- The bolt still have one degree of freedom left.

Select 2 faces

12. Adding more bolts:

- Rotate around to the other side of the sub-assembly1.

- <u>Hold</u> the <u>CONTROL</u> key and drag the default-bolt to make a copy and place it on the right of the Part2.

- Hold the Control key again, drag the copy of the default bolt to the mating hole as indicated. Look for the smart-mate symbol before releasing the mouse button. Click the Flip Mate Alignment if needed (arrow).

Hold the Control key while dragging

- Once again, it would be easier to use the standard mates for the next step, since we cannot really see the 2 two mating faces very well.

- Click **Mate** .

- Select the **bottom face** of the flange and the **top face** of the Part2.

- Another **coincident** mate is added.

- Click **OK** to exit the mate mode.

Select 2 faces

13. Repeating:

- For practice purposes, we are going to add more instances of the bolts to the other components.

- Keep in mind that fasteners do not have to be fully defined. Each bolt only needs two mates, and even though they still rotate but that will not affect the assembly at all.

- By using one less mate for each component you can reduce the file size of this assembly by about 10%. It will also helps reduce the time that it takes to rebuild the assembly every time a change is applied. In other words, the less mates (and less components), the faster the computer performance.

14. Saving your work:

- Save your work as **Fixture Assemly.sldasm** and overwrite the existing file when prompted.

Questions for Review

Using Smart-Mates

1. When using the smart-mate options, you will need to select the Mate command first.
   - a. True
   - b. False

2. To activate the smart-mates, hold the Alt key while dragging the component.
   - a. True
   - b. False

3. To make a copy of a component and apply smart-mates to it at the same time, hold both key Control & Alt, and then drag the component to its destination.
   - a. True
   - b. False

4. Smart-mates will work with either a set of model edges, faces, or vertices, as mating entities.
   - a. True
   - b. False

5. Smart-mates also work with reference geometry such as planes and axis, as mating entities.
   - a. True
   - b. False

6. To flip the component direction during the smart-mate mode, push the "esc" key.
   - a. True
   - b. False

7. Using the Alt + Drag option, the tab key is used to flip the mate alignment (still holding the mouse button, release the Alt key and push Tab).
   - a. True
   - b. False

8. Hold the Control key while dragging a component to make a copy and smart-mate it at the same time.
   - a. True
   - b. False

7. TRUE
8. TRUE
5. TRUE
6. FALSE
3. FALSE
4. TRUE
1. FALSE
2. TRUE

Level 1 - Final Exam

<u>Files location:</u> Training Files folder.
Bottom Up Assembly Folder.
Copy the entire folder to your
Desktop.

1. Starting a new Assembly document:

- Select **File / New / Assem**. (Assembly)
from either the Template or the
Tutorial folder.

2. Inserting the Fixed component:

- Click the **Insert Component** command from the Assembly toolbar.

- Locate the **Molded Housing** and place it on the assembly's origin.

Note: *To show the Origin symbol, click **View / Origins.***

3. Inserting the other components:

- Insert the rest of the components as labeled, from the Bottom Up Assembly folder into the assembly.

Support Arm

Mirror/Copy Support Arm

End Cap

Mirrored Cover-Plate1

Cover Plate

Label

Spring

Nose

Molded Housing

Mirror Label

Mirror Cover-Plate2

Mirror Cover Plate3

4. Mating the components:

- Assign the Mate conditions such as Concentric, Coincident, etc., to assemble the components.

- The finished assembly should look like the one pictured below.

5. Verifying the position of the Spring:

- Select the Right Plane and click Section View.

- Position the Spring approximately as shown to avoid assembly's interferences.

- Click-off the section view option when finished.

Avoid interferences
between the Housing
and the Spring

- Add a **Distance** Mate and a **Coincident** Mates between the Planes of the Molded Housing and the Spring components.

6. Creating the Assembly Exploded View:

- Click or Select **Insert / Exploded View**.

- Select a component either from the Feature tree or directly from the Graphics area.

- Drag one of the three Drag-Handles to move the component along the direction you wish to move.

- Repeat the same step to explode all components.

- For editing, right click on any of the steps on one of the Explode-Steps and select Edit-Step.

Drag the Blue-Ring to rotate, then drag the Blue-Arrow head to move.

Note: *The finished exploded view can be edited by accessing the ConfigurationManager under the Default Configuration.*

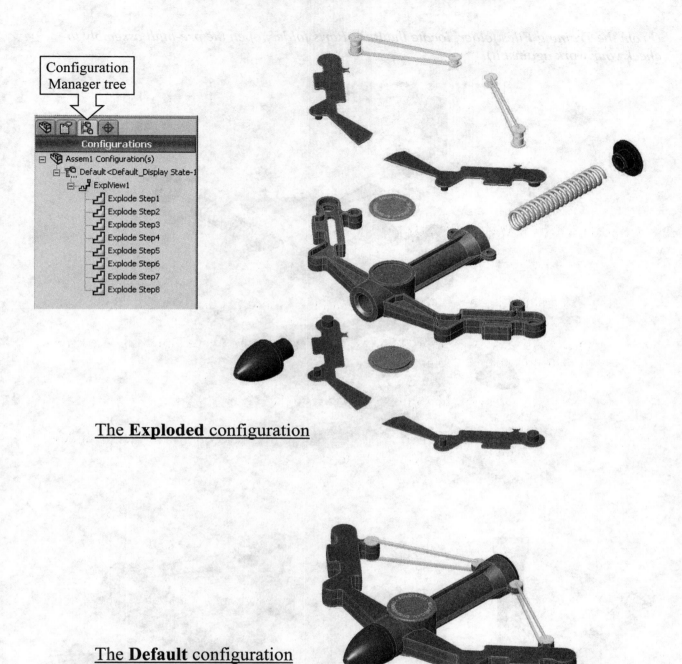

Configuration Manager tree

The **Exploded** configuration

The **Default** configuration

7. Saving your work:

- Select **File / Save As**.

- Enter **L1 Final Exam** for the name of the file.

- Click **Save**.

(From the Training Files folder, locate the Built-Parts folder; open the pre-built assembly to check your work against it).

CHAPTER 12

Layout Assembly

Layout Assembly

- You can design an assembly from the top-down using layout sketches. You can construct one or more sketches showing where each assembly component belongs. Then, you can create and modify the design before you create any parts. In addition, you can see the assembly motions ahead of time and how the components are going to behave when they are being moved around.

- The major advantage of designing an assembly using a layout sketch is that if you change the layout sketch, the assembly and its parts are automatically updated. You can make changes quickly, and in just one place.

- In a Layout Assembly, blocks are created from each sketch to help handle them more efficiently. A block is created by grouping the sketch entities, dimensions, callouts, etc., into one unit and then saving them as a Block. A block can easily be moved, positioned, or re-used in other assembly documents.

- In layout-based assembly design, you can switch back and forth between top-down and bottom-up design methods. You can create, edit, and delete parts and blocks at any point in the design cycle without any history-based restrictions. This is particularly useful during the conceptual design process, when you frequently experiment with and make changes to the assembly structure and components.

- This chapter will guide you through the use of Layout Assembly, as well as making new blocks and converting them to 3D models.

Assembly Motions
Layout Assembly

Dimensioning Standards: **ANSI**
Units: **INCHES** – 3 Decimals

Tools Needed:

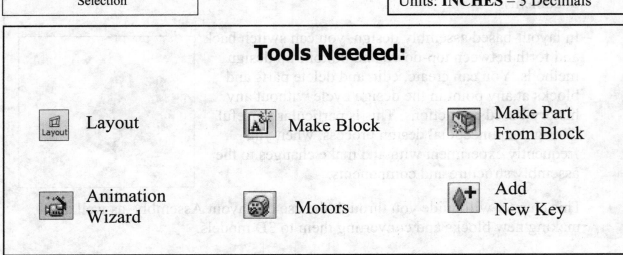

Layout   Make Block   Make Part From Block

Animation Wizard   Motors   Add New Key

1. Opening an assembly document:

- Browse to the Training Files folder and open the document named: **Layout Assembly.sldasm**.

2. Activating the layout mode:

- In order to see the motions in the Layout mode, each sketch must be converted into a Block.

- In a block, a set of sketch entities and Dimensions are grouped into one unit or one block so that they can be moved, positioned easily, or re-used in other assembly documents.

Block 2

Block 1

- Click the **Layout** button on the Layout tab, next to the Assembly toolbar (arrow).

Block 3

NOTE: *Recreate the mates if needed.*

3. Creating a new sketch:

- Sketch the profile below and add the dimensions as shown.

Ø.710
Ø.395
R2.000
Tangent
3.000

Ø.710
Ø.395
R2.000
3.000

4. Making a Block:

- A block is created by grouping the Sketch entities, dimensions, callouts, etc., into one unit and then saving them as a Block.

- Box-select the entire profile, click the **Make Block** button from the pop up toolbar – OR – select **Tools / Block / Make** from the pull down menus.

Make Block

5. Setting the Insertion Point:

- Each block should have an Insertion Point (or Handle Point), which will allow the block to move and position more easily.

Manipulator symbol

Drag the Manipulator to here

- Expand the **Insertion Point** option (arrow) and drag the Blue Manipulator symbol and place it on the center of the middle circle.

- Click **OK** ✓ .

6. Editing a block:

- To edit a block simply double click on one of its sketch entities - or - Right click one of the lines and select: **Edit Block** (arrow).

- Click-Off the Edit Block button on the Layout tool bar when finished (arrow).

Coincident

- Ensure that the Edit Block mode is off.

- Add a **Coincident** relation between the centers of the 2 small circles as indicated.

7. Adding dimensions:

- Add a **6.000 in** dimension to define the spacing between the 2 blocks.

Note: _Dimension from the vertical centerline of the 1st block to the center of the 4th block as noted below._

Dimension to centerline (Try adding the dimension <u>from</u> the centerpoint of the circle <u>to</u> the centerline).

6.000

8. Testing the relations between the blocks:

- Drag one of the vertices of the new part to see how the blocks respond.

6.000

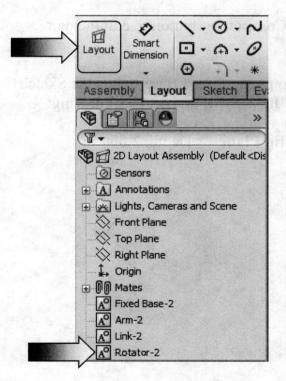

- **Click-off** the Layout command (arrow).

- Rename the new block to: **Rotator** (arrow).

- So far we have 4 different blocks, created as 2D-sketches in the assembly environment. The next step is to convert these blocks into 3D solid parts.

9. Converting a Block into a Component:

- Right click the name of the 1st block (Fixed Base) select **Make Part from Block**.

- Select the **On Block** option under the Block to Part Constraint dialog.

- Click **OK** .

- A new part is created on the Feature tree and it can be edited using the Top Down assembly method, as described in the next few steps.

Project: Creates a part that is projected from the plane of the block in the layout sketch, but not constrained to be co-planar with. In the assembly, you can drag the part in a direction normal to the plane of the block.

On Block: Constrains the part to be co-planar with the plane of the block in the layout sketch.

10. Extruding the Fixed Base:

- Click the **Edit Component** button to edit the part Fixed Base.

- **Expand** the component Fixed Base, select the Sketch1, click **Extruded Boss/Base**, and set the following:

* Type: **Mid Plane**   * Depth: **2.000 in**

- Click **OK** .

11. Adding fillets:

- Click the **Fillet/ Round** command.

- Enter **.500 in** for radius.

- Select the **2 edges** As indicated.

- Click **OK** .

Select 2 edges

12. Shelling the part:

- Click the **Shell** command from the Features toolbar.

- Enter **.250 in** for wall thickness.

- Select the **7 faces** as noted.

Select 7 faces on the left and right sides

- Click **OK** .

13. Adding a hole:

- Click the **Extruded Cut** command.

- Select **Though All** for both Direction1 and Direction2.

- Click in the **Selected-Contour** selection box and select the **circle** as shown.

- Click **OK** ✓ .

Select this circle...

- Click off the **Edit Component** command , the first part is completed.

14. Converting the next block: (Repeating from step no. 8)

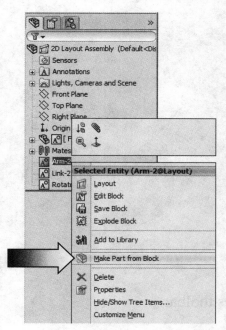

- Right click on the block named **Arm** and select **Make Part from Block**.

- Select the **On Block** option once again, from the **Block to Part Constraint** section.

- A new part is created on the Feature Tree and it can be edited using the same method as the last one.

- Click **OK** ✓.

15. Extruding the Arm:

- Select the part **Arm** from the Feature tree and click the **Edit Component** button.

- **Expand** the part **Arm**, select its sketch and click **Extruded Boss/Base**.

- Set the following:

　　* Type: **Mid Plane**

　　* Depth: **1.400 in**

- Click **OK** ✓.

Note: _There should be a .050" of clearance on each side of this part, measured from the opening of the Fixed Base._

16. Adding a cut:

- Select the **Front** plane of the Part Arm and sketch the profile as shown.

- Use **Convert Entities** If needed and add the relations/dimensions to fully define the sketch.

- Select the **Extruded Cut** command from the Features toolbar.

- Set the following:

  * Type: **Mid Plane**

  * Depth: **.900 in**

- Click **OK** ✅ .

Note: _Make any adjustments if necessary to ensure proper fits between the components so that they can move freely._

- **EXIT** the **Edit Component** mode 🖼️ .

17. Repeating:

- Repeat either the **step 8** or **step 13** and convert the next two blocks the same way.

- Make the part **Link .800 in** thick as shown.

- Extrude with the **Mid Plane** type to keep the Link on the center of the Arm.

- **EXIT** the **Edit Component** mode .

18. Using the Extrude-From option:

- The Extrude-From option allows a sketch to be extruded from a different location rather than from its own sketch plane. This new "location" can be either a plane, a surface of a part, or an offset distance which the user can control.

- Select the part **Rotator** and click **Edit Component**.

- Set the following:

1. Extrude From:

* **Offset**

* **.400 in**

* **Reverse Direction**

2. Direction 1:

* **Blind**

* **.500 in**

* **Reverse Direction**

3. Selected Contour:

* Select the sketch of the **Rotator**.

* Click **OK**.

* **EXIT** the **Edit Component**.

19. Hiding the sketches:

- For clarity, hide all sketches of the components.

- Right click on one of the sketch entities and select HIDE.

*- Note: Make any adjustments if necessary to make sure the components can be moved freely. Use the **Interference Detection** option and check for interferences, if any.*

20. Viewing the Assembly Motions:

- Drag the part **Rotator** back and forth to see how the components will move.

- Keep the part Fixed Base fixed and recreate any mates if necessary.

21. Saving your work:

- Save the assembly document as **Layout Assembly.sldasm**

SolidWorks Animator – The Basics

- You can use animation motion studies to simulate the motion of assemblies.

- The following techniques can be used to create animated motion studies:

  * Create a basic animation by dragging the timeline and moving components.
  * Use the Animation Wizard to create animations or to add rotation, explodes, or collapses to existing motion studies.
  * Create camera-based animations and use motors or other simulation elements to drive the motion.

- This exercise discusses the use of all techniques mentioned above.

1. Opening an existing Assembly document:

- Open the file named: **Egg-Beater.sldasm** from the Training Files folder.

- Click the **Motion Study** tab to switch to the SolidWorks-Animation program (Motion Study1).

Motion Study Tab

2. Adding a Rotary Motor:

- Click the **Motor** icon from the **Motion Manager** toolbar.

- Under **Motion Type**, click the **Rotary Motor** option (arrow).

- Select the **Circular edge** of the Main Gear as indicated, for **Direction**.

- Click **Reverse direction** (arrow).

- Under **Motion**, select **Constant Speed**.

- Set the speed to: **30 RPM** (arrow).

- Click **OK** .

Select this circular edge
(of the blue wheel)
for direction

3. Viewing the rotary motions:

- Click the **Calculate** button on the **Motion Manager** (arrow).

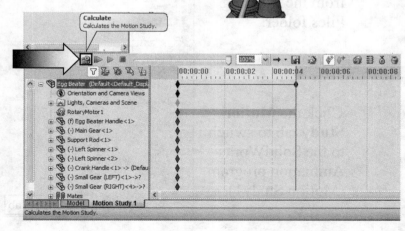

- The motor plays back the animation and by default, stops at the 5-second timeline.

4. Using the Animation Wizard:

- Click the **Animation Wizard** button on the **Motion Manager** toolbar.

- Select the **Rotate Model** Option from the **Animate Type** dialog.

- As noted in this dialog box, in order to animate the Explode or Collapse of an assembly, an exploded view must be created prior to making the animation.

- Click **Next** [Next >] .

- For **Axis of Rotation**, select the **Y-axis**.

- For **Number of Rotation**, enter **1**.

- Select the **Clockwise** option.

- Click **Next** [Next >] .

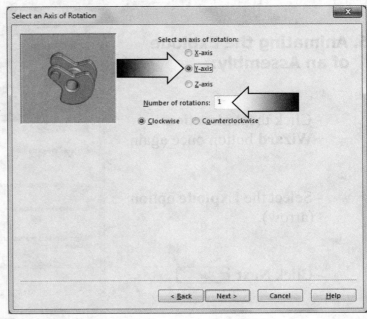

- To control the speed of the animation, the duration should be set (in seconds).

    * **Duration: 5** (arrow)

- To delay the movement at the beginning of the animation, set:

    * **Start time: 6** seconds

- This puts one-second of delay time after the last movement before animating the next.

- Click **Finish** Finish .

- Click **Calculate** to view the rotated animation.

5. Animating the Explode of an Assembly:

- Click the **Animation-Wizard** button once again.

- Select the **Explode** option (arrow).

- Click **Next** Next > .

- Use the same speed as the last time

     * **Duration: 5 seconds** (arrow).

- Also put one-second of delay time at the end of the last movement.

     * **Start Time: 12 seconds** (arrow).

- Click **Finish** [Finish] .

- Click **Calculate** to view the new animated movements.

- To view the entire animation, click:

Play from Start.

6. Animating the Collapse of the Assembly:

- Click the **Animation Wizard** button on the **Motion-Manager** toolbar.

- Select the **Collapse** option from the **Animate Type** dialog.

- Click **Next** ⟨ Next > ⟩ .

- Set the **Duration** to: **5 seconds**.

- Set the **Start Time** to: **18 seconds**.

- Click **Finish** ⟨ Finish ⟩ .

- Click **Calculate** to view the new animated movements.

- Click the **Play from Start** button to view the entire animation.
Notice the change in the view? We now need to change the view orientation.

7. Changing the View Orientation of the assembly at 17-second:

- Drag the timeline to **17-second position**.

- From the MotionManager tree, right click on **Orientation and Camera Views** and un-select the **Disable View Key Creation** (arrow).

- Click the **Add/Update Key** (below).

- This key will allow modifications to the steps recorded earlier.

Add/Update Key
Creates a new key with the selected item's current attributes, or updates an existing key.

- Press the **F** key on the keyboard to change to the full screen – or – click Zoom to fit.

- The change in the view orientation from a zoomed-in position to a full-screen has just been recorded. To update the animation, press **Calculate.**

- The animation plays back showing the new Zoomed position.

Note: _This last step demonstrated that a key point(s) can be inserted at any time during the creation of the animation to modify when the view change should occur. Other attributes like colors, lights, cameras, shading, etc., can also be defined the same way._

- When the animation reaches the 23 second timeline, the assembly is shown as collapsed. We'll need to add another key and change the view orientation to full screen once again.

8. Changing the View Orientation of the Assembly at 23 second:

- Make sure the timeline is moved to **23 second position**.

- Click the **Add/Update Key** button on the MotionManager toolbar.

Note:

In order to capture the changes in different positions, a new key should be added each time. We will need to go back to the full screen so that more details can be viewed.

- Press the **F** key on the keyboard to change to the full screen – or – click Zoom to fit.

Zoom to Fit ⟶

- Similar to the previous step, the change in the view orientation has just been captured.

- To update the animation, press **Calculate.**

- The system plays back the animation showing the new zoom to fit position.

- Save your work before going to the next steps.

Calculate
Calculates the Motion Study.

9. Creating the Flashing effects:

- Move the timeline to **3-second position**.

- Click the **Add/Update Key** button.

- We are going to make the Handle flash 3 times.

- Right click the part **Egg-Beater-Handle**
from the Animation tree, go to
Component Display and
select **Wireframe**.

- Click **Calculate** .

- At this point, the Handle
turns into Wireframe when
the animation reaches the
3 second timeline and stays
that way until the end.

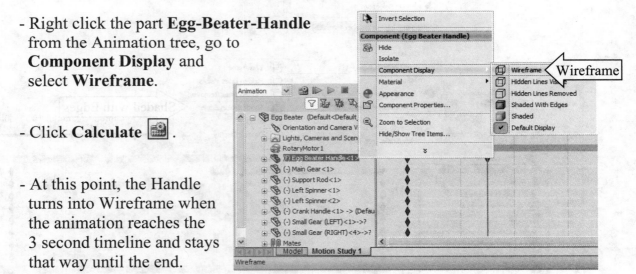

- Hover the cursor over the key point to display its key properties.

Place the mouse cursor over this key

- Next, move the timeline to the **3.5 second position**.

- This time we are going to change the Handle back to shaded mode.

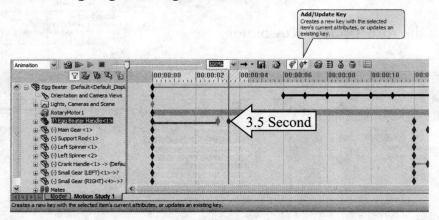

- Right click on the part **Egg Beater Handle**, go to **Component Display**, and select **Shaded with Edges**.

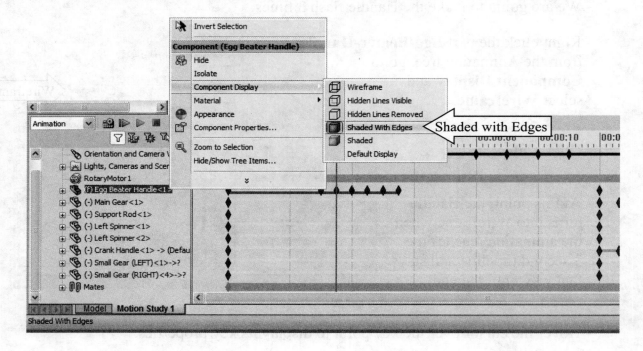

- Click **Calculate** 📷 .

- Since the change only happens within ½ of a second, the handle looks like it was flashing.

- Repeat the same step a few times, to make the flashing effect look more realistic.

4-second = Wireframe

3.5-second = Shaded with Edges

3-second = Wireframe

4.5-second = Wireframe

5-second = Shaded with Edges

5.5-second = Wireframe

- Use the times chart listed above and repeat the step number 9 at least 3 more times.

10. Looping the animation:

- Click the Playback Mode arrow and select **Playback Mode: Reciprocate** (arrow).

- Click **Play From Start** to view the entire animation again.

11. Saving the animation as AVI: (Audio Visual Interleaving):

- Click the **Save Animation** icon on the Motion Manager toolbar.

- Use the default name (Egg Beater) and other default settings.

- Click **Save**.

- The **Image Size** and **Aspect Ratio** (grayed-out) adjusts size and shape of the display. It becomes available when the renderer is PhotoWorks buffer.

- **Compression** ratios impact image quality. Use lower compression ratios to produce smaller file sizes of lesser image quality.

12. Viewing the Egg Beater AVI with Windows Media Player:

- **Exit** the SolidWorks program, locate and launch your **Windows Media Player**.

- **Open** the **Egg Beater.AVI** from Windows Media Player.

- Click the **Play** button to view the animated AVI file.

- To loop the animation in Windows Media Player, select **Repeat** from the Play dropdown menu.

- Also try changing the **Play Speed** from **Normal** to **Fast** and Play the animation again.

- **Close** and **exit** the Window Media Player.

CHAPTER 13

Working with Sketch Pictures

Working with Sketch Pictures
Using the Spline tool

- A digital image can be used as a reference to model a part.
Each image can be placed on its own planes, so several images can be inserted to help define the shape of the model from different orientations.

- The formats such as jpg, tif, bmp, gif, png, etc., are supported in SolidWorks. They can be inserted and converted into a sketch, so that a feature can be made from it.

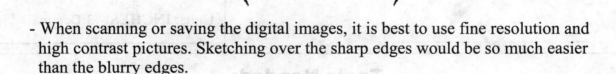

- When scanning or saving the digital images, it is best to use fine resolution and high contrast pictures. Sketching over the sharp edges would be so much easier than the blurry edges.

- Splines are often used to do the tracing of the images due to its flexibilities in manipulating the shapes, and splines offer a set of control tools to assist you with creating and maintaining the smoothness of the curves.

- The digital or scanned image can be scaled to size and reposition with reference to the origin so that dimensions can be added for accuracy.

Working with Sketch Pictures
Using Splines

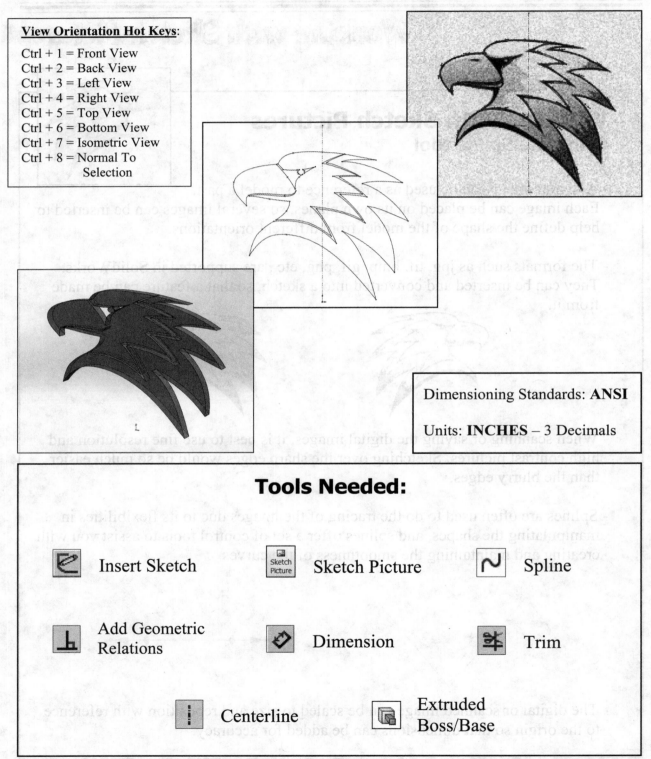

View Orientation Hot Keys:

Ctrl + 1 = Front View
Ctrl + 2 = Back View
Ctrl + 3 = Left View
Ctrl + 4 = Right View
Ctrl + 5 = Top View
Ctrl + 6 = Bottom View
Ctrl + 7 = Isometric View
Ctrl + 8 = Normal To
           Selection

Dimensioning Standards: **ANSI**

Units: **INCHES** – 3 Decimals

Tools Needed:

Insert Sketch		Sketch Picture		Spline	
Add Geometric Relations		Dimension		Trim	
Centerline		Extruded Boss/Base			

1. Inserting the scanned image:

- The scanned image must be inserted into an active sketch.

- Select the <u>Front</u> plane and open a new sketch.

- From the **Tools** menu, click **Sketch Tools / Sketch Picture**

- Browse to the Training Files folder and select the file named: **Eagle Head.jpg** and open it.

- The lower left corner of the image is placed on the origin.

- The image size and locations appear on the properties tree, we will modify those dimensions in the next step.

Origin

2. Positioning and sizing the scanned image:

- Sketch a **vertical centerline** to help centering the image

- Double click the image to activate it.

- Enter the following dimensions to re-position and re-size the image:

  * X = **-1.825in**.
  * Y = **-0.300in**.
  * Angle = **0deg**.
  * Width = **3.600in**.
  * Height = **3.000in**.

- Be sure to enable the **Lock Aspect Ratio** checkbox.

- Click **OK**.

Splines:

- A spline is a sketch entity that gets its shape from a set of spline points. This tool is great for modeling free-form shapes that required a little more "flexibilities" than other curve tools.

- During the creation of a spline, each click creates a spline point and these points can be added or deleted when needed.

- Try to use as few spline points as possible in the general, long curving areas. Only use more spline points on tighter, smaller radiuses.

- Use the spline handles to drag freely, or hold the ALT key to drag symmetrically. The spline handles are used to change the direction and magnitude of the tangency at a spine point.

- Use the Control Polygons in place of the spline handles. Drag its control points to manipulate the spline.

- The Curvature Combs displays the curvature of the spline in a form of a series of lines called a comb. The length of the lines represents the curvature. The longer the line, the larger the curvature, and smaller the radius.

- Inflection Points or Markers are used to show where the inflection changes in a spline, whether it is convex or concave.

3. Tracing the image with the spline tool:

- The sketch should still be active at this time, select the Spline command from the Sketch toolbar.

- Keep in mind that the simpler the spline, the easier to manipulate it. So we are going to create one spline with two or three spline points each time, and then adjust it to match the outline of the image as close as possible. (Zoom in a little closer).

- Start at "point 1", and "point 2", then "point 3" as indicated.

- Push the **Escape** key when done.

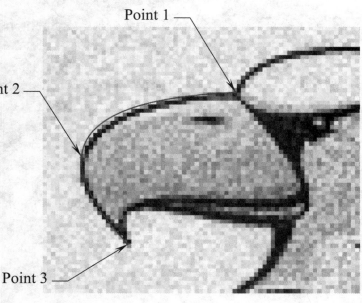

- Zoom in even closer so that You can adjust the spline a little easier.

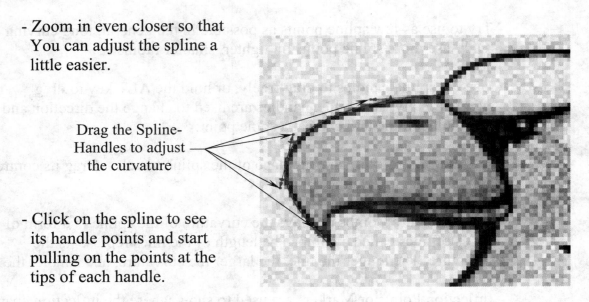

Drag the Spline-Handles to adjust the curvature

- Click on the spline to see its handle points and start pulling on the points at the tips of each handle.

- It may take some getting used to, so work on a small area each time. Create only one spline each time, and each spline should have two or three points only.

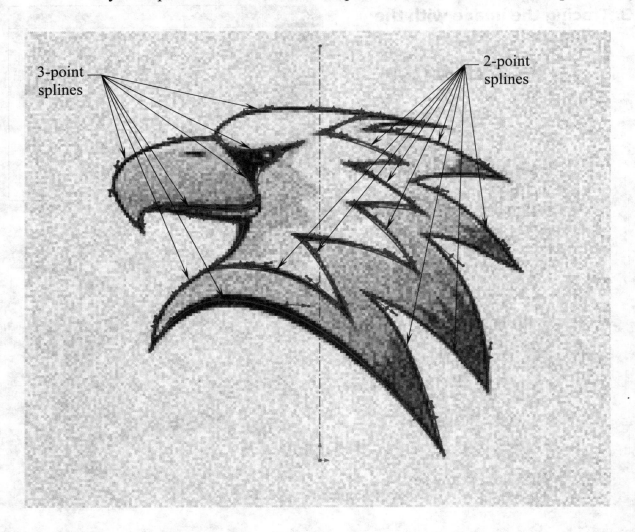

3-point splines

2-point splines

- There should be a small gap
around the sketch (as noted),
so that a single sketch
can be extruded
into a feature.

Gaps

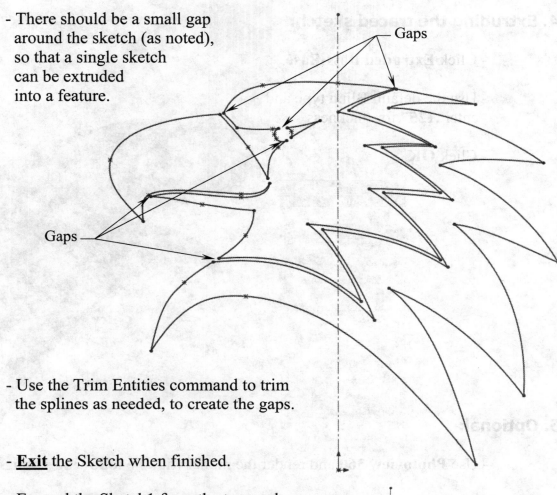

Gaps

- Use the Trim Entities command to trim
the splines as needed, to create the gaps.

- **Exit** the Sketch when finished.

- Expand the Sketch1 from the tree and
Suppress the Sketch Picture.

4. Extruding the traced sketch:

- Click **Extruded Boss-Base**.

- Use the default Blind type and enter **.125"** for thickness

- Click **OK**.

5. Optional:

- Use **Photoview 360** and render the model with the following settings:

- Appearances: **Glass / Clear Thick Gloss / Clear Thick Glass**

- Scene: **Studio Scenes / Reflective Floor Black**.

- Lighting: **Green
              Brown
              Blue**

- Output Image Quality:
  1280 X 1024

6. Saving your work:

- Save your work as:
Eagle Head_Sketch Picture.

Questions for Review

Working with Sketch Pictures

1. A digital image can be inserted into a sketch to reference a model.
   - a. True
   - b. False

2. Most picture formats are supported such as: bmp, jpg, gif, tif, png.
   - a. True
   - b. False

3. A digital image can be copied and pasted into a sketch plane, and used as a background for tracing.
   - a. True
   - b. False

4. A scanned picture should be scanned as low-resolution and has multi-colors is best for tracing.
   - a. True
   - b. False

5. To open a digital image, you should use the command Sketch Picture to insert it into a plane.
   - a. True
   - b. False

6. A digital image can be opened in SolidWorks like any part or assembly file.
   - a. True
   - b. False

7. The spline command creates curves that are fixed and cannot be changed or manipulated.
   - a. True
   - b. False

8. To see the spline handles, simply click on the spline.
   - a. True
   - b. False

7. FALSE   8. TRUE
5. TRUE   6. FALSE
3. FALSE   4. FALSE
1. TRUE   2. TRUE

CHAPTER 13 (cont.)

Working with MultiBody Parts

MultiBody Parts
Creating Mates and Exploded Views

- Use the **Insert Part** command to insert a base part into another part document.

- When you insert a part into another part, it becomes a MultiBody Part, and the part you insert becomes a Solid Body.

- If the inserted part contains mate references, you can use them to position the inserted part.

- There are 3 options available to help locate a solid body: Constraints, Translate, and Rotate. You can move or rotate the body after it is placed in the graphics area. A feature Body-Move/Copy is then added to the FeatureManager design tree.

- The inserted body can also be constrained with the mate options. Some of the standard mates are available in the part mode to help position the solid bodies.

- An exploded view is created after all solid bodies are positioned. Exploded views are stored in the ConfigurationManager. They can be edited, deleted, or more than one exploded views can be created, if needed.

- This chapter will guide you through the use of multibodies parts, where an existing part document with a number of solid bodies is used. Other parts will then get inserted into the same document and constrained with some mates. After all solid bodies are positioned, an exploded view will be created in the same part mode, and the Solid Bodies folder is used to help keep track of the number of solid bodies exist in the part document.

MultiBody Parts
Creating Mates and Exploded Views

Dimensioning Standards: **ANSI**
Units: **INCHES** – 3 Decimals

Tools Needed:

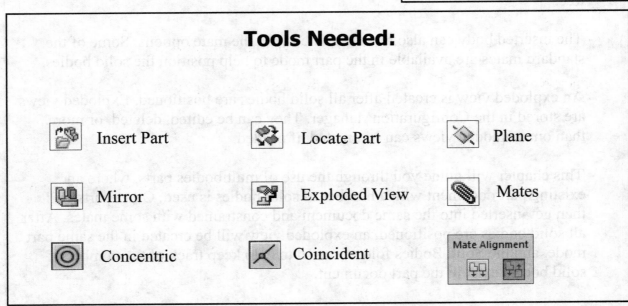

Insert Part

Locate Part

Plane

Mirror

Exploded View

Mates

Concentric

Coincident

Mate Alignment

1. Opening a part document:

- Go to **File / Open**.

- Browse to the Training Files folder. Locate the part document named: **MultiBodies Parts** and open it.

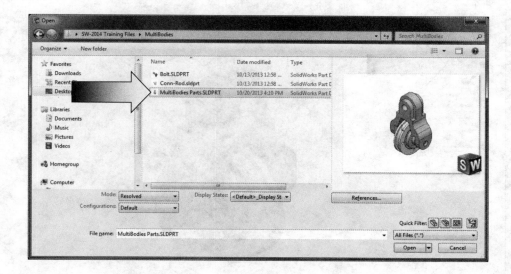

- When opening a non-SolidWorks native document, the program will prompt you with a couple of options such as Import Diagnostics or Feature-Recognition. We will not discuss these options in this chapter but focus on the use of MultiBodies instead.

- If prompted, click **No** to cancel the Import Diagnostics option.

- Click **No** once again to cancel the Feature Recognition options

2. Creating an exploded view:

- We are going to create an exploded view so that a new configuration is made and the collapse / explode views can be toggled back and forth in the future.

- Select **Insert/ Exploded View**.

- The Exploded dialog appears similar to the one seen in the assembly mode.

- Select the **Imported2** solid body either from the graphics area from the feature tree.

- Drag the **Green** arrow head upward to approximately **10 inches**.

- Right click anywhere in the graphics area and select: **Box Selection**.

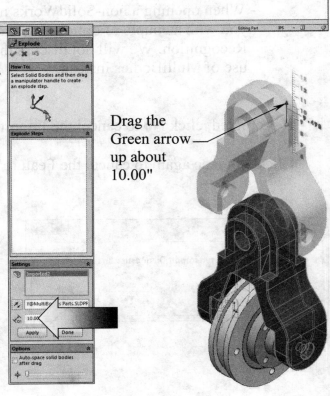

Drag the Green arrow up about 10.00"

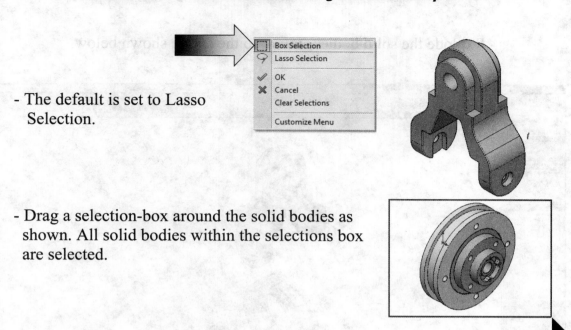

- The default is set to Lasso Selection.

- Drag a selection-box around the solid bodies as shown. All solid bodies within the selections box are selected.

- The outer pulley (Imported1) should not be part of this group, so we are going to unselect it before exploding this group of solid bodies.

- Either hold the Control key and click the Imported1 body to exclude it from the group, or delete it from the list under the Settings section.

Remove Importd1 from the selection

- An alternate method is to select the bodies-to-explode from the Solid Bodies folder, on the FeatureManager tree.

- Explode the solid bodies similar to the image shown below.

3. Collapsing the solid bodies:

- Switch to the ConfigurationManager tree (arrow).

- Expand the Default configuration to see the ExpView1. Right click on ExpView1 and select **Collapse** (arrow).

- The solid bodies are collapsed to their initial stage. We'll toggle back and forth between the Collapse and Explode modes while adding more parts in the next few steps.

- Switch back to the FeatureManager tree by clicking on its tab.

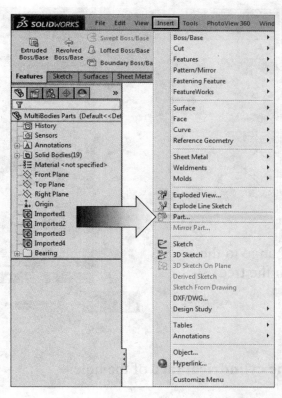

4. Inserting another part:

- Other parts can be inserted into an existing part document. Once inserted they will become Solid Bodies, and the original part becomes a Multibody Part.

- Click **Insert / Part**.

- Select the part document named: **Conn-Rod.sldprt** from the same training files directory and open it.

- Place the new part on the right side of the others, approx. as shown below.

- The **Insert Part** dialog box appears.

- Select the following options:

    * **Solid Bodies**

    * **Planes**

    * **Locate Part with Move/ Copy feature**

- Uncheck all other checkboxes.

- Click **OK**.

5. Constraining the solid bodies:

- By clicking OK from the previous step the **Locate Part** section is activated.

- Click the **Constraints** button to switch to the Mate Settings mode (arrow).

(Click the Translate / Rotate button to change to the Constraints section if it is not visible on the tree).

Adding a Concentric mate:

- Select the **shaft body** of the bolt and the **cylindrical face** of the hole.

- A **Concentric** mate is created and the bolt moves to the same center with the hole.

- Click the **Add** button (arrow) to save the mate in its mate group below.

Select the shaft body and the hole

Adding a Coincident mate:

- Select the 1st **planar face** (face1) as indicated.

- Select the 2nd **planar face** (face2) as noted.

Select face 1

- A **Coincident** mate is created and the 2 selected faces are now coincide or occupying the same place.

Select face 2

- To help keep the file size smaller, we are going to leave the 3rd degree of freedom open. The last mate does not really needed for the purpose of the lesson.

- Select **View / Planes** to hide all the planes in the Imported1 solid body (arrow).

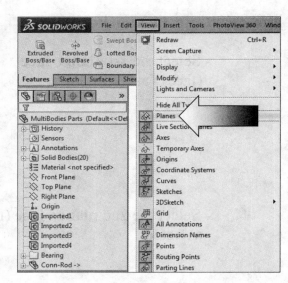

6. Creating a new mirror plane:

- Change to the **Features** tool tab and select the **Plane** command from the Reference Geometry drop down arrow.

- Two **planar surfaces** are needed to create a Mid Plane.

- Select the outer most **left** and **right** faces of the main housing as noted. A Mid Plane is created in the middle of the 2 selected faces.

Select face 1 (Left side)

Select face 2 (Right side)

7. Creating a mirror body:

- Click the **Mirror** command from the Features tool tab.

- Select the **new plane** for **Mirror Face / Plane** (arrow).

- Expand the **Bodies to Mirror** section.

- Expand the **Solid Bodies folder** from the FeatureManager tree and select the **Conn-Rod** from the list.

- **Clear** the **Merge Solids** checkbox and click **OK**.

- **Edit** the Exploded view and move the solid bodies to the positions approx. as shown.

- Right click on
ExplView1and
select **Collapse**.
We will now insert
the bolt into this
document.

- Switch back to the
FeatureManager
tree (arrow).

Optional:

- The FeatureManager tree can be split to display
any combination of:

  * FeatureManager Design tree
  * PropertyManager tree
  * ConfigurationManager
  * DimXpertManager

- Move the mouse pointer under the FeatureManager tab
until it changes to ⇕, drag the split bar down half way
to split it into two panes. Show the FeatureManager tree
on top and the ConfigurationManager below it as shown.

8. Inserting another part:

- The Bolt is going to be inserted into the same part document, it will become another solid body, and the part document is called Multi-Body Part.

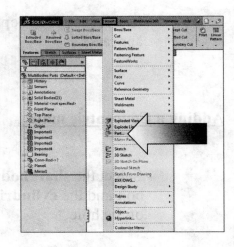

- Click **Insert / Part**.

- Select the part **Bolt.sldprt** from the previous training files folder.

- Place the new part on the right side of the main housing.

- Click **YES** to change the units of the new part to match the units of the MultiBody part.

- Select the **3 checkboxes** as noted and click **OK**.

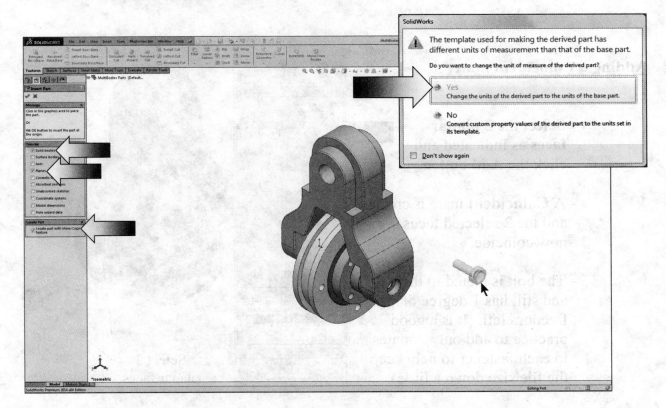

- The **Locate Part** options appears.

Adding a Concentric mate:

- Select the **shaft body** of the bolt and the **cylindrical face** of the hole.

- A **Concentric** mate is created and the bolt moves to the same center with the hole.

Select 2 cylindrical faces

- Click the **Add** button (arrow) to save the mate in its mates group below.

Adding a Coincident mate:

- Select the 2 **planar-faces** as indicated and click the **Add** button.

- A **Coincident** mate is created and the 2 selected faces are now coincide.

- The bolt is mated to the hole and still has 1 degree of freedom left. (It is a good practice to add only 2 mates to each fastener to help keep the file size down a little).

Select 2 planar faces

9. Adding another instance of the bolt:

- A second instance of the bolt is needed on the opposite side of the main housing.

- Click **Insert / Part**.

- Select the part **Bolt.sldprt** once again from the previous directory.

- Rotate the view and place the new part on the left side on the of the main housing.

Adding a Concentric mate:

- Select the body of the bolt and the side hole of the main housing to add a **Concentric** mate.

- Click the **Anti-Aligned** button to flip the bolt 180 degrees (arrow), and then click the **Add** button to save the new mate in its Mates group.

Select 2 cylindrical faces

Anti-Aligned

Adding a Coincident mate:

- Select the 2 **planar-faces** as indicated.

- The 2 selected faces are constrained to share the same location.

- Click the **Add** button to save the new mate.

- Click **OK** to exit the Locate Part mode.

Select 2 planar faces

10. Editing the exploded view:

- Switch to the ConfigurationManager.

- Expand the Default configuration. Right click the **ExpView1** and select **Edit Feature** (arrow).

- Select the bolt on the right.

- Drag the head of the **Red arrow** to move the bolt along the X direction.

NOTE: _Enter a dimension* if a precise distance is preferred._

Settings
< Bolt > <Imported1>
X@MultiBodies Parts.SLDPRT
-225.00mm
Apply   Done

* If distance is used: Select a direction arrow (red), enter a dimension then click Apply and Done.

- Select the bolt on the left.

- Drag the head of the **Red arrow** to the left to move the bolt along the -X direction.

- Click **OK** to exit the exploded View mode.

11. Saving your work:

- Click **File / Save As**.

- Enter: **MultiBodies Parts** for the name of the file.

- Click **Save**.

- Close all documents.

CHAPTER 13 (cont.)

PhotoView 360 Basics

PhotoView 360 enables the user to create photo-realistic renderings of the SolidWorks models. The rendered image incorporates the appearances, lighting, scene, and decals included with the model. PhotoView 360 is available with SolidWorks Pro or SolidWorks Premium only.

- Open the document named **Supersonic Green Aircraft** from the Training Files folder.

1. Activating the PhotoView 360 Add-In:

- Click **Tools / Add-Ins**...

- Select the **PhotoView 360** checkbox.

- Click **OK**.

NOTE:

Enable the checkbox on the right of the PhotoView 360 add-in if you wish to have it available at startup. Otherwise only activate it for each use.

2. Setting the Appearance: (right click the Sketch tab and enable the Render tools).

- Click the **Edit Appearance** button from the Render tool tab (arrow).

- Expand the **Painted** folder, the **Car** folder (arrows) and double click the **Metallic Cool Grey** appearance to apply it to the model. Click **OK** to close.

3. Setting the Scene:

- Click the **Edit Scene** button from the Render tool tab (arrow).

- Expand the **Scenes** folder, the **Basic Scenes** folder (arrows) and <u>double click</u> the **Backdrop - Studio Room** scene to apply it. Set the other settings as noted.

4. Setting the Image Quality options:

- Click the **Options** button from the Render tool tab (arrow).

- Set the **Output Image** to **1920x1080** from the drop down list.
- Set the other options as indicated with the arrows. Click **OK** to close.

5. Rendering the image:

- Click the **Final Rende**r button from the Render tool tab (arrow).

6. Saving the image:

- Select the **Best Fit** option from the drop down list and click **Save Image** (arrows).

- Select the **JPEG** format from the Save-as-Type drop down list.

- Enter a file name and click **OK**.

NOTE:

- *Different file formats may reduce the quality of the image and at the same time, it may increase or decrease the size of the file.*

Save Image

SW-2013 Basic Training Files ► Renderings

Organize ▼   New folder

Favorites
   Desktop
   Downloads
   Recent Places

Libraries
   Documents
   Music
   Pictures
   Videos

Name   Date modified   Type   Size

No items match your search.

File name: Supersonic Green Aircraft

Save as type: JPEG (*.JPG)

Flexible Precision Image Format (*.flx)
Targa (*.tga)
Windows BMP (*.BMP)
Radiance High Dynamic Range HDR (*.hdr)
JPEG 2000 (*.jp2)
JPEG 2000 16-Bit (*.jp2)
JPEG 2000 16-Bit Lossless (*.jp2)
JPEG (*.JPG)
Portable Network Graphic PNG (*.png)
Portable Network Graphic PNG 16-bit (*.png)
SGI RGB (*.SGI)
Tagged Image Format File TIF (*.tif)
16-Bit TIF (*.tif)
16-Bit Uncompr. TIF (*.tif)
OpenEXR Half 16-bit (*.exr)
OpenEXR Float 32-bit (*.exr)
OpenEXR Tiled Half 16-bit (*.exr)
OpenEXR Tiled Float 32-bit (*.exr)

Hide Folders

- Close all documents when finished.

Designed by a CSWP student

Designed by a CSWP student

Designed by a CSWP student

Designed by a CSWP student

CHAPTER 14

Drawing Preparations

Customizing the Document Template

- Custom settings and parameters such as: ANSI standards, units, number of decimal places, dimensions and note fonts, arrow styles and sizes, line styles and line weights, image quality, etc., can be set and saved in the document template for use with the current drawing or at any time in the future.

- All Document Templates are normally stored either in the templates folder or in the Tutorial folder:

  * (C:\Program Files\SolidWorks Corp\ SolidWorks\Data\Templates)
  * (C:\Program Files\SolidWorks Corp\ SolidWorks\Lang\English\Tutorial)

- By default, there are 2 "layers" in every new drawing. The "top layer" is called the **Sheet**, and the "bottom layer" is called the **Sheet Format**.

- The **Sheet** layer is used to create the drawing views and annotations. The **Sheet-Format** layer contains the title block information, revision changes, BOM-anchor, etc.

- The 2 layers can be toggled back and forth by using the FeatureManager tree, or by right clicking anywhere in the drawing and selecting: Edit Sheet Format / Edit Sheet.

- When the settings are done they will get saved in the Document Template with the extension: **.drwdot** (Drawing Document Template).

- This chapter will guide us through the settings and the preparations needed prior to creating a drawing.

Drawing Preparations

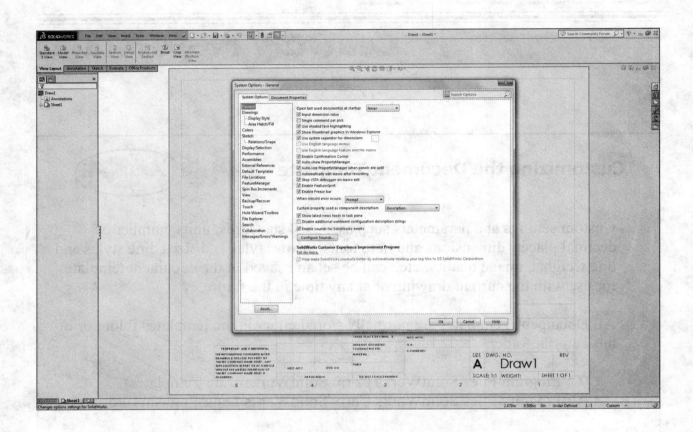

Dimensioning Standards: **ANSI**	Third Angle Projection
Units: **INCHES** – 3 Decimals	

Tools Needed:

 New Drawing

 Options...

Edit Sheet Format   Edit Sheet   Drawing Templates (*.drwdot)

1. Setting up a new drawing:

- Select **File / New / Draw** (or Drawing) / **OK** [OK] .

- Change the option Novice to **Advanced** as noted.

Change to
Advanced

- By clicking on either **Advanced** or **Novice** (Circled), you can switch to the appropriate dialog box.

- Set the following options:

    * **Scale: 1:2**

    * **Third Angle Projection**

    * View Label and Datum Label both set to A.

- Under Standard Sheet Size, choose: **C-Landscape**.

- Uncheck the **Only Show Standard Format** checkbox (arrow).

- Click **OK** [OK]

- The SolidWorks Drawing User Interface

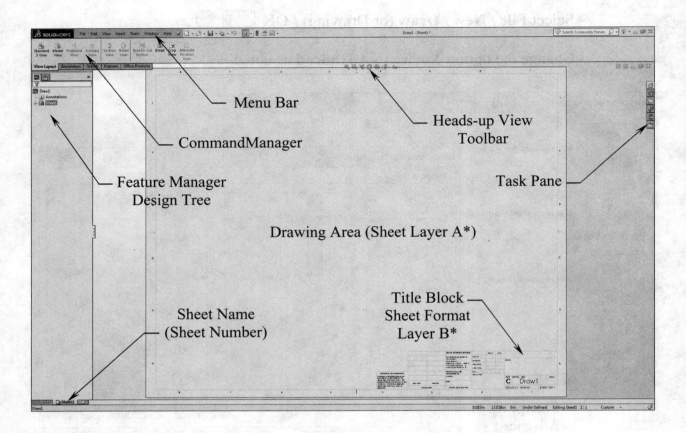

Menu Bar

Heads-up View Toolbar

CommandManager

Feature Manager Design Tree

Task Pane

Drawing Area (Sheet Layer A*)

Sheet Name (Sheet Number)

Title Block — Sheet Format Layer B*

*A. By default, the **Sheet** layer is active and placed over the **Sheet Format** layer.

- The **Sheet** layer is used to create drawing views, dimensions, and annotations.

* B. The "bottom layer" is called the **Sheet Format** layer, which is where the revision block, the title block and its information are stored.

- The Sheet Format layer includes some links to the system properties and the custom properties.

- OLE objects (company's logo) such as .Bmp or .Tif can be embedded here.

- SolidWorks drawings can have different Sheet Formats or none at all.

- Formats or title blocks created from other CAD programs can be opened in SolidWorks using either DXF or DWG file types, and saved as SolidWorks' Sheet Format.

2. Switching to the Sheet Format layer:

- Right click in the drawing and select **Edit Sheet Format**.

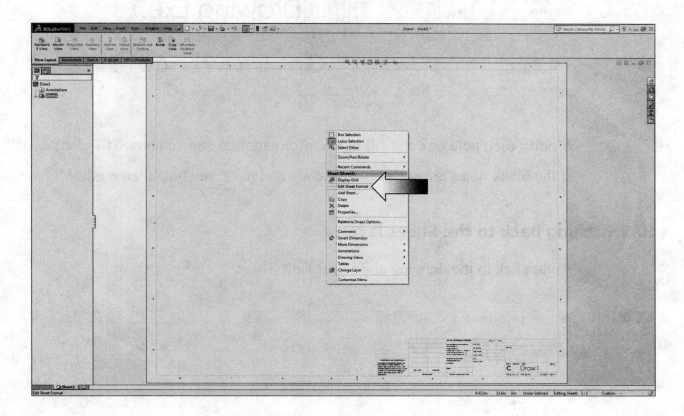

- Using the SolidWorks drawing templates, there are "blank notes" already created for each field within the title block.

- Double click the blank note in the Company-Name field and enter: **SolidWorks.**

Double click on the blank note to modify it...

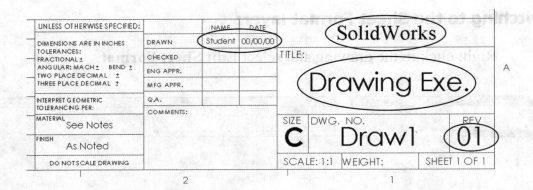

- Modify each note box and fill in the information as shown above (Circled).

- If the blank notes are not available, copy and paste any note then modify it.

3. Switching back to the Sheet layer:

- Right click in the drawing and select **Edit Sheet**.

- The Sheet layer is brought to the top, all information within the Sheet Format layer is kept on the bottom layer.

4. Setting up the Drawing Options:

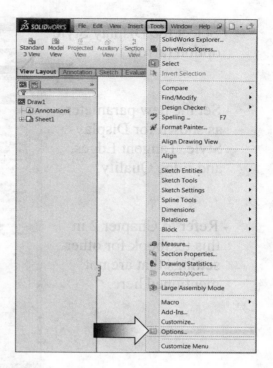

- Go to **Tools / Options**.

- Select the **Drawings** options from the list.

- Enable and/or disable the drawing options by clicking on the check boxes as shown below.

NOTE:

For further information about these options, please refer to Chapter 2 in the: SolidWorks 2012 Part I - Basic Tools textbook (Essential Parts, Assemblies and Drawings).

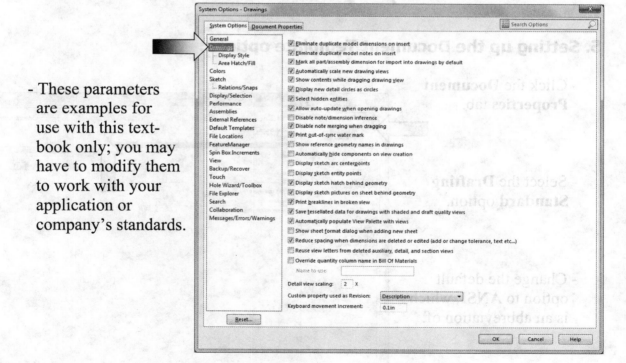

- These parameters are examples for use with this text-book only; you may have to modify them to work with your application or company's standards.

- The parameters that you are setting here will be saved as the default system options, and they will affect the current as well as all future documents.

- Once again, enable only the check boxes as shown in the dialog above.

- Select the Display Style
  option (arrow).

- Set the new parameters
  as shown for Display-
  Style, Tangent Edges,
  and Edge Quality.

- Refer to Chapter 2 in
  this textbook for other
  settings that are not
  mentioned here.

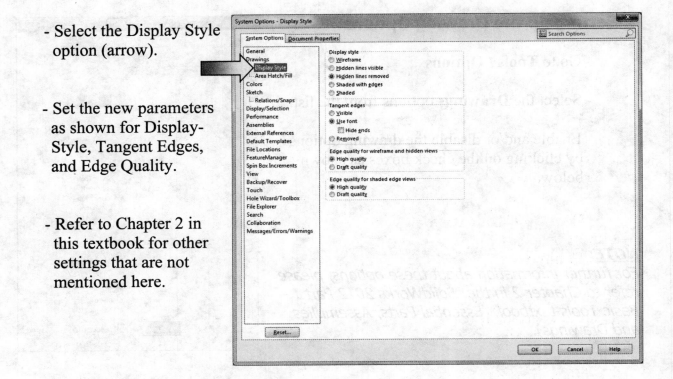

5. Setting up the Document Template options:

- Click the **Document
  Properties** tab.

- Select the **Drafting
  Standard** option.

- Change the default
  option to **ANSI**, which
  is an abbreviation of:

       American
       National
       Standards
       Institute.

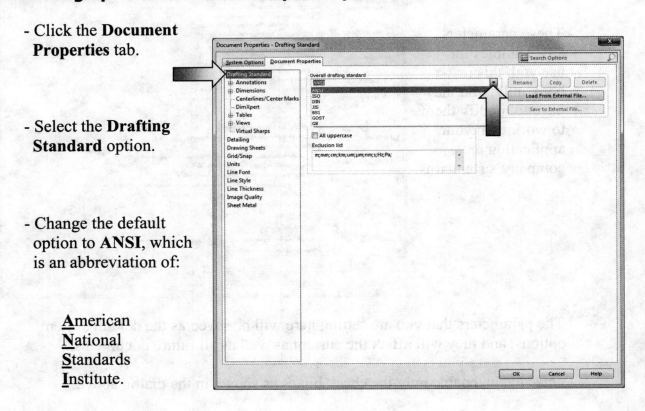

- Select the **Annotations** option (arrow).

- Set the new parameters as shown.

- Click the **Font** button and select the following:

  Century Gothic
  Regular
  13 points

- Set the Note, Dimension, Surface Finish, Weld-Symbol, Tables, and Balloon to match the settings for Annotations.

- Select the **Dimensions** option (arrow).

- Set the parameter in this section to match the ones shown in this dialog box.

- If the Dual Dimension Display is selected, be sure to set the number of decimal places for both of your Primary and Secondary dimensions.

NOTE: Skip to the Units option below, if you need to change your Primary unit from Millimeter to Inches, or vice versa.

- Select the **Centerlines/ Center Marks** option.

- Set the options as indicated for Centerline Extension, Center Marks Size and Slot Center-Marks.

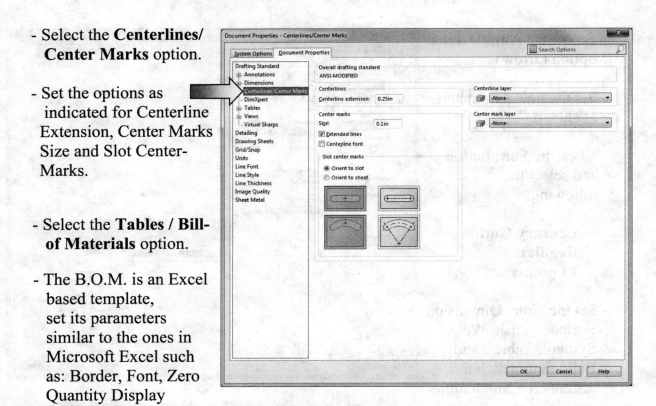

- Select the **Tables / Bill-of Materials** option.

- The B.O.M. is an Excel based template,
  set its parameters similar to the ones in Microsoft Excel such as: Border, Font, Zero Quantity Display
  Missing Component, Leading and Trailing Zeros, etc.

- **Leading Zeros:**
  * Standard: Leading zeros appear according to the overall drafting standard.
  * Show: Shows zeros before decimal point are shown.
  * Remove: Leading zeros do not appear.

- **Trailing Zeros:**
  * Smart: Trailing zeros are timed for whole metric values.
  * Standard: Trailing zeros appear according to ASME standard.
  * Show: Trailing zeros are displayed according to the decimal places specified in Units.
  * Remove: Trailing zeros do not appear.

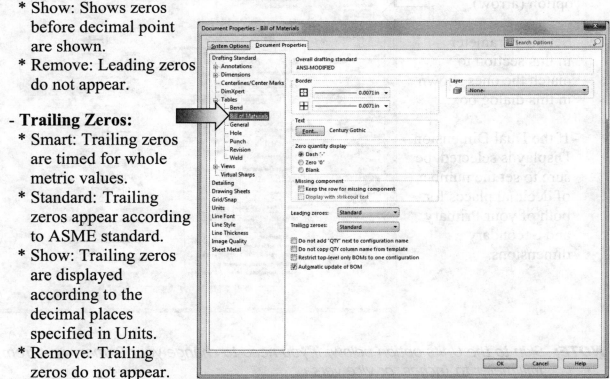

- Select the **Tables /
Revision** option.

- Set the document-level
drafting settings for
revision table like:
Border, Font,
Alphabet Numerical
Control, Multiple Sheet
Style and Layer.

- Select the **View Label /
Detail** option.

- Set the options for:
ANSI View Standard,
Circle, Fonts, Label
and Border.

- Select the **View Label /
Section** option.

- Set the Line Style, Line
Thickness, Fonts, Label,
Scale, Layer, and
Section Arrow
Size.

Standard Display

Alternate Display

- Select the **Detailing**
option.

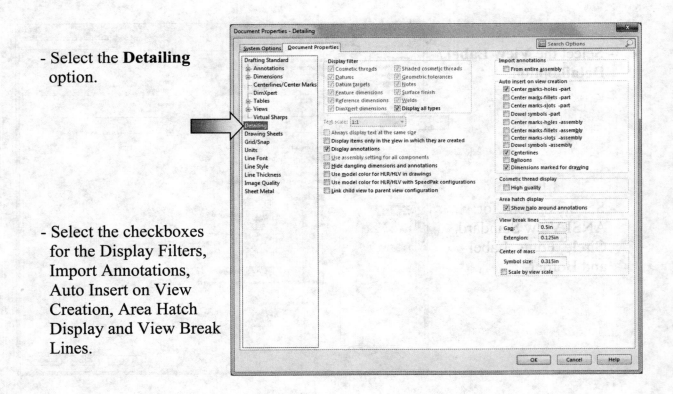

- Select the checkboxes
for the Display Filters,
Import Annotations,
Auto Insert on View
Creation, Area Hatch
Display and View Break
Lines.

- Select the **Drawing-Sheet** option.

- Enable the checkbox: **Use Different Sheet Format** if sheet 2 uses a different (or partial) title block.

- This property lets you automatically have one sheet format for the first sheet and a separate sheet format for all additional sheet.

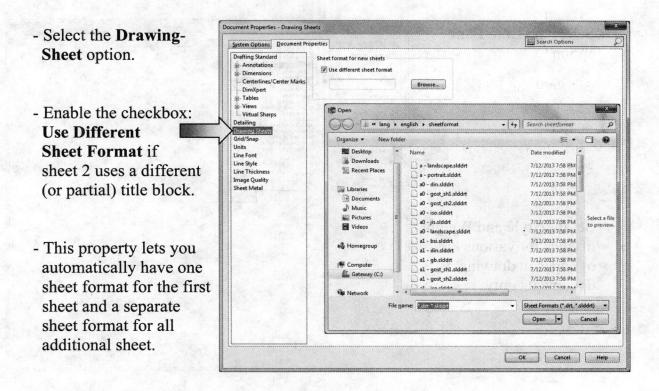

- Select the **Units** option.

- Click the **IPS (Inch, Pound, Second)** system.

- Set the Length Units to: **3 Decimal Places (.123)**

- Other options can be set to meet your company's standards.

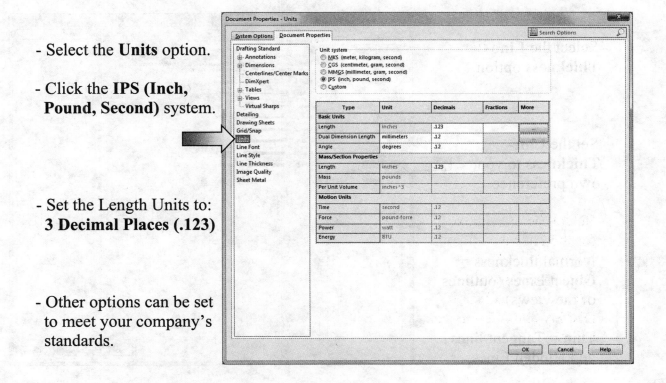

- Select the **Line Font** option.

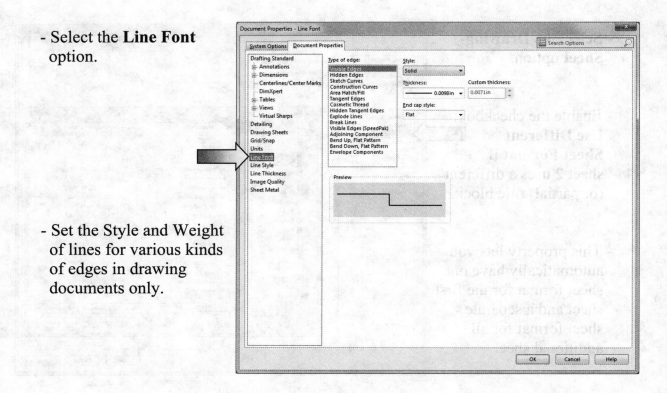

- Set the Style and Weight of lines for various kinds of edges in drawing documents only.

- Select the **Line-Thickness** option.

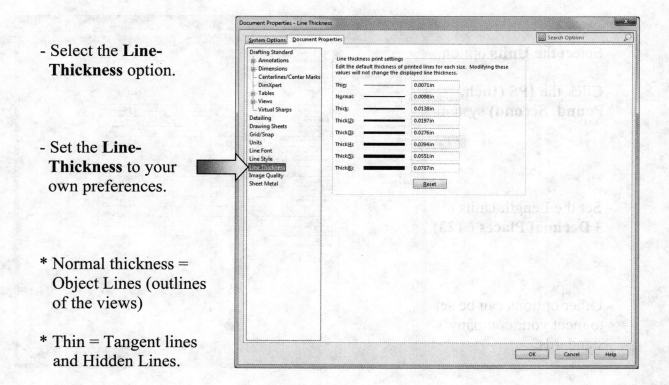

- Set the **Line-Thickness** to your own preferences.

* Normal thickness = Object Lines (outlines of the views)

* Thin = Tangent lines and Hidden Lines.

- Select the **Image-Quality** option.

- Drag the Deviations' Slider to the right to improve the shaded quality (0.00800in Deviation).

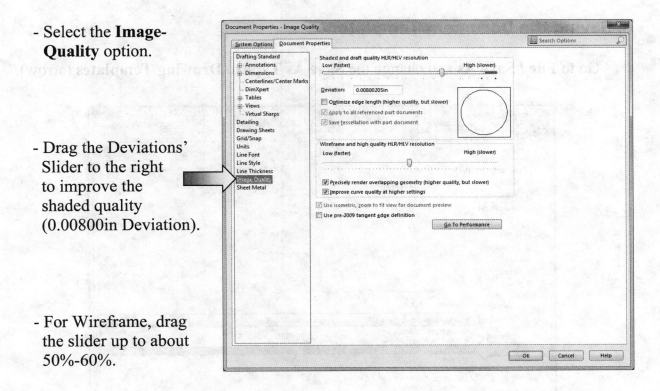

- For Wireframe, drag the slider up to about 50%-60%.

- Select the **Sheet Metal** option.

- Set the colors for Bend-Lines, Form Features, Hems, Model Edges, Flat Pattern Sketch-Color, and Bounding Box.

- Click **OK** OK .

- These settings control the tessellation of curved surfaces for shaded rendering output. A higher resolution setting results in slower model rebuilding but more accurate curves.

6. Saving the Document Template:

- Go to **File / Save As** and change the **Save As Type** to **Drawing Templates** (arrow).

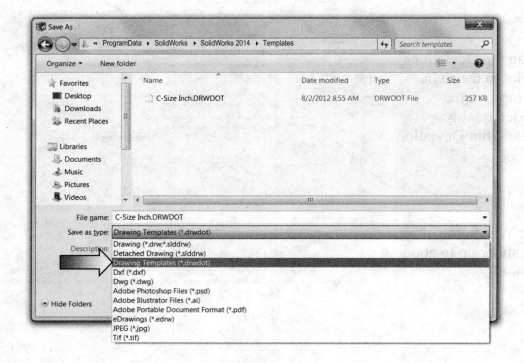

- SolidWorks automatically switches to the **Templates** folder (or **Tutorial** folder), where all SolidWorks templates are stored.

- Enter a name for your new template (i.e. C-Size Inch).

- Click **Save**.

- The Drawing Template can now be used to create new drawings.

- To verify if the Template has been saved properly, click **File / New**, change the option Novice to Advance, and look for the new Template (arrow).

- **Close** the document template.

Questions for Review

Drawing Preperations

1. Custom settings and parameters can be set and saved in the Document Template.
   - a. True
   - b. False

2. Document Templates are normally stored either in: (C:\Program Files\SolidWorks Corp\ SolidWorks\Data\Templates) OR (C:\Program Files\SolidWorks Corp\Lang\English\ Tutorial).
   - a. True
   - b. False

3. To access the sheet format and edit the information in the title block:
   - a. Right click in the drawing and select Edit Sheet Format.
   - b. Right click the Sheet Format icon from the Feature Tree and select Edit Sheet-Format.
   - c. All of the above.

4. The **Sheet** layer is where the Title Block information and Revisions changes are stored.
   - a. True
   - b. False

5. The **Sheet Format** layer is used to create the drawing views, dimensions, and annotations.
   - a. True
   - b. False

6. Information in the Title Block and Revision Block are Fixed, they cannot be modified.
   - a. True
   - b. False

7. The Document Template is saved with the file Extension:
   - a. DWG
   - b. DXF
   - c. SLDPRT
   - d. DRWDOT
   - e. SLDDRW

1. TRUE 2. TRUE 3. C 4. FALSE 5. FALSE 6. FALSE 7. D

CHAPTER 15

Assembly Drawings

Assembly Drawings
Links Assembly

- Assembly drawings are created in the same way as part drawings, the same drawing tools and commands are used to create the drawing views and annotations. In an assembly drawing all components are shown together as assembled or as exploded.

- The standard drawing views like the Front, Top, Right, and Isometric views can be created with the same drawing tools, or they can be dragged and dropped from the View Pallet.

- When a cross section view is created, it will be cross hatched automatically and the hatch patterns that represents the material of the part can be added and easily edited as well.

- A parts list or a Bill of Materials (B.O.M.) is created to report the details of the components such as:

* Materials.

* Vendors.

* Quantities.

* Part numbers, etc.

4	004-12345	Single Link	4
3	003-12345	Pin Head	6
2	002-12345	Alignment Pin	6
1	001-12345	Double Link	3
ITEM NO.	PART NUMBER	DESCRIPTION	QTY.

- The components will then be labeled with Balloons (or Dash Numbers) for verification against the Bill of Materials.

- This chapter discusses the basics of creating an assembly drawing using SolidWorks 2014.

Links Assembly
Assembly Drawings

ITEM NO.	PART NUMBER	DESCRIPTION	QTY.
1	004-12345	Double Link	3
2	003-12345	Alignment Pin	6
3	002-12345	Pin Head	6
4	001-12345	Single Link	4

SolidWorks

TITLE:
LINKS ASSEMBLY

C | 001-12345 | 01

Dimensioning Standards: **ANSI**	Third Angle Projection
Units: **INCHES** – 3 Decimals	

Tools Needed:

 New Drawing
Draw

 Model View

 Shaded View

 Balloon

 Bill of Materials

 Properties...

1. Creating a new drawing:

- Select **File / New / Draw** (or Drawing) / **OK**.

- Under Standard Sheet Size, select **C-Landscape** for paper size.

A = 8.5"	x	11.00"	(Landscape)
B = 17.00"	x	11.00"	(Landscape)
C = 22.00"	x	17.00"	(Landscape)
D = 34.00"	x	22.00"	(Landscape)
E = 44.00"	x	34.00"	(Landscape)

- Enable **Display Sheet Format** checkbox to display the revision and title blocks.

- Click **OK** [OK] .

- The Drawing template appears in the graphics area.

- Right click in the drawing and select **Properties**.

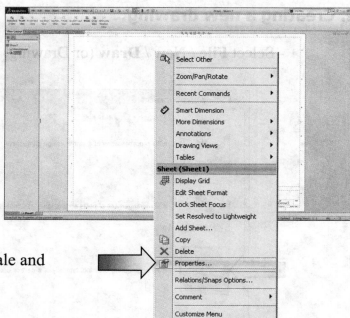

- Set the Drawing Views Scale and Angle of Projection:

(3rd **Angle = U.S. OR 1st = Europe & Asia**).

(**3rd Angle = U.S. OR 1st = Europe & Asia**).

- Set **Scale** to **1:1** (full scale)

- Set **Type of Projection** to: **Third Angle**

- Click **OK** .

2. Editing the Sheet Format:

- Right click inside the drawing and select **Edit-Sheet-Format**.

- The **Format** layer is brought up to the top.

3. Setting up the anchor point to attach the B.O.M.:

- Zoom in on the lower right side of the title block.

- Right click on the end point of the line (as shown) and select **Set-As-Anchor / Bill Of Materials**.

- Double click each blank note and fill out the information in the Title Block as shown.

4. Switching back to the Sheet layer:

- Right click inside the drawing and select **Edit-Sheet.**

- **Change the Drawing Paper's color:**

- Select **Tools / Options / System Options / Colors / Drawing Paper Colors / Edit**.

- Select the **White** color and also enable: **Use Specified Color for Drawings Paper-Color** option.

5. Opening an existing assembly document:

- Click the **Model View** command from the View Layout toolbar.

- Click the **Browse** button, from the Training Files folder, locate and open the **Links Assembly** document.

- There are several different methods to create the drawing views; in this lesson, we will discuss the use of the **Model-View** command first.

- Select the **Isometric** view button (arrow) and place the drawing view approximately as shown.

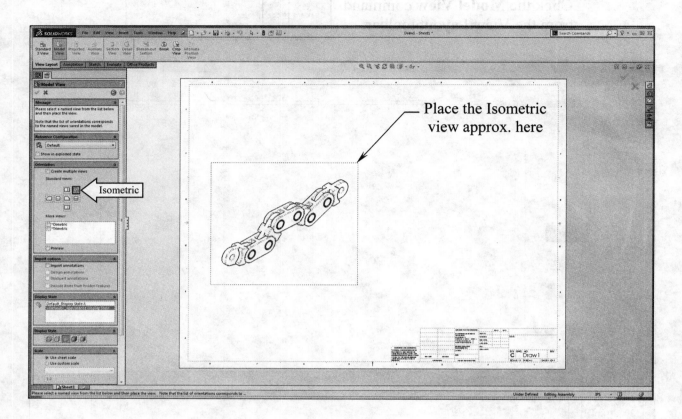

Place the Isometric view approx. here

Isometric

- The drawing view scale will be changed in the next couple of steps.

- The isometric view is created based on the default orientations of the last saved assembly document.

<u>NOTE:</u>

*If the Assembly document is already opened, press **Ctrl + Tab** to toggle back and forth between the Drawing and the Assembly documents.*

6. Switching to the Exploded View state:

- Right click on the drawing view's border and select **Properties**.

(In the newer releases of SolidWorks, the Explode option is also available on the top left of the properties tree).

Right click on the drawing view border and select Properties...

- Enable the **Show In - Exploded State** check box.

- The exploded checkbox is only available if an exploded view has been created earlier in the assembly level.

- Click **OK** [OK] .

7. Changing the Scale of the Isometric Exploded view:

- Click the drawing view border to access the Properties tree.

- Select **User Defined** under the Scale section.

- Enter **3:2 (or 1.5 to 1)** for Custom Scale.

Notes:

- When changing the Scale from the Properties tree, only the selected drawing view(s) will be affected.

- To change the scale of all drawing views on the same sheet, right click on the drawing, select Properties, and change the scale from there.

- The Scale can be pre-set and saved in the Drawing Template.

8. Creating the 2nd Isometric View:

- Click the **Model View** command.

- Click **Next** ➡, select the ISOMETRIC view button (arrow) under the Orientation Section.

- Place the drawing view approximately as shown.

- Click **OK** ✓.

Place the Isometric view approx. here

Drawing view border ➡

Note:

The drawing view borders appear on the screen but not on the printouts.

9. Changing Scale:

- Set the Scale option to: **Use Custom Scale**.

- Select from the list: **User Define**.

- Enter **3:2** for custom scale. (Use 1:1 if preferred).

- Click **OK** .

10. Switching to Shaded view:

- Sometimes for clarity, a drawing view is changed to shaded instead of wireframe.

- The shaded view will be printed as shaded. To change the shading of more than one view at the same time, hold the control key, select the borders of the views then change the shading.

- Select the Isometric view border .

- Click **Shaded** or select **View / Display / Shaded with Edges**.

- The Isometric view is now shown as Shaded with Edges.

11. Creating a Bill Of Materials (B.O.M.):

- Click the Isometric view's border.

- Select **Insert / Tables / Bill Of Materials** – OR – Click the B.O.M. command from the **Tables** button.

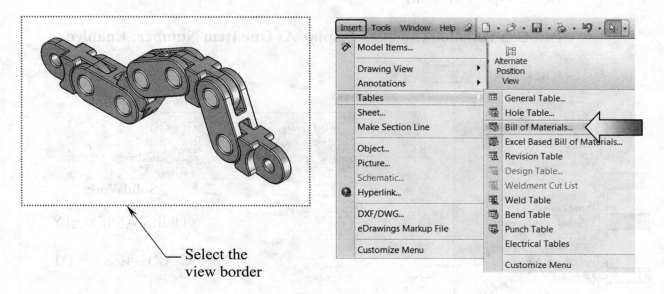

Select the view border

- A BOM is created automatically and the information in the assembly document is populated with item numbers, description, quantities and part numbers.

- When the Bill Of Materials properties tree appears, select **Bom-Standard** (Circled) from the Table Template list (Circled) and Click **Open** [Open].

12. Selecting the B.O.M. options:

- Table Template: **BOM Standard.**

- Attach to Anchor Point*: **Enabled**.

- BOM Type: **Parts only**.

- Part Configuration Grouping **Display As One Item Number: Enabled**.

- Click **OK** [OK].

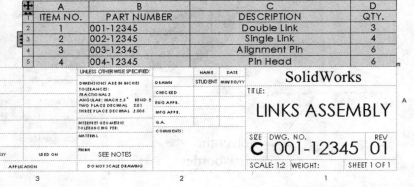

	A	B	C	D
	ITEM NO.	PART NUMBER	DESCRIPTION	QTY.
2	1	001-12345	Double Link	3
3	2	002-12345	Single Link	4
4	3	003-12345	Alignment Pin	6
5	4	004-12345	Pin Head	6

- The Bill Of Materials is created and anchored to the lower right corner of the title block, where the anchor point was set earlier.

* The Anchor point is set and saved in the Sheet Format layer. To change the location of the anchor point, first right click anywhere in the drawing and select Edit Sheet Format then right click on one of the end points of a line and select: Set-As-Anchor / Bill of Material.

- To change the anchor corner, click anywhere in the B.O.M, click the 4-way cursor on the upper left corner and select the stationary corner where you want to anchor the table (use the Bottom Right option for this lesson).

13. Modifying the B.O.M.:

- Double-click on the B.O.M. table to edit its content.

- Transfer the Part Number column over to the Description column.

- **To transfer Cell-By-Cell:**

  In the Part Number column, double-click in a cell and select **Keep Link**.

  Press **Control + X** (Cut).

  Enter a New Part Number.

  Double-click a cell in the Description column and press **Control+V** (Paste) or simply re-enter the part name.

	A	B	C	D
1	ITEM NO.	PART NUMBER	DESCRIPTION	QTY.
2	1	Double Link	Double Click	3
3	2	Alignment Pin		6
4	3	Pin Head		6
5	4	Single Link		4

- Click OK or click anywhere in the drawing when finished with editing. The BOM is updated accordingly.

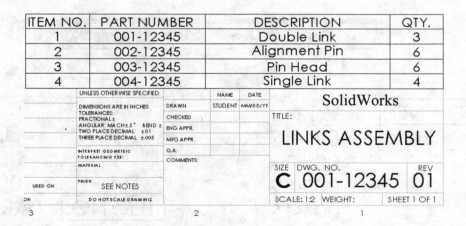

ITEM NO.	PART NUMBER	DESCRIPTION	QTY.
1	001-12345	Double Link	3
2	002-12345	Alignment Pin	6
3	003-12345	Pin Head	6
4	004-12345	Single Link	4

Note: *Refer to SolidWorks Online Help to learn more about customizing the B.O.M and how to create Custom Properties such as Part Numbers, Materials, etc.*

14. Reversing the column headers:

- Click anywhere in the B.O.M. table to access its **Properties**.

Click anywhere in the BOM to access its Properties…

Assembly Structure and Preview pane

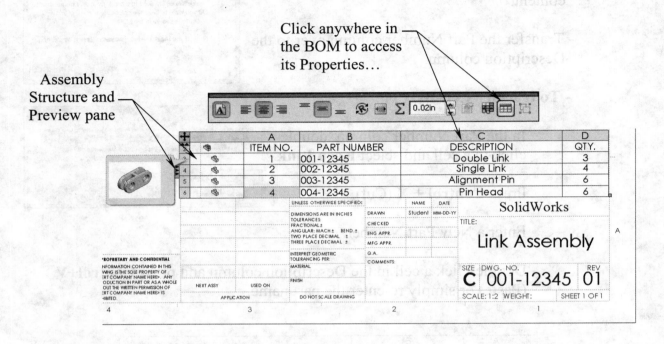

- Click the Assembly Structure arrow-tab to see the preview of the components.

- The Formatting toolbar pops up on top of the BOM.

- Click the **Table Header** button.

Table Header Top/Bottom

- Click **OK** ⊘.

Table Header set to Top

Table Header set to Bottom

15. Adding Balloon callouts:

- Click or select **Insert / Annotations / Balloon**.

- Click on the **edge** of the Single-Link. The system places a balloon on the part.

- The Item Number matches the one in the B.O.M. automatically.

- Click on the Double Link, the Alignment Pins, and Pin Heads to assign balloons to them.

Notes:

Balloons are similar to notes; they can have multiple leaders or attachment points. To copy the leader line, hold down the CONTROL key and drag the tip of one of the arrows.

16. Changing the balloon style:

- Hold down the CONTROL key and select all balloons, the balloon Properties tree appears on the left side of the screen.

- Select **Circular Split Line** under the Style menu.

- Select **2 Character** size.

- Click **OK** ✅.

> 💡 **Circular Split Line**
>
> - The Upper Number represents the Item-Number.
> - The Lower Number represents the Quantity.

Item Number

Quantity

NOTE: *To switch from Circular Split Lines to the number of places (X), activate the Quantity checkbox, then select the Placement and the X denotation options.*

17. Saving your work:

- Select **File / Save As / Links-Assembly / Save**.

Questions for Review

Assembly Drawings

1. The drawing's paper size can be selected or changed at any time.
   - a. True
   - b. False

2. The First or Third angle projection can be selected in the sheet setup.
   - a. True
   - b. False

3. To access the sheet format and edit the information in the title block:
   - a. Right click in the drawing and select Edit Sheet Format
   - b. Right click the Sheet Format icon from the Feature Tree and select: Edit Sheet Format.
   - c. All of the above.

4. The BOM anchor point should be set on the Sheet Format not on the drawing sheet.
   - a. True
   - b. False

5. A Model View command is used to create Isometric views.
   - a. True
   - b. False

6. The Drawing views scale can be changed individually or all at the same time.
   - a. True
   - b. False

7. A Bill of Materials (BOM) can automatically be generated using Excel embedded features.
   - a. True
   - b. False

8. The Balloon callouts are linked to the Bill of Materials and driven by the order of the Feature Manager Tree.
   - a. True
   - b. b. False

8. TRUE	9. TRUE
5. TRUE	7. TRUE
3. C	4. TRUE
1. TRUE	2. TRUE

Exercise: Assembly Drawings

Go to: Training Files folder.
        Mini Vise folder.

1. Create an Assembly Drawing
   from the components provided.

2. Create a Bill Of Materials and
   modify the Part Number and the
   Description columns as shown.

ITEM NO.	PART NUMBER	DESCRIPTION	QTY.
1	001-12345	Base	1
2	002-23456	Slide Jaw	1
3	003-34567	Lead Screw	1
4	004-45678	Crank Handle	1
5	005-56789	Crank Handle Knob	1

3. Save your work as: **Mini Vise Assembly.slddrw**

Exercise: Assembly Drawings

File Location:
Training Files folder
Egg Beater.sldasm

ITEM NO.	PART NUMBER	DESCRIPTION	QTY.
1	010-8980	Egg Beater Handle	1
2	010-8981	Main Gear	1
3	010-8982	Support Rod	1
4	010-8983	Right Spinner	1
5	010-8984	Left Spinner	1
6	010-8985	Crank Handle	1
7	010-8986	Small Gear (RIGHT)	1
8	010-8987	Small Gear (LEFT)	1

1. Create an Assembly Drawing with 5 views.

2. Add Balloons and a Bill Of Materials.

3. Save your work as: **Egg Beater Assembly**.

CHAPTER 15 (cont.)

Alternate Position Views

Assembly Drawings
Alternate Position Views

- Assembly drawings are created in the same way as part drawings, except for all components that are shown together as assembled or exploded.

- A Bill of Materials is created to specify the details of the components, such as: Part Number, Material, Weight, Vendor, etc.

- The BOM template can be modified to have more columns, rows, or different headers.

- Balloons are also created on the same drawing to help identify the parts from its list (B.O.M). These balloons are linked to the Bill of Materials parametrically, and the order of the balloon numbers is driven by the Assembly's Feature tree.

Alternate Position Views

- The Alternate Position View allows users to superimpose one drawing view precisely on another (open/close position as an example).

- The alternate position(s) is shown with phantom lines.

- Dimension between the primary view and the Alternate Position View can be added to the same drawing view.

- More than one Alternate Position View can be created in a drawing.

- Section, Detail, Broken, and Crop views are currently not supported.

Alternate Position Views
Assembly Drawings

ITEM NO.	PART NUMBER	DESCRIPTION	QTY.
1	011-4221	Base Stand	1
2	012-4221	Arm Connector	1
3	013-4221	Arm	1
4	014-4221	Connecting Arm	1
5	015-4221	Gate	1
6	016-4221	Gate Support	1
7	017-4221	Connector Joint	1
8	018-4221	Double Joint	1

SOLIDTRANS

GATE ASSEMBLY

C 06-20-2004 01

Dimensioning Standards: **ANSI**	Third Angle Projection
Units: **INCHES** – 3 Decimals	

Tools Needed:

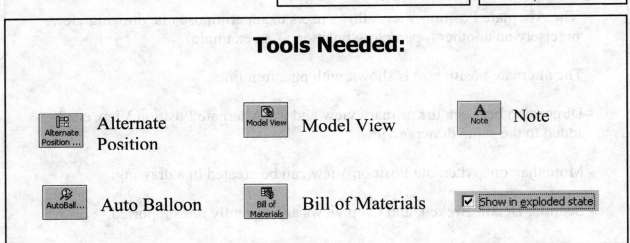

Alternate Position

Model View

Note

Auto Balloon

Bill of Materials

☑ Show in exploded state

1. Creating a new drawing:

- Select **File / New / Draw** (or Drawing) / **OK**.

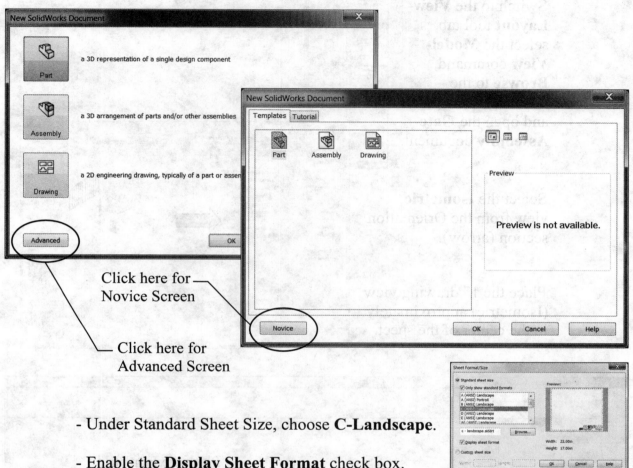

Click here for
Novice Screen

Click here for
Advanced Screen

- Under Standard Sheet Size, choose **C-Landscape**.

- Enable the **Display Sheet Format** check box.

- Click **OK** [OK].

- Right click in the drawing
  and select **Properties.**

- Set **Scale** to **1:1**
  (full scale)

- Set **Type of Projection** to:
  Third Angle [○ Third angle] .

- Click **OK** [OK].

2. Creating the Isometric Drawing View:

- Switch to the **View-Layout** tool tab, select the **Model-View** command, **Browse** to the Training Files folder and open the **Gate-Assembly** document.

- Select the **Isometric** view from the Orientation section (arrow).

- Place the 1st drawing view (Isometric) approximately in the center of the sheet.

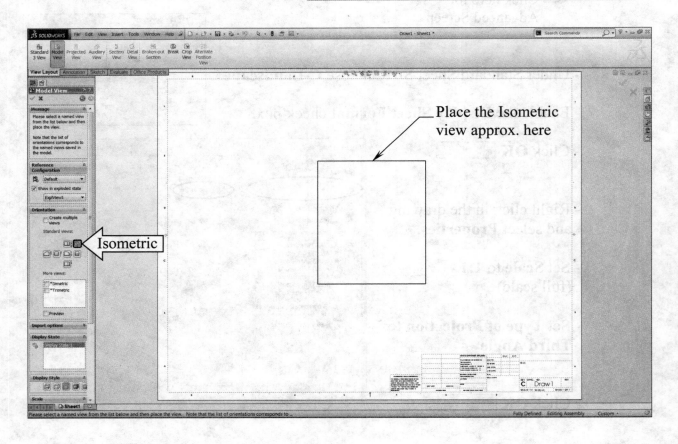

Place the Isometric view approx. here

Isometric

3. Changing the Drawing View Scale:

- Click on the drawing view border and change the Scale to:

* **Use Custom Scale.**

* **User Defined.**

* **Scale 1:3**

- Click **OK** ✅ .

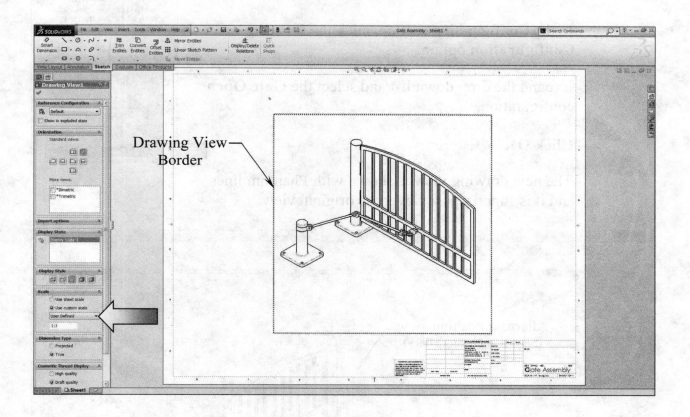

- The Isometric View is scaled to (1:3) or 1/3 time the actual size.

- When selecting the User Defined option you can enter your own scale, if the scale option that you want is not on the list.

- The scale in the Sheet properties is linked to the scale callout in the title block (page 14-25). Changing the scale in the Properties will automatically update the one in the title block.

4. Creating an Alternate Position drawing view:

Alternate Position View
Adds a view displaying a configuration of a model superimposed on another configuration of the model.

- Use Alternate Position Views to shows different positions of the components in an assembly.

- From the Drawing Toolbar, click [Alternate Position...] or select **Insert / Drawing View / Alternate Position View**.

- In the Configuration section, click the **Existing-Configuration** option.

- Expand the drop down list and select the **Gate Open** configuration.

- Click **OK** ✓.

- The new drawing view is shown with Phantom lines and it is superimposed over the original view.

Alternate Position

Message

Select New configuration, click OK or Enter and define the new configuration parameters.
Or
Select Existing configuration and click OK or Enter.

Configuration

○ New configuration

AltPosition_Default_1

● Existing configuration

Gate Open

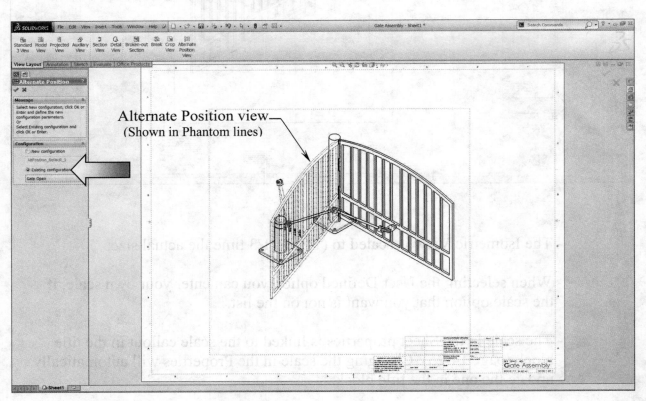

Alternate Position view
(Shown in Phantom lines)

5. Adding the Top Drawing view:

- From the Drawing Toolbar, click **Model View** or select: **Insert / Drawing View / Model**.

- Click the **NEXT** arrow.

- Select the **TOP** view from the Orientation dialog.

- Place the Top drawing view approximately as shown.

- Click **OK** ✅.

- For clarity, change the view line style to Tangent Edges With Font. (Right click on the view's border, select Tangent Edge, and then click Tangent Edges with Font).

6. Creating the 2nd Alternate Position View:

- Click the Top Drawing View's Border to activate.

- Click 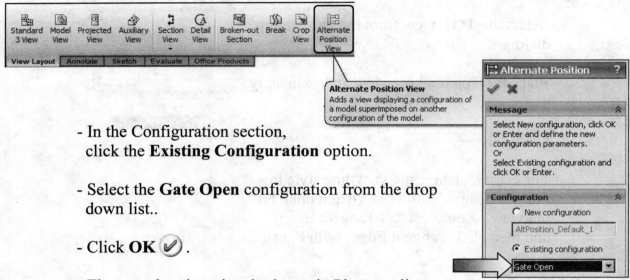 or select **Insert / Drawing View / Alternate Position**.

- In the Configuration section,
click the **Existing Configuration** option.

- Select the **Gate Open** configuration from the drop
down list..

- Click **OK** ✓ .

- The new drawing view is shown in Phantom lines
and is superimposed over the original view.

7. Adding Text / Annotations:

- Select the Top drawing view's Border to activate the view and then click **Note** [Note].

- Add the notes: **Top View** and **Isometric View** as shown.

- Use the options in the Formatting toolbar to modify the text.

- Highlight the text and change it to match the settings below:

| * Century Gothic | * 28 Points |
| * Bold | * Underline |

8. Creating an Exploded Isometric view:

- Click or select **Insert / Drawing View / Model**.

- Click the **NEXT** arrow ➡ .

- Select the **Isometric** view from the Orientation dialog.

- Place the Isometric view on the upper right side of the sheet.

- On the upper left corner of the Properties tree, enable the **Show-In Exploded State** checkbox (Arrow).

- Set the scale of the view to **1:8**.

NOTE:
The exploded view must be already created in the assembly for this option to be available in the drawing.

- Click **OK** ▭ OK ▭ .

9. Adding Auto-Balloons to the Exploded view:

- Switch to the **Annotation** tool tab.

- Select the Isometric drawing view's border.

- Click or select **Insert / Annotations / AutoBalloon**.

AutoBalloon
Adds balloons for all components in the selected views.

- In the Auto Balloon properties tree, set the following:

* Balloon Layout: **Square**

* Ignore Multiple Instances: **Enable**

* Style: **Circular**

* Size: **2 Character**

* Balloon Text: **Item Number**

- Click **OK** [OK] .

10. Adding a Bill of Materials to the Drawing:

- Click [Bill of Materials] or select **Insert / Tables / Bill Of Materials**.

- Select **Bom-Standard** under Table Templates.

- **Disable** Attached To Anchor.

- Select **Parts Only** for BOM Type.

- Click **OK** [OK].

	A	B	C	D
	ITEM NO.	PART NUMBER	DESCRIPTION	QTY.
2	1	011-4321	Base Stand	1
3	2	012-4321	Arm Connector	1
4	3	013-4321	Arm	1
5	4	014-4321	Connecting-Arm	1
6	5	015-4321	Gate	1
7	6	016-4321	Gate Support	1
8	7	017-4321	Connector Joint	1
9	8	018-4321	Double Joint	1

- Modify the BOM
if needed to add
part numbers
and Descriptions.

11. Saving a copy of your work:

- Click **File / Save As.**

- Enter **Gate Assembly.slddrw** for the name of the file and click **Save.**

Questions for Review

Assembly Drawings

1. The Alternate Position command can also be selected from Insert / Drawing View / Alternate Position.
   - a. True
   - b. False

2. The Alternate Position command precisely places a drawing view on top of another view.
   - a. True
   - b. False

3. The types of views that are not currently supported to work with Alternate Position are:
   - a. Broken and Crop Views
   - b. Detail View
   - c. Section View
   - d. All of the above.

4. Dimensions or annotations cannot be added to the superimposed view.
   - a. True
   - b. False

5. The Line Style for use in the Alternate Position view is:
   - a. Solid line
   - b. Dashed line
   - c. Phantom line
   - d. Centerline

6. In order to show the assembly exploded view on a drawing, an exploded view configuration must be created first in the main assembly.
   - a. True
   - b. False

7. Balloons and Auto Balloons can also be selected from: Insert / Annotations / (Auto) Balloon.
   - a. True
   - b. False

8. The Bill of Materials contents can be modified to include the Material Column.
   - a. True
   - b. False

7. TRUE	8. TRUE
5. C	6. TRUE
3. D	4. FALSE
1. TRUE	2. TRUE

CHAPTER 16

Drawing Views

Drawing Views
Machined Block

- When creating an engineering drawing, one of the first things to do is to layout the drawing views such as:

    * The standard Front, Top, Right, and Isometric views.

    * Other views like Detail, Cross section, Auxiliary views, etc., can be created or projected from the 4 standard views.

- Most of the drawing views in SolidWorks are automatically aligned with one another (default alignments); each one can only be moved along the direction that was defined for that particular view (vertical, horizontal, or at projected angle).

- Dimensions and annotations will then be added to the drawing views.

- The dimensions created in the part will be inserted into the drawing views, so that their association between the model and the drawing views can be maintained. Changes done to these dimensions will update all drawing views and the solid model as well;

- Configurations are also used in this lesson to create some specific views.

- This chapter will guide you through the creation of some of the most commonly used drawing views in an engineering drawing like: 3 Standard views, Section views, Detail views, Projected views, Auxiliary views, Broken Out Section views, and Cross Hatch patterns.

Machined Block
Drawing Views Creation

Dimensioning Standards: **ANSI**	Third Angle Projection
Units: **INCHES** – 3 Decimals	

Tools Needed:

 New Drawing

 Model View

 Projected View

 Auxiliary View

 Detail View

 Section View

 Broken Out Section

 Area Hatch Fill

 Note

1. Creating a new drawing:

- Select **File / New / Drawing** template.

- Choose **D-Landscape** under Standard Sheet Size. (34.00 in. X 22.00 in.)

- Enable the **Display Sheet Format** check box to include the title block.

- Click **OK**.

- If the options above are not available, right click inside the drawing and select Properties.

- Select the **Third Angle** option under Type of Projection.

- Set the default view scale to **1:2**.

- The Units can be changed later on.

- The drawing template comes with 2 default "layers":

  * The "Front layer" is called the **Sheet** layer, where drawings are created.

  * The "Back layer" is called the **Sheet Format,** where the title block and the revision information are stored.

2. Editing the Sheet Format:

- Zoom in on the Title Block area. We are going to first fill out the information in the title block.

- Right click in the drawing area and select **Edit Sheet Format.**

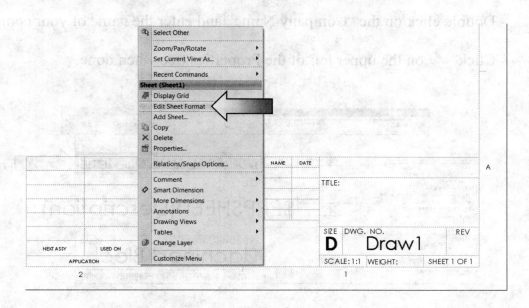

- The Sheet Format is brought up on top.

- New annotation and sketch lines can now be added.

- Any existing text or lines can now be modified.

- Notice the link to properties text strings: "$PRPS". Some of the annotations have already been linked to the part's properties.

3. Modifying the existing text:

- Double click on the "Company Name" and enter the name of your company.

- Click ✅ on the upper left of the Properties tree when done.

4. Adding the Title of the drawing:

- Double click on the PropertyLink in the Title area ($PRPSHEET:{Description})

- Type **Machined Block** for the title of the drawing.

- Enter the information as shown in the title block for the other areas.

- Click **OK** ✅.

5. Switching back to the drawing Sheet:

- Right click in the drawing and select **Edit Sheet**.

- The Drawing Sheet "layer" is brought back up on top.

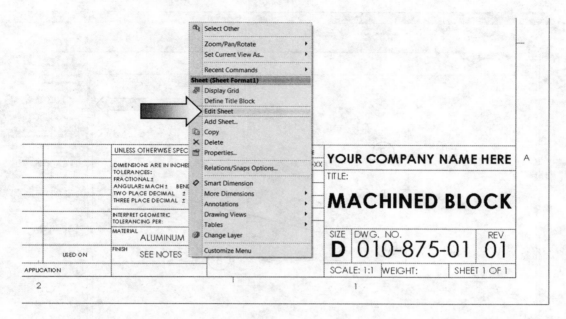

6. Accessing the View-Palette:

- The **View Palette** is located on the right side of the screen in the Task Pane area, click on its icon to access it.

Note: *If the drawing views are not visible on the View Palette window, click the Browse button and open the part Machined block.*

- The standard drawing views like the Front, Right, Top, Back, Left, Bottom, Current, Isometric, and Sheet Metal Flat-Pattern views are contained within the View Palette window.

- These drawing views can be dragged into the drawing sheet to create the drawing views.

- The **Auto Start Projected View** checkbox should be selected by default.

7. Using the View Palette:

- Click/Hold/Drag the Front view from the View-Palette (arrow) and drop it on the drawing sheet, approximately as shown. Make sure the Auto-Start projected view checkbox is enabled (arrow).

(Disable the Dimensions Marked For Drawing option under: Tools/Options/Document Prop/Detailing).

- After the Front view is placed (position 1), move the mouse cursor upward, a preview image of the Top view appears, click in an approximate spot above the Front view to place the Top view (position number 2); repeat the same step for the Right view (position 3).

- All of the views from the View-Palette can be added to the drawing by using the same method.

- Click **OK** ✔ when you are finished with the first three views.

8. Adding an Isometric view:

- Click or select **Insert / Drawing View / Model View**.

- Click the NEXT arrow.

- Select **Isometric** (Arrow) from the Model View properties tree and place it approximately as shown.

Click the view border to activate it...

- Changing the view scale:

- Click the border of the isometric view to activate.

- From the FeatureManager tree select: **Use Custom Scale** option and set the scale to **1:2**.

- Click **OK**.

9. Moving the drawing view(s):

- Position the mouse cursor over the border of the Front view and "Click/Hold/ Drag" to move, all 3 views will move at the same time. By default, the Top and the Right views are automatically aligned with the Front view.

- When moving either the Right or the Top view, notice they will only move along the default vertical or horizontal directions. These are the default alignments when creating the standard drawing views.

10. Breaking the alignments between the views:

- Right click inside the Top view or on its dotted border and select: **Alignment / Break-Alignment***.

- The Top view is no longer locked to the default direction, it can be moved freely.

- Dependent views like Projected Views, Auxiliary Views, Section views, etc. will be aligned automatically with the views from where they were created. Their alignments can be broken or also reverted back to their default alignments.

- Independent views can also be aligned with other drawing views by using the same alignment options as shown above.

* To re-align a drawing view:

- Right click on the view's border and select **Alignment / Default-Alignment**.

11. Creating a Detail View:

- Click or select **Insert / Drawing View / Detail**.

- Sketch a circle approximately as shown on the Top drawing view.

- The system creates a Detail view automatically at the default 2 to1 scale.

> ☼ **Detail View** ⒼA
>
> This command uses a circle to show a portion of a view, at an enlarged scale.

DETAIL A

- Place the detail view on the left side of the Top view.

Sketch Circle

12. Using the Detail View options:

- While creating the Detail view, the following can be controlled:

- Change Per-Standard style to **With Leader**.

- Enable **Full Outline**.

- Use Custom scale of **2:1**.

- Click **OK** ✓.

DETAIL A
SCALE 2 : 1

13. Creating a Projected View:

- Click on the Front view's border to activate.

> **Projected View**
>
> This command creates projected views from any orthographic view.

- Click ⊞ or select **Insert / Drawing View / Projected**.

- The preview of a projected left side view is attached to the mouse cursor, place it on the left side of the Front view.

Click view's border

- Notice this view is also aligned automatically to the horizontal axis of the Front view. It can only be moved from left to right.

- For the purpose of this lesson, we will keep all of the default alignments the way SolidWorks creates them. (To break these default alignments at anytime, simply right click on their dotted borders and pick Break-Alignment).

- This left side view can also be dragged and dropped from the View Palette.

14. Creating an Auxiliary View:

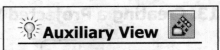

Auxiliary View

This command creates a view normal to a reference edge in an existing view.

- Select the Angled-Edge as indicated.

- Click or select **Insert / Drawing View / Auxiliary**.

- The system creates an Auxiliary view and attaches it onto your cursor.

- Place the Auxiliary view approximately as shown.

DETAIL A

Select Edge

- The Auxiliary view is also aligned to the edge from which it was originally projected.

- The projection arrow can be toggled on and off from the Properties tree (arrow).

Drawing View6

Reference Configuration
Default

Arrow
B
Flip direction

Display State

- Use the Break-Alignment option if needed to rearrange the drawing views to different locations.

15. Creating a Section View:

- Click or select **Insert / Drawing View / Section**.

> ### 💡 Section Views 🔁
>
> This command creates a cut through a view, using single or multiple lines to show the interior details.
> The sectioned surfaces are fully crosshatched automatically.

Section Line

- Position the Section Line on the center of the hole on the right.

- The preview of a section view appears, move the mouse cursor to the right-side and click **OK** (the check button) to place it.

- The Section view is aligned horizontally with the view from which it was created and the cross-hatched are added automatically.

- To change the direction of the cut:

* Double Click on the section line and click Rebuild – OR –
* Enable Flip Direction checkbox in the FeatureManager tree (arrow).

Place the section line here & click OK

SECTION C-C

16. Showing the hidden lines in a drawing view:

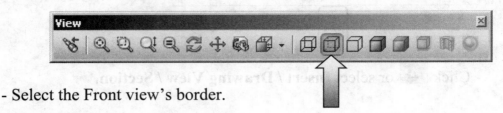

- Select the Front view's border.

- Click or select **View / Display / Hidden Lines Visible**.

- The hidden lines are now visible.

Click on the View's border to activate it.

17. Creating a Broken-Out-Section:

- Sketch a <u>closed</u> free-form shape on the Front view, around the area as shown (use either the Line or the Spline command to create the profile).

- Select the entire *Closed Profile.*

- Click [icon] or select **Insert / Drawing View / Broken-Out-Section**.

Closed Profile

Broken Out Section View

Creates a partial cut, using a closed profile, at a specified depth to display the inner details of a drawing view.

- Enable the **Preview** check box in the Properties tree ☑ Preview

- Enter **.500** in. for Depth [0.500in]

- Click **OK** ✅.

18. Adding a Cutaway view: (Previously created as a Configuration in the model).

- Click 🖼 or select **Insert / Drawing View / Model**...

- Click on one of the view borders, the Model View Properties tree appears.

- Select **Isometric** (arrow) under Orientation window; use **Custom Scale** of **1:2**.

- Place the new Isometric view below the other isometric view.

19. Changing Configurations: (From Default to Cutaway View).

- Click the Isometric view's border.

- On the Properties tree, select the **Cutaway View** configuration from the list.

- Click **OK** [OK] .

- The **Cutaway View** configuration is activated and the extruded-cut feature that was created earlier in the model, is now shown here.

- Since the cutout was created in the model, there is no crosshatch on any of the sectioned faces.

- Crosshatch is added at the drawing level and will not appeared in the model.

- The hatch lines are added next...

20. Adding crosshatch to the sectioned surfaces:

- Crosshatch is added automatically when section views are made in the drawing, since the cut was created in the model, we will have to add the hatch manually.

- Hold down the CONTROL key and select the 3 faces as indicated.

- Click or **Insert / Annotations / Area Hatch/Fill.**

- Set the parameters indicated in the dialog box.

Select 3 faces

- The Cutaway View is crosshatched.

21. Modifying the crosshatch properties:

- Zoom in on the **Section C-C**.

- Click inside the hatch area, the **Area Hatch / Fill** properties tree appears.

- Clear the Material Crosshatch checkbox.

- Change the hatch pattern to **ANSI38** (Aluminum).

- Scale: **1.500** (Sets the spacing between the hatch lines).

- Angle **00.00 deg**. (Sets the angle of the hatch lines).

- Enable: **Apply Changes Immediately**.

- Click **OK** [OK] .

Change the Hatch Pattern to match the previous settings.

SECTION C-C

- When the hatch pattern is applied locally to the selected view, it does not override the global settings in the system options.

- Change to the same hatch pattern for any views with crosshatch.

22. Saving your work:

- Select **File / Save As /**

- Enter **Machine Block-Drawing Views** for file name and click **Save**.

- The drawing views can also be changed from Wireframe to Shaded .

- The color of the drawing views is driven by the part's color. What you see here in the drawing is how it is going to look when printed (in color).

- Modifying the part's color will update the color of the drawing views automatically.

Geometric Tolerance & Flag Notes

Geometric Tolerance Symbols GCS are used in a Feature Control Frame to add Geometric Tolerances to the parts and drawings.

Symbol	Name	Symbol	Name
∠	Angularity	⊕	Position
↔	Between	⌓	Profile of Any Surface
○	Circularity (Roundness)	↗	Simple Runout
◎	Concentricity and Coaxially	↗	Simple Runout (open)
⌭	Cylindricity	—	Straightness
▱	Flatness	≡	Symmetry
⌒	Profile of Any Line	⌰	Total Runout
//	Parallelism	⌰	Total Runout (open)
⊥	Perpendicularity	To access the symbol libraries, select: **Insert / Annotations / Note**

Modifying Symbols Library

Circle 1-99	Square 1-99	Square/Circle 1-99	Triangle 1-99
1. 1	1. 1	1. 1	1. 1
Circle A-Z	Square A-Z	Square/Circle A-Z	Triangle A-Z
A. A	A. A	A. A	A. A

Modifying & Hole Symbols

Modifying Symbols MC

Symbol	Name	Symbol	Name
℄	Centerline	Ⓣ	Tangent Plane
▫	Degree	(slope up)	Slope (Up)
⌀	Diameter	(slope down)	Slope (Down)
S⌀	Spherical Diameter	(slope inverted up)	Slope (Inverted Up)
±	Plus/Minus	(slope inverted down)	Slope (Inverted Down)
Ⓢ	Regardless of Feature Size	□	Square
Ⓕ	Free State	⊠	Square (BS)
Ⓛ	Least Material Condition	⟨ST⟩	Statistical
Ⓜ	Maximum Material Condition	⌀↰	Flattened Length
Ⓟ	Projected Tolerance Zone	⌐L	Parting Line
Ⓔ	Encompassing		SolidWorks supports **ASME-ANSI Y14.5** Geometric & True Position Tolerancing

⌴ Counterbore (Spot face)   ⌵ Countersunk   ▽ Depth/Deep   ⌀ Diameter

ASME (American Society for Mechanical Engineering)
ANSI Y14.5M (American National Standards Institute)

SYMBOLS DESCRIPTION

ANGULARITY:

The condition of a surface or line, which is at a specified angle (other than 90°) from the datum plane or axis.

BASIC DIMENSION: 1.00

A dimension specified on a drawing as BASIC is a theoretical value used to describe the exact size, shape, or location of a feature. It is used as a basis from which permissible variations are established by tolerance on other dimensions or in notes. A basic dimension can be identified by the abbreviation BSC or more readily by boxing in the dimension.

CIRCULARITY (ROUNDNESS):

A tolerance zone bounded by two concentric circles within which each circular element of the surface must lie.

CONCENTRICITY:

The condition in which the axis of all cross-sectional elements of a feature's surface of revolution are common.

CYLINDRICITY:

The condition of a surface of revolution in which all points of the surface are equidistant from a common axis or for a perfect cylinder.

DATUM:

A point, line, plane, cylinder, etc., assumed to be exact for purposes of computation from which the location or geometric relationship of other features of a part may be established. A datum identification symbol contains a letter (except I, C, and Q) placed inside a rectangular box.

DATUM TARGET:

The datum target symbol is a circle divided into four quadrants. The letter placed in the upper left quadrant identifies it is associated datum feature. The numeral placed in the lower right quadrant identifies the target; the dashed leader line indicates the target on far side.

FLATNESS:

The condition of a surface having all elements in one plane. A flatness tolerance specifies a tolerance zone confined by two parallel planes within which the surface must lie.

MAXIMUM MATERIAL CONDITION: Ⓜ
The condition of a part feature when it contains the maximum amount of material.

LEAST MATERIAL CONDITION: Ⓛ
The condition of a part feature when it contains the least amount of material. The term is opposite from maximum material condition.

PARALLELISM: //
The condition of a surface or axis which is equidistant at all points from a datum plane or axis.

PERPENDICULARITY: ⊥
The condition of a surface, line, or axis, which is at a right angle (90°) from a datum plane or datum axis.

PROFILE OF ANY LINE: ⌒
The condition limiting the amount of profile variation along a line element of a feature.

PROFILE OF ANY SURFACE: ⌓
Similar to profile of any line, but this condition relates to the entire surface.

PROJECTED TOLERANCE ZONE: Ⓟ
A zone applied to a hole in which a pin, stud, screw, etc. is to be inserted. It controls the perpendicularity of any hole, which controls the fastener's position; this will allow the adjoining parts to be assembled.

REGARDLESS OF FEATURE SIZE: Ⓢ
A condition in which the tolerance of form or condition must be met, regardless of where the feature is within its size tolerance.

RUNOUT: ↗
The maximum permissible surface variation during one complete revolution of the part about the datum axis. This is usually detected with a dial indicator.

STRAIGHTNESS: —
The condition in which a feature of a part must be a straight line.

SYMMETRY: ≡
A condition wherein a part or feature has the same contour and sides of a central plane.

TRUE POSITION: ⊕
This term denotes the theoretically exact position of a feature.

DETAIL A
SCALE 2 : 1

VIEW B-B

SEC VIEW C-C

MACHINED BLOCK

CHAPTER 17

Detailing

Detailing a drawing
Machined Block Details

- After the drawing views are all laid out, they will be detailed with dimensions, tolerances, datums, surface finishes, notes, etc.

- To fully maintain the associations between the model dimensions and the drawing dimensions, the Model Items 🔷 options should be used. If a dimension is changed in either modes (from the solid model or in the drawing) they will both be updated automatically.

- When a dimension appears in gray color it means that the dimension is being added in the drawing and it does not exist in the model. This dimension is called a Reference dimension.

- SolidWorks uses different colors for different types of dimensions such as:
    * Black dimensions = Sketch dimensions (driving).
    * Gray dimensions = Reference dimensions (driven).
    * Blue dimensions = Feature dimensions (driving)
    * Magenta dimensions = Dimensions linked to Design Tables (driving).

- For certain types of holes, the Hole-Callout option 🔲 should be used to accurately call out the hole type, depth, diameter, etc...

- The Geometric Tolerance option 🔲 helps control the accuracy and the precision of the features. Both Tolerance and Precision options can be easily created and controlled from the FeatureManager tree.

- This chapter discusses most of the tools used in detailing an engineering drawing, including importing dimensions from the model, and adding the GD&T to the drawing (Geometric Dimensions and Tolerancing).

Machined Block
Detailing

| Dimensioning Standards: **ANSI** | Third Angle Projection |
| Units: **INCHES** – 3 Decimals | |

Tools Needed:

	Model Dimensions		Geometric Tolerance		Datum Feature Symbol
	Surface Finish		Hole Callout		Note

1. Opening the previous file:

- Click **File / Open** and open the document **Machined Block** from the CD.

2. Inserting dimensions from the model:

- Dimensions previously created in the model can be inserted into the drawing.

- Click the **Right** drawing view's border.

- Click or select **Insert / Model Items**.

- For Source/Destination: **Entire Model**.

- Under Dimensions: Enable **Eliminate Duplicates**.

- Under Options: Select **Use Dimension Placement in Sketch**.

- Click **OK** ✓.

Select the Right drawing view's border

- The dimensions that were created earlier from the model into the selected drawing view.

3. Re-arranging the new dimensions: Zoom in 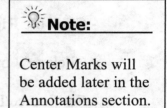 on the Right drawing view.

- Keep only the hole location dimensions and delete the others. The hole types and sizes will be added later. Also add any missing dimensions manually.

Note:

Center Marks will be added later in the Annotations section.

4. Inserting dimensions into the Section view:

- Select the Section view's border.

- Click or select **Insert / Model Items**.

- The previous settings (arrow) should still be selected.

- Click **OK** ✓

- Some of the dimensions are missing due to the use of the relations in the model.

SECTION C-C

- The dimensions from the model are imported into the Section view.

- Use the Smart Dimension tool to add any missing dimensions.

- These dimensions are attached to the drawing view and will move with the view.

- If any of these dimensions are changed, both the model and the drawing views will also change accordingly.

SECTION C-C

5. Repeating step 4: Insert the model's dimensions into the Top view.

6. Adding dimensions to the Auxiliary view:

- Add any missing dimensions to the drawing view using the Smart Dimension command.

NOTE: *To add the Centerline symbol, select the Note command from the Annotation tab, click the Add Symbol button, then select the Centerline option from the list.*

See note

VIEW B

7. Adding the Center Marks:

- Zoom in 🔍 on the Detail View.

- Click ⌖ or select **Insert / Annotations / Center Mark**.

- Click on the edge of each hole to add Center Marks. The system places a Center Mark in the center of the hole.

Click on the circular edge to add Center Mark (skip this step if the center marks are already added).

DETAIL A
SCALE 2 : 1

8. Adding center marks to the other holes:

- Click or select **Insert / Annotations / Center Mark**.

- Add a center mark to other holes by clicking on their circular edges.

9. Adding the Datum Feature Symbols:

- Click or select **Insert / Annotations / Datum Feature Symbol**.

- Select edge 1 and place **Datum A** as shown.

- Select edge 2 and place **Datum B** as shown.

🔆 Datum Feature

A symbolic language used on engineering drawings for explicitly describing nominal geometry and its allowable variation.

Edge 2

Edge 1

Datum Reference & Geometric Tolerance Examples

FEATURE CONTROL FRAME

SEPARATORS

CHARACTERISTIC SYMBOL (POSITION)

TOLERANCE ZONE SHAPE (DIAMETER)

TOLERANCE

PRIMARY DATUM

MAXIMUM MATERIAL CONDITION MODIFIER

SECONDARY DATUM

REGARDLESS OF FEATURE SIZE MODIFIER

TERTIARY DATUM

LEAST MATERIAL CONDITION MODIFIER

💡 FEATURE CONTROL FRAMES

A feature control frame symbolizes the tolerance requirements for a feature of a part. It can be added to a drawing note for a feature tolerance, or can be specified by running a leader line from the feature control frame directly to the feature.
The box may be attached to an extension line from the feature or it can be placed on a dimension line. A feature can have more than one feature control frame, depending on its requirements.

Placement of Feature Control Frame

10. Adding hole specifications using the Hole-Callout:

- Click or select **Insert / Annotations / Hole Callout**.

- Select the edge of the C'bore and place the callout below the hole.

- The system creates a callout that includes the diameter and the depth of the hole and the C'bore.

Select Edge

Ø.625 THRU
⊔.875 ⤓.250

11. Adding Geometric Tolerances:

- Geometric dimensioning and tolerancing (GD&T) is used to define the nominal (theoretically perfect) geometry of parts and assemblies to define the allowable variation in form and possibly size of individual features and to define the allowable variation between features. Dimensioning and tolerancing and geometric dimensioning and tolerancing specifications are used as follows:

* Dimensioning specifications define the nominal, as-modeled or as-intended geometry. One example is a basic dimension.

* Tolerancing specifications define the allowable variation for the form and possibly the size of individual features and the allowable variation in orientation and location between features. Two examples are linear dimensions and feature control frames using a datum reference.

Select Edge

- Zoom in on the Front drawing view.

- Select the upper edge as shown.

- Click or select **Insert / Annotations / Geometric Tolerance**.

- The Geometric Tolerance Property appears.

- Click the **Symbol Library** dropdown list.

- Select **Parallelism** ⫽ from the **Symbol** library list.

- Enter **.010** under Tolerance 1.

- Enter **A** under Primary reference datum (arrow).

- Click **OK** OK .

12. Align the Geometric Tolerance:

- Drag the Control Frame towards the left side until it snaps to the horizontal alignment with the upper edge, then release the mouse button.

13. Attaching the Geometric Tolerance to the Driving dimension:

- Select the C'bore dimension. By pre-selecting a dimension, the geometric-tolerance will automatically be attached to this dimension.

Ø.625 THRU
⌴.875 ⯯.250

- Click or select **Insert / Annotation / Geometric Tolerance**.

- Click the **Symbol Library** dropdown list ▾.

- Select **Perpendicularity** ⟂ from the Symbol library list.

- Enter **.005** under Tolerance 1.

- Enter **B** under Secondary reference datum.

- Click **OK**   OK   .

- The Geometric Tolerance frame is attached to the driving dimension.

Ø.625 THRU
⌴.875 ⯯.250

⟂ | .005 | B

14. Adding Tolerance/Precision to dimensions:

- Select the dimension **.500** (circled).

- The dimension properties tree pops up, select **Bilateral** under the Tolerance/ Precision section.

VIEW B

- Enter **.000 in**. for Max variation.

- Enter **.005 in**. for Min variation.

- Click **OK** ✅.

15. Adding Symmetric tolerance to a dimension:

- Select the width dimension **1.250** (circled) and the dimension properties tree appears .

- Choose **Symmetric** under Tolerance/Precision list (arrow).

- Enter **.003 in**. for Maximum Variation.

- Click **OK** ✅.

- Repeat step 15 and add a Symmetric tolerance to the height dimension: (**2.000 ±.003**).

- For practice purposes: Add other types of tolerance to some other dimensions such as Min – Max, Basic, Fit, etc..

16. Adding Surface Finish callouts:

- Surface finish is an industrial process that alters the surface of a manufactured item to achieve a certain property. Finishing processes such as machining, grinding, or buffing, may be applied to improve appearance and other surface flaws, and control the surface friction.

- Zoom in on the Section C-C.

- Select the edge as indicated.

- Click ✓ or select **Insert / Annotations / Surface Finish**.

- Choose **Machining-Required** ✓ under Symbol.

- Under **Maximum Roughness**, enter: **125**

- Under Leader, select: **Bent leader.**

- Click **OK** ✅.

SECTION C-C

17. Adding non-parametric callouts:

- Click and add a diameter dimension to one circle.

- The dimension properties tree appears .

- Enter **4X** before <MOD-DIA>… or enter **4 PLCS** under callout.

- Click **OK** .

18. Inserting Notes:

- Zoom in on the upper left side of the drawing.

- Click **A** or select **Insert /Annotations / Note**.

- Click on an upper left area, approximately as shown, and a note box appears.

NOTE: *To prevent the note from moving, right click in the drawing and select: **Lock-Sheet-Focus**.*

Note box —

DETAIL A
SCALE 2 : 1

- Enter the notes below:

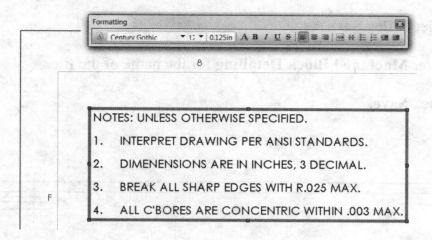

- Click **OK** ✅ when you are finished typing.

19. Changing document's font:

- Double click anywhere inside the note area to activate.

- Highlight the entire note and select the following:

- Font: **Century Gothic**.

- Point size: **14**.

- Alignment: **Left**.

- Click **OK** ✅.

20. Saving your work:

- Select **File / Save As**.

- Enter **Machined Block Detailing** for the name of the file.

- Click **Save**.

Questions for Review

Drawing & Detailing

1. Existing text in the title block can be edited when the Sheet-Format is active.
   - a. True
   - b. False

2. The standard drawing views can be created using the following method:
   - a. Use Insert / Drawing views menu
   - b. Use the Model-View command
   - c. Drag and drop from an open window
   - d. All of the above

3. View alignments can be broken or re-aligned.
   - a. True
   - b. False

4. The Detail-View scale cannot be changed or controlled locally.
   - a. True
   - b. False

5. The Projected view command projects and creates the Top, Bottom, Left, and Right views from another view.
   - a. True
   - b. False

6. To create an Auxiliary view, an edge has to be selected, not a face or a surface.
   - a. True
   - b. False

7. Only a single line can be used to create a Section view. The System doesn't support a multi-line section option.
   - a. True
   - b. False

8. Hidden lines in a drawing view can be turned ON / OFF locally and globally.
   - a. True
   - b. False

9. Configurations created in the model cannot be shown in the drawings.
   - a. True
   - b. False

9. FALSE
7. FALSE   8. TRUE
5. TRUE   6. TRUE
3. TRUE   4. FALSE
1. TRUE   2. D

Exercise: Detailing I

1. <u>Create</u> the **part** <u>and</u> the **drawing** as shown.

⚠2 The Counter-Bore dimensions are measured from the Top planar surface.

3. Dimensions are in inches, 3 decimal places.

4. The part is symmetrical about the Top reference plane.

   (To create the "Back-Isometric-View" from the model: hold the Shift key and push the Up arrow key twice. This should rotate the part 180°, and then insert this view to the drawing using the Current View option).

Front Isometric View

Back Isometric View

2X ⌀ .500 THRU
⌴ ⌀.875▽.425

2.000

2.000

⌀1.250 THRU

R.063 TYP

1.500

.250

.795

2X R1.000

2.000

2X 10.00°

.750

1.125

4.000

5. Save your work as: **Clamp Block**.

Exercise: Detailing II

1. <u>Open</u> the part named **Base Mount Block** from the Training Files folder
2. Create a drawing using the provided details.
3. Create the Virtual-Sharps where needed prior to adding the Ordinate Dimensions.
   (To add the Virtual Sharps: Hold the Control key, select the 2 lines, and click the Sketch-Point command).

4. Save your work as: **Base Mount Block_EXE**.

Fastener Callouts

Right Hand Threads
Threads lean to the left

PITCH (Expressed as Threads Per Inch or TPI)

Left Hand Threads
Threads lean to the right

.500 – 13 UNC – 2 A

Nominal Size
(Express as a 3-place decimal)

TPI
(Threads Per Inch)

Unified National
(Threads Series)

External Threads
(or B = Internal Threads)

Class of Fit
1 = Loose
2 = Average
3 = Tight

Threads Coarseness
F = Fine
EF = Extra Fine
C = Coarse

Thread Nomenclature

.500 TYP

125

4.000

2.000

1.500

.500

0

4.000
3.500
3.000

2.000

1.000
.500

0

SECTION C-C

CHAPTER 18

Sheet Metal Drawings

Sheet Metal Drawings
Post Cap

- When a *sheet metal Drawing* is made from a *sheet metal Part*, the SolidWorks software automatically creates a Flat Pattern view for use in conjunction with the Model View command.

- Any drawing views can be toggled to show the flattened stage, along with the bend lines. By accessing the Properties of the view, you can change from Default (Folded) to Flattened.

- By default, the Bend Lines are visible in the Flat Pattern but the Bend-Regions are not. To show the bend-regions, open the sheet metal part and right click the **Flat-Pattern** in the FeatureManager design tree, select **Edit Feature** and clear **Merge Faces**. You may have to rebuild the drawing to see the tangent edges.

- Both of the Folded and Flat Pattern drawing views can be shown on the same drawing sheet if needed. The dimensions and annotations can then be added to define the views.

- Changes done to the Sheet Metal part **will** reflect in the drawing views and the drawing itself can also be changed to update the sheet metal part as well. To prevent this from happening several options are available, refer to the Online Help from within the SolidWorks software for more details.

- This exercise will guide you through the basics of creating a sheet metal drawing and the use of the Default/Flat-Pattern configurations.

Post Cap
Sheet Metal Drawings

Dimensioning Standards: **ANSI**
Units: **INCHES** – 3 Decimals

Third Angle Projection

Tools Needed:

New Drawing
Draw

Model View

Detail View

Model Items

Horizontal Ordinate
Vertical Ordinate

Properties...

1. Starting a new drawing:

- Select **File / New / Draw** and click **OK**.

- *NOTE: If you have already created and saved a template, you can browse and select the same template for this drawing.*

- Click the **Cancel** button (arrow) to exit the insert part mode. The drawing paper size, drawing view scale, and the projection angle must be set first.

- If the Sheet Properties dialog does not appear, right click in the default paper and select Properties.

- Set **Scale** to **1** to **1** and set **Type of Projection** to **Third Angle**.

- Select **C-Lanscape** sheet size.

- Enable **Display Sheet Format** and click **OK** [OK] .

- Go to **Tools / Options** and change the **Units** to **IPS** (Inch / Pound / Second).

2. Creating the 3 Standard Views:

- Select **the Model View** command from the View Layout tab.

- Click the **Browse** `Browse...` button, from the Training CD locate and open the part named **Post Cap**.

- Once a part is selected SolidWorks automatically switches to the ProjectedView mode.

- Start by placing the Front view approximately as shown and then create the other 3 views as labeled.

- Click **OK** to stop the projection.

3. Re-arranging the drawing views:

- Re-arrange the drawing views to the approximate positions by dragging on their borders. A flat-pattern view will be placed on the right side of the drawing.

Drag the view' border to move

4. Creating the Flat Pattern drawing view:

- Select the **Model View** command , click Next , select the **Flat-Pattern** view (Arrow) from the list and place it approximately as shown.

- Bend notes must be turned off <u>prior</u> to creating the Flat Pattern view (**Tools/Option/ Document Properties/Sheet Metal**).

Bend notes

5. Creating a Detail view:

- Click the **Detail View** command and sketch a Circle approximately as shown.

- Use the **Connected** option and **Custom Scale** of **2:1** (arrows).

Add Centerlines

6. Adding the Ordinate dimensions:

- Click the small arrow below **Smart Dimension** to access its options, and select: **Horizontal Ordinate Dimension** (arrow).

NOTE: *Ordinate dimensions are a group of dimensions measured from a zero point. They are reference dimensions and their values cannot be used to change the model.*

- Starting at the Vertical Centerline, add the Horizontal Ordinate dimensions as shown here.

- Click the drop down arrow under Smart Dimension and select: **Horizontal Ordinate Dimension**

Start the Horizontal here

Start the Vertical here

RECTANGULAR RELIEF
1/2 MAT'L THICKNESS

- Add the Vertical Ordinate dimensions as shown in the drawing view above.

7. Adding the Model dimensions:

- Select the Front view's border to activate it.

- On the **Annotation** tab, click the **Model Items** button, select: **Entire Model** and **Eliminate Duplicates**.

- Click **OK** ✅.

- Modify the dimensions and add the depth and the thickness callouts as shown.

4.000

.060
MAT'L THK

1.500

2X Ø .225
THRU BOTH WALLS

5.000

2.500

1.000

2.000

- Repeat step 6 and add the Model Dimensions to the Right drawing view.

- Add the annotations below the dimension text (Circled).

- Continue adding Model Dimensions to the Top drawing view.

- Add annotations as needed.

8. Creating the Isometric Flat Pattern view:

- Click the **Model View** command from the View Layout tab .

- Click the **Next button** , select the Isometric View from the menu and place it below the flat-pattern view.

- A drawing view can also be copied and pasted using Ctrl+C and Ctrl+V.

- Under the Reference Configuration section change the **Default** configuration to **SM-Flat-Pattern** configuration (arrow).

- Click **OK**   OK   .

- The flat pattern of the sheet metal part appears. The bend lines and bend regions are also visible in this view.

9. Showing /Hiding the Bend Lines:

- Click the DrawingManager tab (arrow), scroll down the tree and expand the last drawing view in the FeatureManager tree (click the **+** symbol).

- Expand the Flat Pattern feature.

- Right click on the Bend-Lines and select **Show**.

10. Saving your work:

- Select **File / Save As**.

- Enter **Post Cap.slddrw** for the name of the file.

- Click **Save**.

CHAPTER 18 (cont.)

2D to 3D Conversion

2D to 3D
Converting 2D AutoCAD files to 3D SolidWorks Parts

- The 2D to 3D options allow sketches and/or drawings created in SolidWorks or other CAD programs, like AutoCAD, to be converted into 3D solids.

- The sketches can be created in SolidWorks or imported as a DWG or DXF from other CAD sources. In either case, the sketch or the drawing should be a single sketch imported into a part template.

- The drawing can be Cut and Pasted into a sketch in a part template or can be imported into SolidWorks as a sketch in a part template, using the SolidWorks DXF/DWG import options.

- Once the drawing is imported or a sketch is created, follow the four easy steps to convert your sketch into a solid:

    * Edit the sketch.   * Extract the sketches (Front, Top, Right...)
    * Align the sketches.   * Extrude the sketch.

- This chapter and its exercises will guide you through some of the easiest techniques in converting an AutoCad 2D drawing into a SolidWorks 3D model, as well as using a built-in utility program called DXF/DWG Import by SolidWorks.

2D to 3D Conversions
Converting 2D AutoCAD DWG to 3D SolidWorks Model

Dimensioning Standards: **ANSI**	Third Angle Projection
Units: **INCHES** – 3 Decimals	

Tools Needed:

Front	Top	Right	Left
Bottom	Back	Auxiliary	Create New Sketch
Repair Sketch	Align Sketch	Extrude	Cut

1. Creating the drawing in AutoCAD®:

- The orthographic views below have already been created in AutoCAD.

- The drawing has also been saved as **2Dto3D.dwg**.

2. Opening the AutoCAD drawing from SolidWorks:

- In SolidWorks, click **File / Open**.

- Change the Files of Type to **Dwg** (*dwg), select the file **2Dto3D** and **open**.

- In the DXF / DWG Import dialog box select: **Import To New Part**.

- Click Next Next > .

Import to a New Part as 2D Sketch

- In the Document Settings dialog box, select **All Selected Layers** and **Add-Constraints** checkboxes.

- Click **Next** [Next >] .

- In the Drawing Layer Mapping dialog, select / set the following:

  * Merge points closer than **0.001**

  * White Background: **Enabled**.

- Click Finish [Finish] .

- The AutoCad drawing is placed on the SolidWorks' Front plane as a sketch.

- A 2D-To-3D toolbar pops up on the screen. (The 2D-To-3D toolbar can be toggled on/off under View / Toolbars / 2D-To-3D).

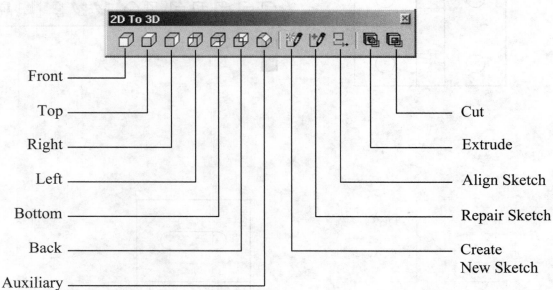

Front

Top

Right

Left

Bottom

Back

Auxiliary

Cut

Extrude

Align Sketch

Repair Sketch

Create
New Sketch

3. Converting the sketches:

- Drag select (click-hold-drag) the Front view.

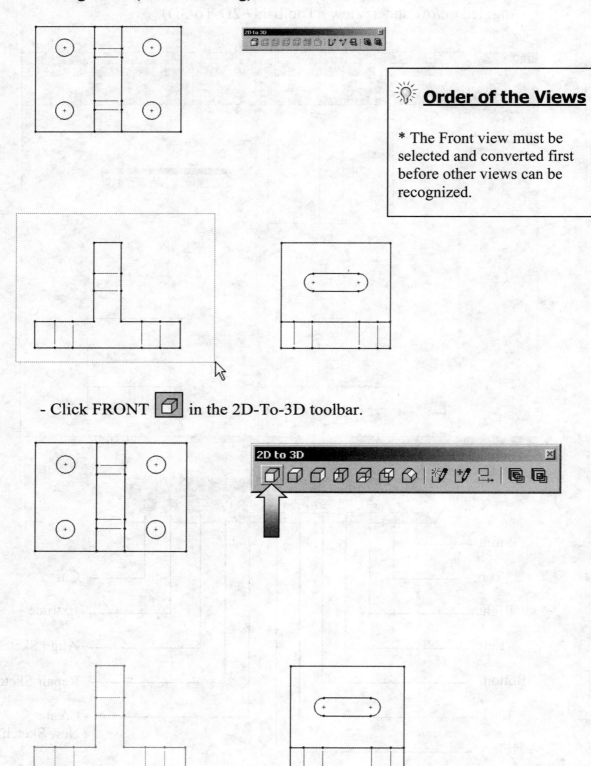

> ### 💡 Order of the Views
>
> * The Front view must be selected and converted first before other views can be recognized.

- Click FRONT [icon] in the 2D-To-3D toolbar.

- The Front view is converted and turned into gray color.

- Drag select (click-hold-drag) the Top view.

- Click TOP ⬜ in the 2D-To-3D toolbar.

- The Top view is converted and rotated 90°.

The Top view is
converted and
rotated 90°

- Drag select (click-hold-drag) the Right view.

- Click RIGHT ⬜ in the 2D-To-3D toolbar.

- The Right view is converted and rotated 90°.

The Right view is
converted and
rotated 90°

- Change to the Isometric view (or press Ctrl + 8), the next step is to align the sketches before making the extrusions.

4. Aligning the three views:

- While holding the CONTROL key, select the **left-edge** of the Top view and the *left-edge* of the Right view as shown.

- Click Align Sketch on the 2D-To-3D tool bar.

- The 2 selected views are aligned.

- Change to the Right view to verify the result of the alignment.

Select 2 edges

- Repeating the step 4:

- Repeat step number 4 and align the 2 bottom lines between the Front and the Right views.

Align the 2 bottom lines.

5. Extruding the Base Feature:

- Select the profile of the Front view. (Right click on one of the lines and pick: **Select Chain**).

- The Select Chain option selects all connecting entities, regardless of their conditions.

Right click and pick — **Select Chain**.

- Click Extrude on the 2D-To-3D toolbar or select **Tools / Sketch Tools / 2D-To-3D / Extrude**.

* <u>For Start Condition:</u>

Change the Sketch Plane option to **Vertex** and select the point as indicated.

Extrude From:
Select this Vertex

* <u>For End Condition:</u>

Change the Direction 1 to **Up To Vertex** and select the point as indicated.

Extrude To:
Select this Vertex

- The solid feature is created from an imported drawing and is centered between the three views.

6. Creating the first Cut extrude, the 4 Holes:

- Select the **four circles** and press **Cut** on the 2D-To-3D toolbar.

Hold CONTROL key and select the 4 Circles.

- Change the Direction 1 to **Through All**.

- Click **OK** .

- The Cut feature is created; rotate the part to verify the result.

7. Create the second Cut extrude, the Center Slot:

- Right click on one of the lines of the slot and pick **Select-Chain**.

- Press **Convert To Cut** on the 2D-To-3D toolbar.

Right click on one of the lines and pick: **Select-Chain.**

- Change the Direction 1 to **Through All**.

- Click **OK** .

- The Slot feature is created; rotate the model to check out the cut.

8. Hiding the Front sketch:

- Right click on one of the lines of the Front sketch and select **Hide.**

Right click on one of the
lines and select **HIDE**.

- The AutoCAD drawing has been converted into SolidWorks 3D solid model.

9. Saving your work as 2D to 3D:

- Click **File / Save As**.

- Enter **2D to 3D** for the name of the file.

- Click **Save**.

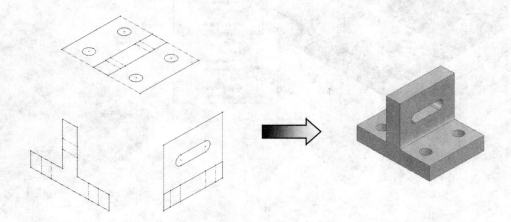

Questions for Review

2D To 3D Conversion

1. The 2D to 3D option allows sketches created in SolidWorks or other CAD software to be converted into 3D solid models.
    a. True
    b. False

2. Both .DXF and .DWG formats are supported for 2D to 3D conversion.
    a. True
    b. False

3. A .DWG document can be inserted into a new SolidWorks drawing or to a new part as a sketch.
    a. True
    b. False

4. The Front view does not have be selected and converted first, no sequence is required.
    a. True
    b. False

5. After the views are converted, they should be aligned with each other.
    a. True
    b. False

6. To select all sketch entities in a view press Control + A.
    a. True
    b. False

7. Before extruding, one view should be selected and a line or a dimension should be used to specify the depth.
    a. True
    b. False

8. A closed sketch profile can be used to make an Extruded-Cut only, not an Extruded-Boss.
    a. True
    b. False

7. True   8. False
5. True   6. False
3. True   4. False
1. True   2. True

Exercise: Modeling & Detailing III

1. Create the **part** and **drawing** as shown.
2. Dimensions are in inches, 3 decimal.
3. All connected edges are tangent.
4. Save the solid model and drawing as: **2D to 3D Part**.

1.000

.748

Ø1.575

Ø.748
THRU

R.787

R.630

R.866

A

R2.126

A

R1.811

40.00°

2.989
REF

1.890

20.00°

R2.677

1.310 REF

R.433
THRU

R.866

.984

Ø1.122
THRU

R.433
THRU

Ø1.732

R1.378

R.630

2.244
REF

5.827

.400

SECTION A

CHAPTER 18 (cont.)

e-Drawings

eDrawing & 3D Drawing View

Soft-lock Assembly

eDrawing:

- eDrawing is one of the most convenient tools in SolidWorks to create, share, and view your 2D or 3D designs.

- The eDrawing Professional allows the user to create eDrawing markup files (***.markup**) that have markups, such as text comments and geometric elements.

- With eDrawing 2014 and SolidWorks® 2014, you can create an eDrawing from any CAD model or assembly from programs like AutoCAD®, Pro/E®, and others.

- The following types of eDrawing files are supported:
    * 3D part files (***.eprt**)
    * 3D assembly files (***.easm**)
    * 2D drawing files (***.edrw**)

3D Drawing View:

- The 3D drawing view mode lets you rotate a drawing view out of its plane so you can see components or edges obscured by other entities. When you rotate a drawing view in 3D drawing view mode, you can save the orientation as a new view orientation.

- 3D drawing view mode is particularly helpful when you want to select an obscured edge for the depth of a broken-out section view. Additionally, while in 3D drawing view mode, you can create a new orientation for another model view. 3D drawing view mode is not available for detail, broken, crop, empty, or detached views.

Soft-Lock Assembly
SolidWorks e-Drawing & 3D Drawing View

SECTION A-A

3D DRAWING VIEW

C   RE2-6002   01

| Dimensioning Standards: **ANSI** | Third Angle Projection |
| Units: **INCHES** – 3 Decimals | |

Tools Needed:

 SolidWorks e-drawing   Play Animation   Stop Animation

 Rotate View   3D Drawing View

1. Opening an existing drawing:

- Click **File / Open**.

- Select **3D Drawing View.slddrw**
  from the Training Files folder and
  open it.

2. Saving as an e-Drawing file type:

- Select **File / Save As.**

- Change the file format
  to **eDrawing** (*.edrw).

- Enter **3D Drawing View**
  as the file name.

- Click the Options button and
  enable **OK to Measure**.

- Click **Save**.

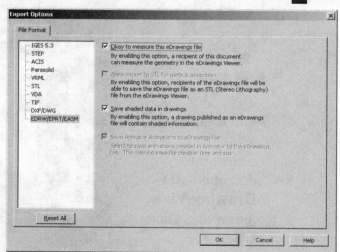

3. Working with eDrawing:

- Close out of SolidWorks and launch the **e-Drawing** program .

- Click **Open** .

- Select the document **3D-Drawing View .edrw** and click **Open**.

- The previously saved drawing is opened in the new User Interface .

- The **eDrawing** toolbar:

- The **Markup** toolbar:

A	Add Text with Leader
A	Add Text without Leader
☁	Add Cloud with Leader
☁	Add Cloud with Text
☁	Add Cloud
\	Add Line
▭	Add Rectangle
⊕	Add Circle
⊙	Add Arc
~	Add Spline
◇	Add Dimension

4. Playing the Animation:

- Click **Play** ▷ Play or select from the menu: **Animation / Continuous Play**.

- The eDrawing animates the drawing views based on the order that was created in SolidWorks.

SECTION A-A

- Click **Stop** Stop or select from the menu: **Animation / Stop**.

- Click **Home** Home to return to the full drawing mode.

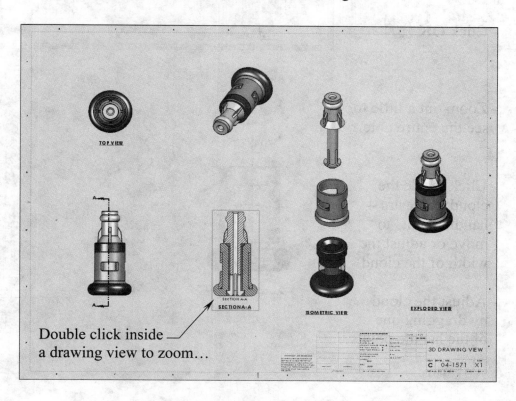

Double click inside
a drawing view to zoom...

- Double click inside the Section view to zoom and fit it to the screen.

5. Adding the markup notes:

- Click the **Markup** button and select the **Cloud-With Leader** command (arrow).

- Click on the **Edge** of the bottom bore hole and place the blank note on the left side.

Click on the edge of
the bore hole

Place the blank
note here

- Enter the note:
Increase the Bore Diameter by .015".

- Click **OK**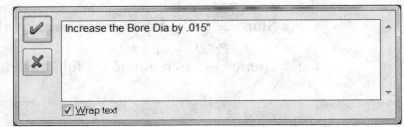

- Zoom out a little to see the entire note.

- Click inside the cloud; there are 4 handle points to move or adjust the width of the cloud.

- Adjust the cloud by dragging one of the handle points.

SECTION A-A
SECTION A-A

Increase the Bore Dia by .015"

Drag handle point

6. Adding a "Stamp":

- Click the Stamp button.

- Locate the DRAFT stamp and drag/drop it on the upper corner of the drawing.

- Click THE **Home** button to return to the full drawing mode.

7. Saving as Executable file type:

- Click **File / Save As**.

- Select **eDrawing Executable Files (*.exe)** from the Save As Type menu & click **Save**.

NOTES:

The .exe files are much larger in size than the standard .edrw.

The .edrw files require eDrawing Viewer or the eDrawing Program itself to view.

Continue...

SolidWorks 2014 - 3D Drawing View

8. Returning to the SolidWorks Program:

- Switch back to the previous SolidWorks drawing (press Alt+ Tab).

- This second half of the lesson discusses the use of the 3D Drawing View command, one of the unique options that allows a flat drawing view to be manipulated and rotated in 3D to make selections of the hidden entities.

- 3D drawing view mode is particularly helpful when you want to select an obscured edge for the depth of a broken-out section view. Additionally, while in 3D drawing view mode, you can create a new orientation for another model view.

9. Using the 3D Drawing View command:

- Create another Top view and then click the drawing view's border to activate.

- Click 3D Drawing View icon from the View toolbar (or under the **View / Modify** menus).

- Select the Rotate tool ⟲ and rotate the Top drawing to a different position approximately as shown.

3D Drawing View pop-up toolbar

Rotate

Click ✔ to keep the new orientation.

Original Drawing View

New 3D Drawing View

10. Saving the New-View orientation:

- Click Save 💾 on the 3D Drawing View pop-up toolbar.

- Enter: **3D Drawing View** in the Named View dialog. This view orientation will be available under **More Views** in the **Model View PropertyManager** the next time you insert a model view.

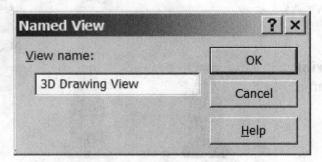

11. Testing out the new view:

- Delete the new view so that we can test out the one that we have just saved.

12. Inserting a Model View:

- Click **Model View**

- Click the **NEXT** arrow.

- In the **Orientation** section, under **More Views**, select: **3D Drawing View**.

- Place the Custom Isometric View approximately as shown.

- Click **OK** ✓.

- Access the properties of the view and click off Show-In-Exploded-State if needed.

13. Saving your work:

- Click **File / Save As**.

- Enter **3D Drawing View** as file name.

- Click **Save**.

CHAPTER 19

Configurations – Part I

Configurations – Part I
Part, Assembly & Drawing

- Configurations is one of the unique options in SolidWorks which allows the users to create multiple variations of a part or assembly within the same document.

- Configurations provide a convenient way to develop and manage families of parts with different dimensions, components, or other parameters.

- In a **Part document**, configurations allow you to create families of parts with different dimensions, features, and custom properties.

- In an **Assembly document**, configurations allow you to create:

  * Simplified versions of the design by suppressing or hiding the components.

  * Families of assemblies with different configurations of the components, parameters, assembly features, dimensions, or configuration-specific custom properties.

- In a **Drawing document**, you can display different views of different configurations that you created earlier in the part or assembly documents by accessing the properties of the drawing view.

- This chapter will guide you through the basics of creating configurations in the part the assembly levels. Later on, these configurations will be called up in a drawing to display the changes that were captured earlier.

Configurations – Part 1
Part, Assembly & Drawing

SECTION A-A

SolidTrans

TITLE
Button Assembly

| SIZE | DWG. NO. | REV |
| C | 001-246 | X1 |

| Dimensioning Standards: **ANSI** | Third Angle Projection |
| Units: **INCHES** – 3 Decimals | |

Tools Needed:

Part document

Assembly document

Drawing document

Add Configuration

| Default |
| Expanded |

1. Opening the existing Assembly Document:

Go to: Training Files folder
Button Assembly folder
Open **Button Assembly.sldasm**

2. Using Configurations in the Part mode:

- From the FeatureManager tree, right click on **Button Spring** and select **Open Part.**

- Change to the **ConfigurationManager** tree.

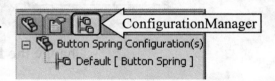

- Right click over the part named Button Spring and select **Add Configuration**.

- Enter **Compressed** under **Configuration Name.**

- Under Comment, enter: **Changed Pitch Dim. from .915 to .415**

- Click **OK** ✅.

3. Changing the Pitch:

- Switch back to the FeatureManager tree. (arrow).

- Expand the **Sweep1** feature (click the + symbol).

- Right click on the **Helix/Spiral1** feature and select **Edit Feature**.

- Change the **Height** dimension to **.415** in.

- Click **OK** .

Default Configuration
(.915 Pitch)

Compressed Configuration
(.415 Pitch)

4. Using Configurations in the Assembly mode:

- Switch back to the Assembly document (**Ctrl + Tab**).

- Change to the **ConfigurationManager** tree.

- Right click over the name of the assembly and select: **Add Configuration**.

- Enter **Expanded** for Configuration Name.

- Click **OK** ✓.

5. Changing the Mate conditions:

- Switch back to the **FeatureManager** tree and expand the Mates group.

- Right click on the mate Coincident8 and select: **Suppress**.

- By suppressing this mate, the Button (upper part) is no longer locked to the Housing and new Mates can be added to re-position it.

6. Adding new Mates:

- Add a **Coincident** Mate between the 2 faces of the two locking features.

Coincident Mate

Default Assembly Configuration

7. Changing Configuration:

- Right click over the part named **Button Spring** and select **Component Properties**.

- From the Component Properties dialog box, select the **Default** Configuration.

- Click **OK** ✓.

Compressed Assembly Configuration

8. Using Configurations in the Drawing:

- Start a New drawing document; Go to **File / New / Draw** (or Drawing).

- Use **C-Landscape** paper size, **Scale: 3:1**

- Create the 4 standard views as shown below (using the **Default** Configuration).

9. Creating a 2nd Isometric view:

- Create another Isometric view and place it approximately as shown.

Note: *Copy and Paste also works; first select the Isometric view and press Ctrl+C, then click anywhere in the drawing and press Ctrl+V).*

10. Changing the Configuration of a drawing view:

- Click the dotted border of the new isometric view.

- Change from the **Default** configuration to **Expanded** configuration (arrow).

- Click **OK** ✅.

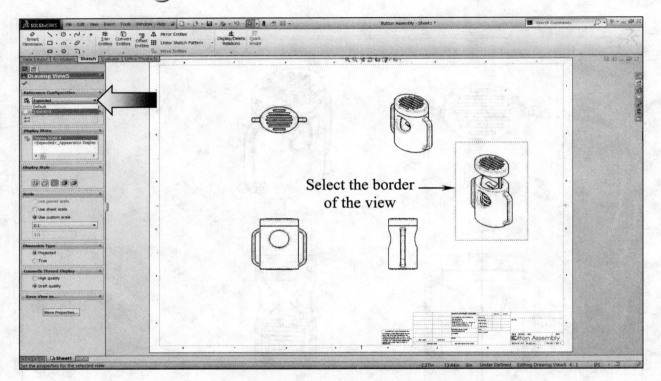

Select the border of the view

- The Expanded configuration is now the active configuration for this specific view.

11. Saving your work:

- Click **File / Save As**.

-Enter **Button Assembly** for the name of the file.

- Click **Save**.

CHAPTER 19 (cont.)

Configurations - Part II

Configurations – Part II
Part / Assembly / Drawing

Configurable Items for Parts:

Part configurations can be used as follows:
* Modify feature dimensions and tolerances.
* Suppress features, equations, and end conditions.
* Assign mass and center of gravity.
* Use different sketch planes, sketch relations, and external sketch relations.
* Set individual face colors.
* Control the configuration of a base part.
* Control the configuration of a split part.
* Control the driving state of sketch dimensions.
* Create derived configurations.
* Define configuration-specific properties.

Configurable Items for Assemblies:

Assembly configurations can be used as follows:
* Change the suppression state (**Suppressed, Resolved**) or visibility (**Hide, Show**) of components.
* Change the referenced configuration of components.
* Change the dimensions of distance or angle mates, or suppression state of mates.
* Modify the dimensions, tolerances, or other parameters of features that belong to the assembly. This includes assembly feature cuts and holes, component patterns, reference geometry, and sketches that belong to the <u>assembly</u> (not to one of the assembly components).
* Assign mass and center of gravity.
* Suppress features that belong to the assembly.
* Define configuration-specific properties, such as end conditions and sketch relations.
* Create derived configurations.
* Change the suppression state of the Simulation folder in the Feature Manager design tree and its simulation elements (Suppressing the folder also suppresses its elements).

Configurations – Part II
Part, Assembly & Drawing

6 Spokes Configuration

7 Spokes Configuration

7 Spokes with Bolts Configuration

| Dimensioning Standards: **ANSI** | Third Angle Projection |
| Units: **INCHES** – 3 Decimals | |

Tools Needed:

 Part document

Assembly document

 Drawing document

Feature Manager

Configuration Manager

Part Configurations

This section discusses the use of Configurations in the part level, where the driving dimensions of the spokes-pattern will be altered to change the number of spokes in the part.

Opening the existing file:

    * Go to the TrainingFiles folder
    * Wheel Assembly folder.
    * **WHEEL.sldprt**

1. Part Configurations:

    - Change to the ConfigurationManager tree:

    - We are going to create a new configuration to capture the change in the Spoke feature.

2. Creating a new configuration:

    - Right click on the name Wheel Configuration and select **Add Configuration**.

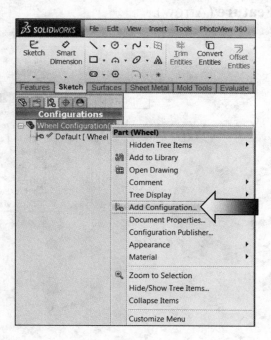

- For Configuration Name, enter:
7 Spokes (arrows).

- Under Description, enter:
Modified the No. of Spokes Pattern.

- Click **OK** .

NOTE:

To display the description in the FeatureManager tree, do the following:

From the FeatureManager tree, right click on the part name, go to Tree-Display, and select:
Show Feature Descriptions.

3. Changing the number of the Spokes:

- Switch back to the FeatureManager tree.

- Right click on the **Spokes Pattern** feature and select **Edit Feature** (Arrow).

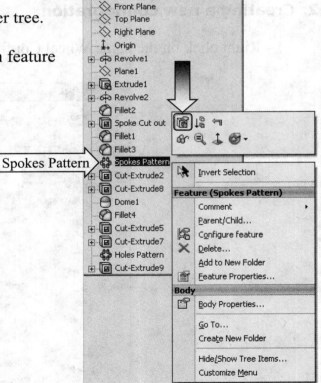

- Change the number of
  instances to **7** (Circled).

- Click **OK** .

NOTE:

*Equations can be used to
change the number of spokes
and achieve the same result.*

4. Viewing the configurations:

- Change to the ConfigurationManager tree.

- Double click on the **Default** configuration to see the
  6-Spokes design.

- Double click on the **7 Spokes** configuration to view
  the new changes.

6 Spokes   **7 Spokes**

5. Saving the part:

- Save the part as a copy and name it: **Wheel.sldprt**

Assembly Configurations

This section discusses the use of Configurations in the assembly level, where a Sub-Assembly is inserted and mated onto the Wheel as a new configuration, and any of the configurations created previously in the part level can be selected to use in the assembly level.

6. Starting a New assembly:

- Click **File / Make Assembly From Part** (arrow).

- Select the Assembly Template from the New SolidWorks Document box.

- Click the Origin Point to place the component. (If the Origin is not visible, enable it from the View / Origins menus).

- The 1st part in the assembly document is the Parent Component, it should be fixed on the origin.

Place the 1st component on the Origin.

7. Assembly Configurations:

- Change to the ConfigurationManager tree.

- Right click on the Assembly's name and select **Add configuration** (Arrow).

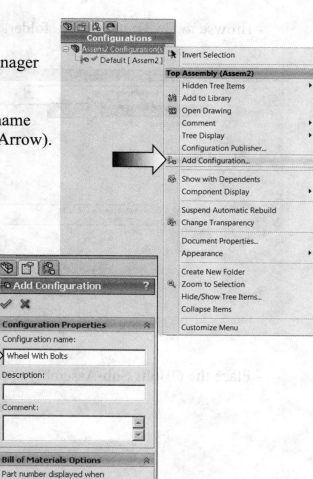

- For Configuration Name, enter: **Wheel With Bolts**.

- Click **OK** ✓.

NOTE:

A set of Bolts, which have been saved earlier as an assembly document, is going to be inserted into the Top Level Assembly and becomes a Sub-Assembly.

8. Inserting the Sub-Assembly:

- Click **Insert Components.**

- Click the [Browse...] button.

- Browse to the Training Files folder, locate and open the **Bolts Sub-Assembly**.

- Place the 6 Bolts Sub-Assembly approximately as shown.

Place the Bolt-Assembly approximately here.

- Go to the View menu and click off the Origins option to hide them.

9. Mating the Sub-Assembly:

- Enable **Temporary Axis** from the **View** menu.

- Click **Mate** or select **Insert / Mate**.

- Select the center Axis of one of the Bolts and the mating Holes (pictured).

Select 2 Axis

- The system selects the Coincident mate automatically.

- Click either **Align** or **Anti-Align**, to flip the Bolts to the proper direction.

- Click **OK**.

- Add a **Coincident** Mate between the Bottom Face of one of the Bolts and its mating surface (pictured).

- Click **OK** ✔.

Coincident Mate the Bolt and its mating face.

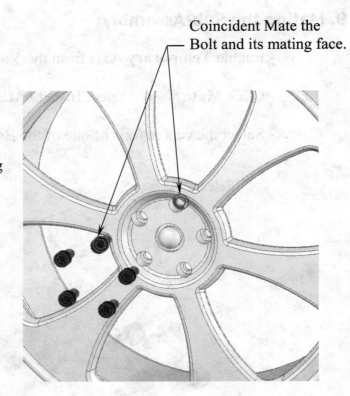

Coincident Mate the next 2 center Axis.

- Add another **Coincident** Mate to the next 2 axis, to fully center the 6 bolts.

The Completed Assembly.

10. Viewing the Assembly Configurations:

- Change to the ConfigurationManager tree.

Wheel With Bolts Configuration

- Double click on the **Default** configuration.

- The Bolts Sub-Assembly is **Suppressed**.

- The **7 Spokes** pattern is displayed.

Default Configuration

- Make any necessary changes to the Number of Spokes pattern by accessing the Component's Properties and its Configurations.

- An assembly exploded view may need to be created for use in the drawing later.

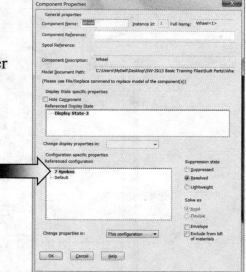

11. Saving your work:

- Save as **Part-Assembly Configurations**.

Drawing Configurations

Change Configurations in Drawing Views

- This section discusses the use of Configurations in the drawing level, where Configurations created previously in the part and assembly levels can be selected for use in the drawing views.

- To change the configuration of the model in a drawing view:

* Right click a drawing view (or hold down **Ctrl** to select multiple drawing views, then right click) and select **Properties**.

- In the dialog box under **Configuration information**, select a different configuration for **Use- named configuration**.

1. Creating an assembly drawing:

- Go to **File / New / Drawing**.

- Use **C-Landscape** paper size.

- Set **Scale** to: **1 to 1**.

- Set the **Projection** to **3rd Angle**.

2. Creating the standard drawing views:

- Select **Model View** command .

- Click **Browse** [Browse...] .

- Select the **Wheel Assembly** and click **Open**.

- Select the **FRONT** view from the Standard Views dialog and place it approximately as shown.

3. Auto-Start the Projected-View:

- If the option **Auto-Start Projected-View** is enabled, SolidWorks will automatically project the next views based on the position of the cursor.

- Place the Top view as pictured.

- Click **OK** .

4. Creating the Aligned Section View:

- Select the Front drawing view's border to activate it.

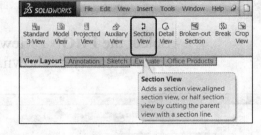

- Select the **Section View** command from the View layout tool tab.

- Click the **Align** button (arrow) and create the section lines in the order shown below.

- Click **OK** to go to the next step.

- **Section Scope**: is an option that allows components to be excluded from the section cut. In other words, when sectioning an assembly drawing view, you will have an option to select which component(s) is going to be effected by this section cut. This option is called Section Scope.

- In the Section Scope dialog box, enable **Auto Hatching** and if necessary, click **Flip Direction**.

SECTION A-A
SCALE 1 : 1

5. Creating the Isometric view:

- Select the **Model View** command

- Click **Next**.

- Select **Isometric** view from the Standard Views list.

- Place the Isometric view on the lower right side of the drawing.

- Click **OK**.

<u>Displaying the Exploded View</u>: (An exploded view must be created from the assembly level prior to showing it in the drawing).

- Right click on the Isometric drawing view's border and select **Properties**.

- Enable the **Show in Exploded State** check box.

The Assembly Exploded view.

6. Changing Configurations:

- Use the **Model View** command and create 2 more Isometric views.

- Right click on the new Isometric drawing view's border and select **Properties**.

- Select the **Default** configuration.

- Set the 2nd Isometric view to the **6-Spokes** configuration (Switch to the Assembly document to modify the configurations).

7. Adding Annotations:

- Click Note **A** and add the call-outs under each drawing views as shown.

* 6 SPOKES CONFIGURATION.

* 7 SPOKES CONFIGURATION.

* 6 SPOKES WITH BOLTS CONFIGURATION.

8. Saving your work:

- Click **File / Save As**.

- Enter: **Drawing Configurations** for the name of the file.

- Click **Save** and close all documents.

CHAPTER 20

Design Tables

Design Tables in Part, Assembly & Drawing

Design Table Parameters	Description (Legal values)
$PARTNUMBER@_____	- For use in a Bill of Materials.
$COMMENT@_____	- Any Description or text string.
$NEVER_EXPAND_IN_BOM@_____	- Yes/No to expand in B.O.M.
$STATE@_____	- Resolved = R, Suppressed = S
$CONFIGURATION@_____	- Configuration Name.
$SHOW@_____	- Has been Obsoleted.
$PRP@_____	- Enter any text string.
$USER_NOTES@_____	- Enter any text string.
$COLOR@_____	- Specifying 32-bit RGB color.
$PARENT@_____	- Parent configuration name.
$TOLERANCE@_____	- Enter tolerance keywords.
$SWMASS@_____	- Enter any decimal legal value.
$SWCOG@_____	- Enter any legal x,y,z value.
$DISPLAYSTATE@_____	- Display state name.

In a Design Table, you will need to define the names of the configurations, specify the parameters that you want to control, and assign values for each parameter. This chapter will guide you through the use of design tables in both the part and assembly levels.

Part, Assembly & Drawing
Design Tables

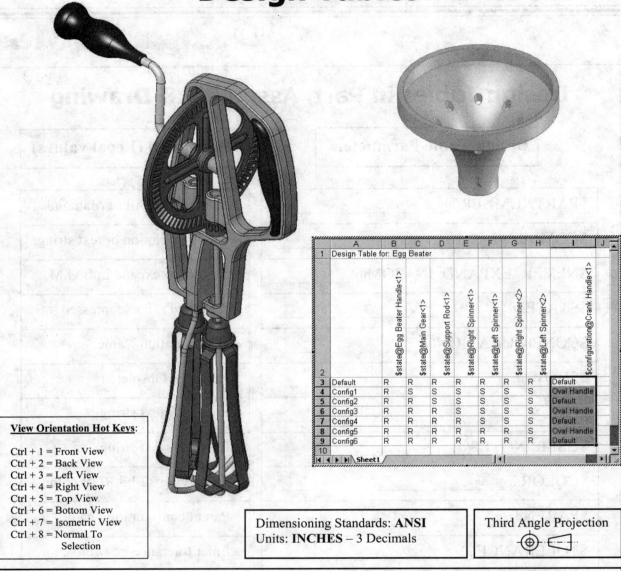

View Orientation Hot Keys:

Ctrl + 1 = Front View
Ctrl + 2 = Back View
Ctrl + 3 = Left View
Ctrl + 4 = Right View
Ctrl + 5 = Top View
Ctrl + 6 = Bottom View
Ctrl + 7 = Isometric View
Ctrl + 8 = Normal To
         Selection

Dimensioning Standards: **ANSI**
Units: **INCHES** – 3 Decimals

Third Angle Projection

Tools Needed:

Design Table   Design Tables / Microsoft Excel

ConfigurationManager

Part - Design Tables

1. Copying the document:

- <u>Go to:</u> The Training Files folder, Design Tables folder **Part Design Table.sldprt**

- **OPEN** a copy of the part document named: **Part Design Table.sldprt**

- This exercise discusses the use of Changing Feature Dimensions and Feature Suppression-States in a Design Table.

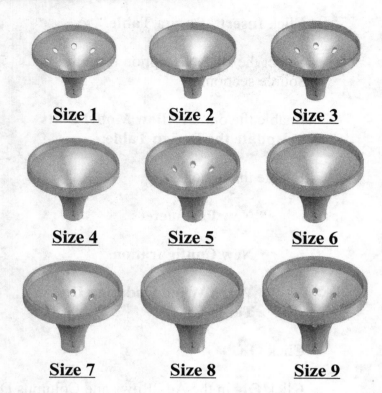

Size 1   Size 2   Size 3

Size 4   Size 5   Size 6

Size 7   Size 8   Size 9

- The names of the dimensions will be used as the column Headers in the design table.

- Go to the **View** menu and enable the option: **Dimension Names** (arrow).

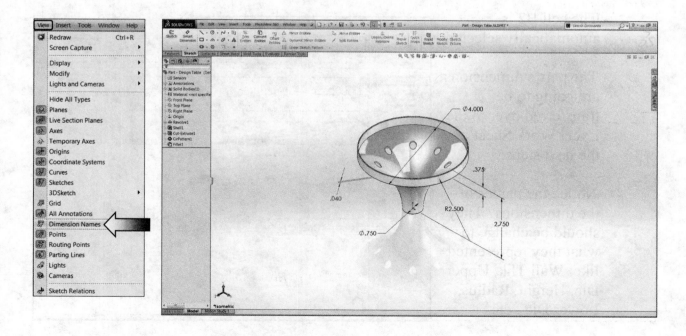

2. Creating a New Design Table:

- Click **Insert / Design Table**.

- Select the **BLANK** option from the Source section.

- Enable the option **Allow Model Edits to Update the Design Table**.

- Enable the options:

    * **New Parameters**

    * **New Configurations**

    * **Warn When Updating Design Table**

- Click **OK** .

- Click **OK** in the Add Rows and Columns Dialog box.

- The Microsoft Excel Work Sheet opens up.

- The cell A1 is filled in with the part's name.

- The cell B2 is automatically selected.

- The part's dimensions are going to be transferred over to the Excel Work Sheet in the next steps.

- Notice the names of the dimensions? They should be change to what they represented like: Wall Thk, Upper Dia, Height, Radius, Lower Dia., etc.

3. Transferring the Dimensions to the Design Table:

- Make sure the cell B2 is selected.

- Double click on the Height DIM 2.750

- The dimension is transferred over to cell B2.

Double click this dimension

- Repeat the same step and transfer the other dimensions in the order as shown.

	A	B	C	D	E	F	G
1	Design Table for: Part - Design Table						
2		Height DIM@Sketch1	Upper DIA@Sketch1	Lower DIA@Sketch1	Side RAD@Sketch1	Side Step@Sketch1	Wall THK@Shell1
3	Size1	2.75	4	0.75	2.5	0.375	0.04
4	Size2						
5	Size3						
6	Size4						
7	Size5						
8	Size6						
9	Size7						
10	Size8						
11	Size9						
12							

- Add configs. names: Size1 thru Size9.

4. Using Excel's Addition Formula:

- Select the cell B3, type the equal sign (=), click the number **2.75** in cell B2, and then enter **+.125**

- Copy the formula to the cells below:

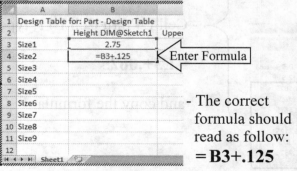

	A	B
1	Design Table for: Part - Design Table	
2		Height DIM@Sketch1
3	Size1	2.75
4	Size2	=B3+.125
5	Size3	
6	Size4	
7	Size5	
8	Size6	
9	Size7	
10	Size8	
11	Size9	
12		

Enter Formula

- The correct formula should read as follow:
=B3+.125

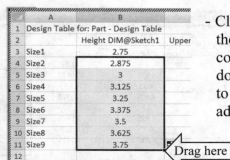

	A	B	
1	Design Table for: Part - Design Table		
2		Height DIM@Sketch1	Upper
3	Size1	2.75	
4	Size2	2.875	
5	Size3	3	
6	Size4	3.125	
7	Size5	3.25	
8	Size6	3.375	
9	Size7	3.5	
10	Size8	3.625	
11	Size9	3.75	
12			

- Click and drag on the bottom right corner of cell B3, down to cell B11 to repeat the addition formula.

Drag here

	A	B	C	D
1	Design Table for: Part - Design Table			
2		Height DIM@Sketch1	Upper DIA@Sketch1	Lower DIA@
3	Size1	2.75	4	0.75
4	Size2	2.875	=C3+125	
5	Size3	3		
6	Size4	3.125		
7	Size5	3.25		
8	Size6	3.375		
9	Size7	3.5		
10	Size8	3.625		
11	Size9	3.75		
12				

	A	B	C	D
1	Design Table for: Part - Design Table			
2		Height DIM@Sketch1	Upper DIA@Sketch1	Lower DIA@
3	Size1	2.75	4	0.75
4	Size2	2.875	4.125	
5	Size3	3	4.25	
6	Size4	3.125	4.375	
7	Size5	3.25	4.5	
8	Size6	3.375	4.625	
9	Size7	3.5	4.75	
10	Size8	3.625	4.875	
11	Size9	3.75	5	

- In cell C4 type:

= **C3+.125**

and copy the formula thru cell C11.

	A	B	C	D
1	Design Table for: Part - Design Table			
2		Height DIM@Sketch1	Upper DIA@Sketch1	Lower DIA@Sketch1
3	Size1	2.75	4	0.75
4	Size2	2.875	4.125	=D3+.0625
5	Size3	3	4.25	
6	Size4	3.125	4.375	
7	Size5	3.25	4.5	
8	Size6	3.375	4.625	
9	Size7	3.5	4.75	
10	Size8	3.625	4.875	
11	Size9	3.75	5	
12				

- Cell D4 thru Cell C11, type:

= **D3+.0625**

and copy the formula.

	A	B	C	D
1	Design Table for: Part - Design Table			
2		Height DIM@Sketch1	Upper DIA@Sketch1	Lower DIA@Sketch1
3	Size1	2.75	4	0.75
4	Size2	2.875	4.125	0.8125
5	Size3	3	4.25	0.875
6	Size4	3.125	4.375	0.9375
7	Size5	3.25	4.5	1
8	Size6	3.375	4.625	1.0625
9	Size7	3.5	4.75	1.125
10	Size8	3.625	4.875	1.1875
11	Size9	3.75	5	1.25
12				

	A	B	C	D	E
1	Design Table for: Part - Design Table				
2		Height DIM@Sketch1	Upper DIA@Sketch1	Lower DIA@Sketch1	Side RAD@Sketch1
3	Size1	2.75	4	0.75	2.5
4	Size2	2.875	4.125	0.8125	=E3+.0625
5	Size3	3	4.25	0.875	
6	Size4	3.125	4.375	0.9375	
7	Size5	3.25	4.5	1	
8	Size6	3.375	4.625	1.0625	
9	Size7	3.5	4.75	1.125	
10	Size8	3.625	4.875	1.1875	
11	Size9	3.75	5	1.25	
12					

- Cell E4 thru Cell E11, type:

= **E3+.0625**

and copy the formula.

	A	B	C	D	E
1	Design Table for: Part - Design Table				
2		Height DIM@Sketch1	Upper DIA@Sketch1	Lower DIA@Sketch1	Side RAD@Sketch1
3	Size1	2.75	4	0.75	2.5
4	Size2	2.875	4.125	0.8125	2.5625
5	Size3	3	4.25	0.875	2.625
6	Size4	3.125	4.375	0.9375	2.6875
7	Size5	3.25	4.5	1	2.75
8	Size6	3.375	4.625	1.0625	2.8125
9	Size7	3.5	4.75	1.125	2.875
10	Size8	3.625	4.875	1.1875	2.9375
11	Size9	3.75	5	1.25	3
12					

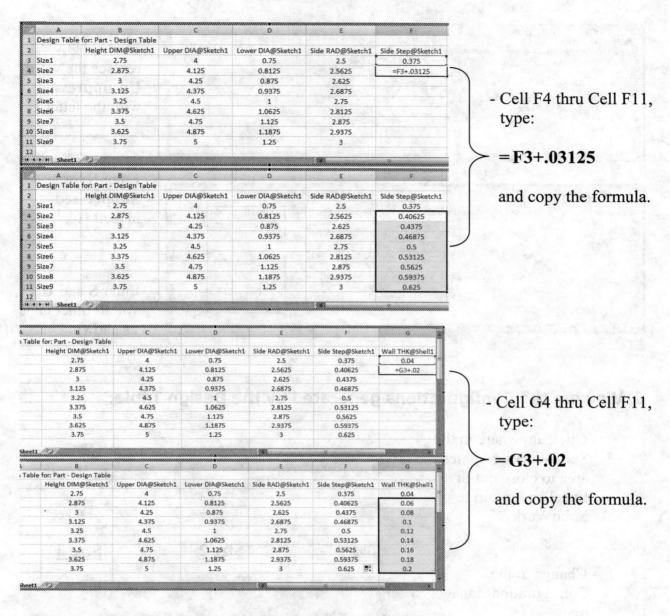

	A	B	C	D	E	F
1	Design Table for: Part - Design Table					
2		Height DIM@Sketch1	Upper DIA@Sketch1	Lower DIA@Sketch1	Side RAD@Sketch1	Side Step@Sketch1
3	Size1	2.75	4	0.75	2.5	0.375
4	Size2	2.875	4.125	0.8125	2.5625	=F3+.03125
5	Size3	3	4.25	0.875	2.625	
6	Size4	3.125	4.375	0.9375	2.6875	
7	Size5	3.25	4.5	1	2.75	
8	Size6	3.375	4.625	1.0625	2.8125	
9	Size7	3.5	4.75	1.125	2.875	
10	Size8	3.625	4.875	1.1875	2.9375	
11	Size9	3.75	5	1.25	3	

- Cell F4 thru Cell F11, type:

$=F3+.03125$

and copy the formula.

	A	B	C	D	E	F
1	Design Table for: Part - Design Table					
2		Height DIM@Sketch1	Upper DIA@Sketch1	Lower DIA@Sketch1	Side RAD@Sketch1	Side Step@Sketch1
3	Size1	2.75	4	0.75	2.5	0.375
4	Size2	2.875	4.125	0.8125	2.5625	0.40625
5	Size3	3	4.25	0.875	2.625	0.4375
6	Size4	3.125	4.375	0.9375	2.6875	0.46875
7	Size5	3.25	4.5	1	2.75	0.5
8	Size6	3.375	4.625	1.0625	2.8125	0.53125
9	Size7	3.5	4.75	1.125	2.875	0.5625
10	Size8	3.625	4.875	1.1875	2.9375	0.59375
11	Size9	3.75	5	1.25	3	0.625

B	C	D	E	F	G
Table for: Part - Design Table					
Height DIM@Sketch1	Upper DIA@Sketch1	Lower DIA@Sketch1	Side RAD@Sketch1	Side Step@Sketch1	Wall THK@Shell1
2.75	4	0.75	2.5	0.375	0.04
2.875	4.125	0.8125	2.5625	0.40625	=G3+.02
3	4.25	0.875	2.625	0.4375	
3.125	4.375	0.9375	2.6875	0.46875	
3.25	4.5	1	2.75	0.5	
3.375	4.625	1.0625	2.8125	0.53125	
3.5	4.75	1.125	2.875	0.5625	
3.625	4.875	1.1875	2.9375	0.59375	
3.75	5	1.25	3	0.625	

- Cell G4 thru Cell F11, type:

$=G3+.02$

and copy the formula.

B	C	D	E	F	G
Table for: Part - Design Table					
Height DIM@Sketch1	Upper DIA@Sketch1	Lower DIA@Sketch1	Side RAD@Sketch1	Side Step@Sketch1	Wall THK@Shell1
2.75	4	0.75	2.5	0.375	0.04
2.875	4.125	0.8125	2.5625	0.40625	0.06
3	4.25	0.875	2.625	0.4375	0.08
3.125	4.375	0.9375	2.6875	0.46875	0.1
3.25	4.5	1	2.75	0.5	0.12
3.375	4.625	1.0625	2.8125	0.53125	0.14
3.5	4.75	1.125	2.875	0.5625	0.16
3.625	4.875	1.1875	2.9375	0.59375	0.18
3.75	5	1.25	3	0.625	0.2

5. Controlling the Suppression-States of the holes:

- Select the cell **H2** and double click on the **CutExtrude1** to transfer to cell H2.

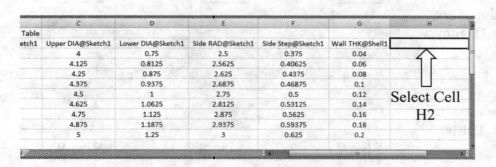

C	D	E	F	G	H
Table					
...tch1 Upper DIA@Sketch1	Lower DIA@Sketch1	Side RAD@Sketch1	Side Step@Sketch1	Wall THK@Shell1	
4	0.75	2.5	0.375	0.04	
4.125	0.8125	2.5625	0.40625	0.06	
4.25	0.875	2.625	0.4375	0.08	
4.375	0.9375	2.6875	0.46875	0.1	
4.5	1	2.75	0.5	0.12	
4.625	1.0625	2.8125	0.53125	0.14	
4.75	1.125	2.875	0.5625	0.16	
4.875	1.1875	2.9375	0.59375	0.18	
5	1.25	3	0.625	0.2	

Select Cell H2

Double click

	Height DIM@Sketch1	Upper DIA@Sketch1	Lower DIA@Sketch1	Side RAD@Sketch1	Side Step@Sketch1	Wall THK@Shell1	$STATE@Cut-Extrude1
1	for: Part - Design Table						
3	2.75	4	0.75	2.5	0.375	0.04	UNSUPPRESSED
4	2.875	4.125	0.8125	2.5625	0.40625	0.06	
5	3	4.25	0.875	2.625	0.4375	0.08	
6	3.125	4.375	0.9375	2.6875	0.46875	0.1	
7	3.25	4.5	1	2.75	0.5	0.12	
8	3.375	4.625	1.0625	2.8125	0.53125	0.14	
9	3.5	4.75	1.125	2.875	0.5625	0.16	
10	3.625	4.875	1.1875	2.9375	0.59375	0.18	
11	3.75	5	1.25	3	0.625	0.2	

- In Cell H3, replace the word **Unsuppressed** with the letter **U**.

	Upper DIA@Sketch1	Lower DIA@Sketch1	Side RAD@Sketch1	Side Step@Sketch1	Wall THK@Shell1	$STATE@Cut-Extrude1
3	4	0.75	2.5	0.375	0.04	U
4	4.125	0.8125	2.5625	0.40625	0.06	S
5	4.25	0.875	2.625	0.4375	0.08	U
6	4.375	0.9375	2.6875	0.46875	0.1	S
7	4.5	1	2.75	0.5	0.12	U
8	4.625	1.0625	2.8125	0.53125	0.14	S
9	4.75	1.125	2.875	0.5625	0.16	U
10	4.875	1.1875	2.9375	0.59375	0.18	S
11	5	1.25	3	0.625	0.2	U

- Enter **S** for: **Suppressed** in Cell H4.

- Enter **S** and **U** for all other cells as shown.

6. Viewing the Configurations generated by the Design Table:

- Click anywhere in the SolidWorks graphics area to close out of Excel and return to SolidWorks.

- Change to the ConfigurationManager tree.

- Double click on Size2 and then other sizes to see the parts that were created by the Design Table.

- Save your work as: **Part - Design Table**.

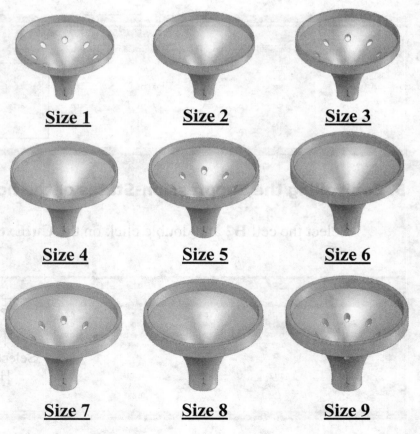

Size 1   Size 2   Size 3

Size 4   Size 5   Size 6

Size 7   Size 8   Size 9

Assembly - Design Tables

1. Copying the Egg Beater Assembly:

- <u>Go to:</u> The Training Files folder
    Design Tables folder
    Egg Beater Assembly Folder.

- Copy the Egg-Beater-Assembly folder to
your computer.

- **Open** the **Egg Beater Assembly.sldasm**

- This exercise discusses the use of the STATE
and CONFIGURATION parameters in a
Design Table.

2. Creating a new Assembly Design Table:

- Select **Insert / New Design Table** Design Table...

- From the property tree, under Source, select **Blank**.

- Under Edit Control, select **Allow Model Edits to Update the Design Table**.

- Under Options, enable **New Parameters**, **New Configs.**, and **Warn When Updating Design Table**.

- Click **OK** ✅.

- A blank Design Table appears and overlays the SolidWorks screen, the toolbars and the pull-down menus are now changed to Microsoft Excel.

- Set the Column Headers to Vertical Alignment.

- Right click the row #2(arrow), select Format Cells, click the Alignment tab and set the Orientation to 90 degrees.

NOTE:
To create a design table, you must define the names of the configurations that you want to create, specify the parameters that you want to control, and assign values for each parameter.

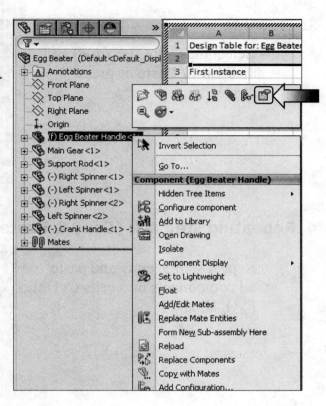

3. Defining the column headers:

- We are going to copy the name of of each component and paste it to the Design Table. They will be used as the Column Headers.

- Right click on the part named Egg Beater Handle and select: **Component Properties** (Arrow).

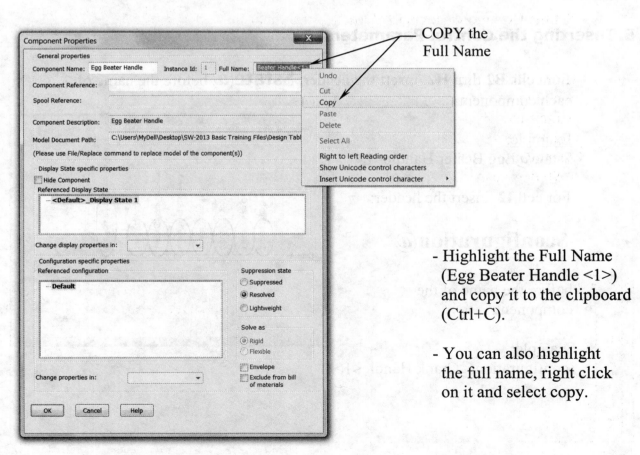

COPY the Full Name

- Highlight the Full Name (Egg Beater Handle <1>) and copy it to the clipboard (Ctrl+C).

- You can also highlight the full name, right click on it and select copy.

- Select the Cell C2 (arrow) and click **Edit / Paste** or press Ctrl+V.

High light and PASTE here.

4. Repeating step #3: (Copy & Paste all components)

- Repeat step 3, copy and paste all components into cells C, D, E, F, G, H, and I.

5. Inserting the Control Parameters:

- For cells **B2** thru **H2**, insert the header: **$state@** before the name of each component.

Example:
$state@Egg Beater Handle<1>

- For cell **I2**, insert the header:

$configuration@

before the name of the component.

Example:
$configuration@Crank Handle<1>

6. Adding the configuration names:

- The actual part numbers can be used here for the name of each configuration.

- Starting at **Cell A4**, (below Default), enter **Config1** thru **Config5** as shown.

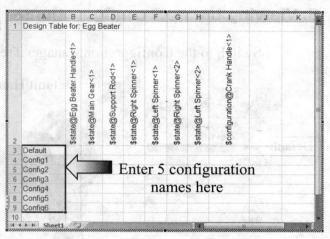

Enter 5 configuration names here

7. Assigning the control values:

- To prevent mistakes, type the letter R and letter S in each cell.

- Enter the values R (Resolved) and S (Suppressed) into their appropriate cells, from column B through column H.

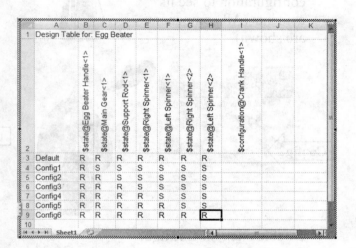

- For Column I, we will enter the names of the configurations instead.

- Select the cell **I3** and enter: **Default**.

- Select the cell **I4** and enter **Oval Handle**.

- Repeat the same step for all 6 configs.

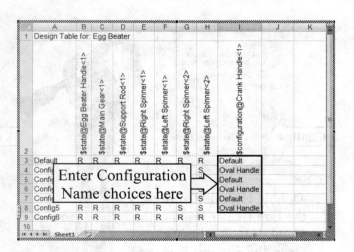

Enter Configuration Name choices here

8. Viewing the new configurations:

- Switch to the ConfigurationManager Tree.

- Double click on **Default** configuration to see its contents (All components are shown).

- Double click on **Config1,** only the Egg Beater Handle and the Crank Handle are shown.

- Double click on **Config2,** the Egg Beater Handle, the Crank Handle, and the Main Gear are resolved.

- Double click on **Config3,** the Egg Beater Handle, the Crank Handle, the Main Gear, and the Support Rod are shown.

- Double click on **Config4,** the Egg Beater Handle, the Crank Handle, the Main Gear, the Support Rod, and the Left Spinner are resolved.

- Double click on **Config5,** the Egg Beater Handle, the Crank Handle, the Main Gear, the Support Rod, the Left Spinner, and the Left Mixer are resolved.

Exercise: Part Design Tables

1. Open the existing document named: **Part Design Tables_EXE** from the Training folder.
2. Create a design table with 3 different sizes using the dimensions provided in the table.
3. Customize the table by merging the cells, adding colors, and borders.
4. Use the instructions on the following pages, if needed.

Design Table for: Part Design Tables_Exe									
	Lower Boss Thickness@Sketch	Upper Boss Thickness@Sketch	Center Hole@Sketch1	Upper Boss Dia@Sketch1	Lower Boss Dia@Sketch1	D1@Revolve1	Bolt Cicle@Sketch2	Hole on Flange@Sketch2	D3@CirPattern1	D1@CirPattern1
Size 1	0.25	0.25	0.5	1	2	360	1.5	0.25	360	4
Size 2	0.375	0.375	0.625	1.25	2.25	360	1.75	0.275	360	4
Size 3	0.5	0.5	0.75	1.5	2.5	360	2	0.3	360	4

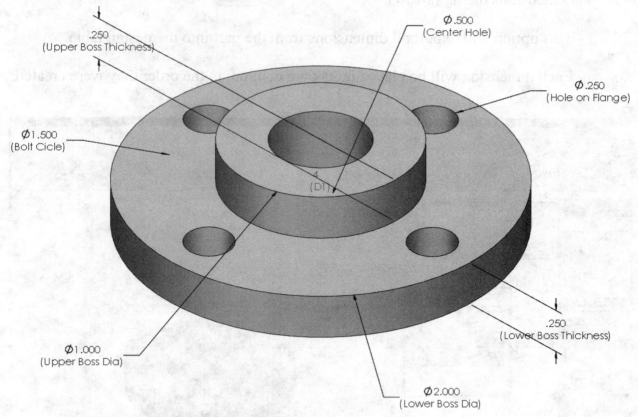

.250
(Upper Boss Thickness)

Ø.500
(Center Hole)

Ø.250
(Hole on Flange)

Ø1.500
(Bolt Cicle)

4
(D1)

.250
(Lower Boss Thickness)

Ø1.000
(Upper Boss Dia)

Ø2.000
(Lower Boss Dia)

1. Opening the Master part file:

- From the training CD, open the part named: **Part Design Tables_Exe**.
The dimensions in this part have been renamed for use in this exercise.

2. Inserting a design table:

- From the **Insert** menu click **Tables / Design-Table**.

- Click the **Auto Create** button (default).

- Leave all other options at their default settings.

- Click **OK**.

3. Adding model dimensions to the table:

- **Select all dimensions** in the Dimensions dialog (arrow).

- This option will export all dimensions from the part into the design table.

- Each dimension will be placed in its own column, in the order they were created.

4. Changing the Configuration names:

- For clarity, change the name Default to **Size 1**.

- Create the next 2 configurations by adding the names **Size 2** and **Size 3**, on cell A4 and A5.

- Enter the **new dimensions** for the next 2 sizes.

5. Viewing the new configurations:

- Click in the background anywhere. SolidWorks report dialog appears showing 3 new configurations have been generated by the design table.

- Double click on the names of the configurations to see the changes for each size.

6. Customizing the table:

- Expand the **Tables** folder, right click on Design Tables and select **Edit Table**.

- Click OK to close the Rows and Columns dialog.

- Highlight the entire Row1 header, right click in the highlighted area and select: **Format Cell**.

- Click the **Fill** tab and select a color for the Row1.

- Change to the **Alignment** tab and enable the **Wrap Text** and **Merge Cells** check-boxes.

- In the **Border** tab, select the **Outline** button.

- Click OK.

- Repeat step 6 for other rows.

7. Saving your work:

- Click File / Save As.

- For file name, enter: **Part Design Table_Exe**.

- Click Save.

- Overwrite the file if prompted.

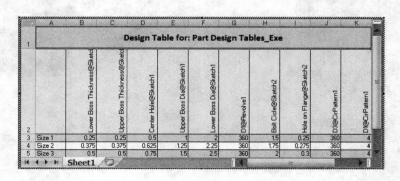

	A	B	C	D	E	F	G	H	I	J	K
1				Design Table for: Part Design Tables_Exe							
2		Lower Boss Thickness@Sketch	Upper Boss Thickness@Sketch	Center Hole@Sketch1	Upper Boss Dia@Sketch1	Lower Boss Dia@Sketch1	D1@Revolve1	Bolt Circle@Sketch2	Hole on Flange@Sketch2	D3@CirPattern1	D1@CirPattern1
3	Size 1	0.25	0.25	0.5	1	2	360	1.5	0.25	360	4
4	Size 2	0.375	0.375	0.625	1.25	2.25	360	1.75	0.275	360	4
5	Size 3	0.5	0.5	0.75	1.5	2.5	360	2	0.3	360	4

Sheet1

Level 2 Final Exam (1of2)

1. Open the existing assembly document named:
   Bottom Up Assembly EXE from the
   Bottom Up Assembly folder.

2. Create an Assembly drawing as shown.
3. Modify the Bill of Materials to match the
   information provided in the BOM.
4. Modify the Balloons to include the Quantity.
5. Save your drawing as:
   L2 Final Assembly Drawing.

ITEM NO.	PART NUMBER	DESCRIPTION	QTY.
1	010-123	Housing	1
2	020-123	Label	2
6	060-123	Cover Plate	4
7	070-123	Nose	1
8	080-123	Spring	1
9	090-123	End Cap	1
11	011-123	Support Arm	2

Level 2 Final Exam (2of2)

1. Open the existing Part document named:
   Nose.sldprt from the previous folder.
2. Create a detailed drawing as shown.
3. Add Dimensions and Geometric Tolerances
   as indicated in each view.

SECTION A-A

4. Add Datums and Annotations as specified.
5. Correct the Model's dimensions to match the drawing.
6. Save your drawing as: **L2 Final Drawing**.

TABLE OF U.S. MEASURES

LENGTH

12 inches	=	1 foot
36 inches	=	1 yard (or 3 feet)
5280 feet	=	1 mile (or 1760 yards)

AREA

144 square inches (in)	=	1 square foot (ft)
9 ft	=	1 square yard (yd)
43,560 ft	=	1 acre (A)
640 A	=	1 square mile (mi)

VOLUME

1728 cubic inches (in³)	=	1 cubic foot (ft)
27 ft	=	1 cubic yard (yd)

LIQUID CAPACITY

8 fluid ounces (fl oz)	=	1 cup (c)
2 c	=	1 pint (pt)
2 pt	=	1 quart (qt)
4 pt	=	1 gallon (gal)

WEIGHT

16 ounces (oz)	=	1 pound (lb)
2000 lb	=	1 ton (t)

TEMPERATURE Degrees Fahrenheit (ºF)

32° F	=	freezing point of water
98.6° F	=	normal body temperature
212° F	=	boiling point of water

TABLE OF METRIC MEASURES

LENGTH

10 millimeters (mm)	=	1 centimeter (cm)
10 cm	=	1 decimeter (dm)
100 cm	=	1 meter (m)
1000 m	=	1 kilometer (km)

AREA

100 square millimeters (mm)	=	1 square centimeter (cm)
10,000 cm	=	1 square meter (m)
10,000 m	=	1 hectare (ha)
1,000,000 m	=	1 square kilometer (km)

VOLUME

1000 cubic millimeters (ml)	=	1 cubic centimeter (cm)
1 cm	=	1 milliliter (mL)
1,000 m	=	1 Liter (L)
1,000,000 cm	=	1 cubic meter (m)

LIQUID CAPACITY

10 deciliters (dL)	=	1 liter (L) - or 1000 mL
1000 L	=	1 kiloliter (kL)

MASS

1000 milligrams (mg)	=	1 gram (g)
1000 g	=	1 kilogram (kg)
1000 kg	=	1 metric ton (t)

TEMPERATURE Degrees Celsius (°C)

0° C	=	freezing point of water
37°C	=	normal body temperature
100° C	=	boiling point of water

SolidWorks 2014

Certified SolidWorks Professional (CSWP)

Certification Practice for the Core Examination

SolidWorks

CERTIFIED
PROFESSIONAL

Courtesy of Paul Tran, Sr. Certified SolidWorks Instructor

Certified-SolidWorks-Professional program (CSWP)
Certification Practice for the Core-Exam

Challenge I: Part Modeling & Modifications

Complete this challenge within 90 minutes

(The following examples are intended to assist you in familiarizing yourself with the structures of the exams and the method in which the questions are asked).

- Create this part in SolidWorks
- Drafting Standards: **ANSI**
- Unit: **Inches, 3 decimals**
- Material: **Cast Alloy Steel**
- Origin: **Arbitrary**
- Density: **0.264 lb/in^3**

1. Creating the 1ˢᵗ revolve body:

- Using the <u>Front</u> plane, sketch the profile shown below.

- Revolve the sketch 1 complete revolution.

- Click **OK** .

2. Creating the 2nd revolve body:

- Open a new sketch on the <u>Front</u> plane.

- Sketch a **rectangle** on the left side of the vertical centerline.

- Add the dimensions shown.

8.000

5.000

Horizontal

1.250

3.000

- Add a horizontal relation to fully define the sketch.

- Revolve the sketch **360 degrees**.

- Click **OK** ✓.

8.000

5.000

1.250

3.000

3. Linking the dimension values:

- To save time on editing features later on, we will link some of the dimensions together.

- From the FeatureManager tree, right click on Annotations and enable both options:

   * **Display Annotations**

   * **Show Feature Dimensions**

- At this point, we will link the two ID dimensions (Ø1.250), by giving them the exact same name.

- Hold the **Control** key and select both **ID** dimensions (circled), then right click on one of them and select: **Link Values** (arrow).

- Enter **ID Holes** for Name and click OK.

- The linked dimensions now have a red link symbol next to their values.

4. Creating the transition wall:

- Select the <u>Front</u> plane and open a new sketch.

- Sketch the profile as shown.

- Add the dimensions and the relations as indicated.

Temporary Axis

Enable the Temporary Axis from the View pull down menu.

R8.750

2.500

Temporary Axis

Collinear with edge of ID

1.061

Front Plane

Collinear with edge of ID

- Extrude the sketch profile using the following parameters:

* **Mid Plane**

* **.750 in**.

* **Merge Result**

- Click **OK** .

5. Creating a recess feature:

- Select the <u>face</u> as indicated and open a new sketch.

Offset 3 entities

Sketch face

.375

.375

- Select the **arc**, the **2 lines**, and click **Offset Entities**.

- Enter **.375"** for offset distance and click OK.

.375

Add 2 lines and trim

- Add 2 more lines as shown and trim them to their nearest intersections.

.375

- Add a sketch fillet of **R.125** to 5 places.

.375

5X R.125

- Enable the Temporary Axis and add the dimensions as shown to fully define this sketch.

1.500   .375   1.875

- Click **Extruded Cut** and use the following parameters:

    * **Blind**

    * **.215 in**.

- Click **OK** .

6. Mirroring the recess feature:

- Select the <u>Front</u> plane for use as the Mirror plane and click the **Mirror** Command from the Features toolbar.

- Select the recess feature either from the graphics area or from the FeatureManager tree.

Select Feature to Mirror

- Click **OK** .

- Turn off the temporary axis.

(Section View)

7. Adding Fillets:

- Click the **Fillet** command and enter **.062"** for radius value.

- Select the **6 edges** as shown.

- Click **OK**.

Select 6 edges

8. Changing dimension values:

- The grading scores are based on the mass of the part after certain changes. At this point, we will change several dimensions and see what the final mass may be.

- Double click on the Transition-Wall to see its dimensions.

- Locate the **2.500"** dimension and change it to **3.250"**.

- Change the dimension
  8.000" to **8.750"**

- Click Rebuild
  or **Control + Q**.

9. Measuring the mass of the part:

- Select **Tools / Mass Properties**.

- Enter the Mass here: _____ pounds.

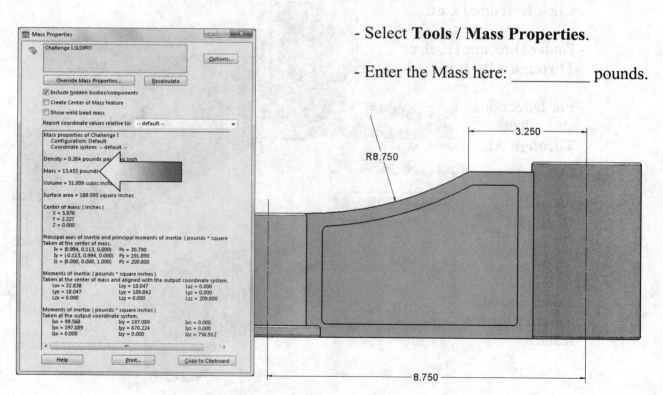

10. Adding the cut features:

- Select the <u>Front</u> plane and open a new sketch.

Collinear
(both sides)

Front Plane

2.186

3.000

1.250

1.250

2.000

1.500

Not Collinear
with edge

- Sketch the 2 rectangles as shown, and add dimensions/relations to fully define the sketch.

- Click **Extruded Cut**.

- Under Direction1, select:
Through All - Both.

- For Direction2 also select:
Through All.

- Click **OK** .

- Rotate the part to verify the cut feature.

11. Adding fillets and chamfers:

- Click the **Fillet** command.

- Enter **.093"** for radius value.

- Select the **4 Edges** as noted.

- Click **OK** .

Select 4 edges

- Click the **Chamfer** command.

- Enter **.080"** for chamfer depth.

- Use the default **45°** angle.

- Select the **8 Edges** as noted.

- Click **OK** .

(By selecting the circular faces of the ID holes, we can reduce the selections to 4 faces, instead of 8 edges)

Select 8 ID edges

12. Adding a recess feature:

- Select the <u>face</u> as indicated and open a new sketch.

- Create an Offset of **.250"** from the **2 edges** as noted.

Offset Entities

Offset Entities

Select Sketch Face

.250

- Add **3 lines** approximately as shown.

- Add the dimensions as indicated in the image below.

- Trim the lines to their closest intersections.

.250

- Add the **sketch fillets** of **R.093"** to **5 places**.

- Make sure the sketch is fully defined.

5X R.093

.250

.300

.400

1.375

- Click **Extruded Cut**.

- Under Direction1, select: **Through All - Both**.

- For Direction2 also select: **Through All**.

- Click **OK** .

- Rotate the part to verify the cut feature.

13. Adding 2 circular bosses:

- Select the <u>Front</u> plane from the FeatureManager tree and open a new sketch.

- Sketch 2 circles and add the dimensions as shown to fully define them.

- Link the diameter dimensions using the Link Values option. Rename them to: **Cir_Bosses**.

- Click **Extruded Boss/Base**.

- Under Direction1, select: **Mid Plane**.

- For extrude depth enter: **2.000in**.

- Click **OK** ✓.

- Change to the Top view (Control + 5) to verify the boss feature.

14. Measuring the mass of the part*:

- Click **Tools / Mass Properties**.

- Locate the mass* (arrow) and enter

  it here _____ lbs.

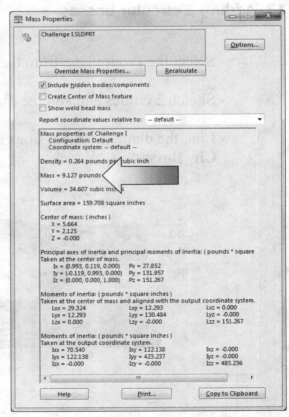

*The mass of an object is the amount of material it contains.
A body with greater mass has more inertia; it needs a greater force to accelerate.
Weight depends on the force of gravity, but mass does not.*

15. Modifying the feature dimensions:

- Locate the diameter dimensions for the 2 ID holes (circled) and change them from: Ø1.250 to Ø **1.500"**.

- Click **Rebuild** or press **Control + Q.**

- Locate the OD dimension (Ø3.000) for the Circular boss on the right side (circled) and change it from Ø3.000" to Ø**2.750"**.

- Click **Rebuild** or press **Control + Q.**

- Did the changes caused any rebuild errors? If so, stop and repair them before to moving forward to the next step.

- Locate the OD dimension
for the circular boss
on the left (circled)
and change it from
Ø2.250 to **2.500"**.

- Click **Rebuild**
or press **Control + Q**.

16. Measuring the mass of the part:

- Click **Tools / Mass Properties**.

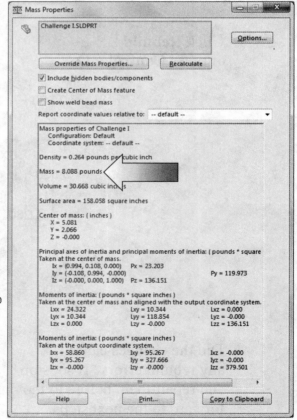

- Locate the mass (arrow) and enter it

here: _____ lbs.

17. Creating the Counter-Bores:

- Click the **Hole-Wizard** command from the Features toolbar.

- Select the following:

* Hole Type: **Counterbore**

* Standard: **Ansi Inch**

* Type: **Binding Head Screw**

* Size: **1/4**

* Fit: **Normal**

* End Condition: **Through All**

Both C'bores are centered on the cir_bosses

* Clear the Near-Side-Countersink box

- Change to the **Positions** tab (circled) and place 2 Counter-bores on the same centers as the circular boss features, click **OK** when finished.

- Create a **Section View** similar to the one shown below to verify the 2 counter bores.

18. Adding a side tab:

- Open a new sketch on the <u>Front</u> plane.

Collinear with edge of ID

⌀.250

1.625

Front Plane

R.325

3.000

- Sketch the profile of the tab as show.

- Add the dimensions and relations needed to fully define the sketch.

- Click **Extruded Boss/Base**.

- Under Direction1, select: **Mid Plane**.

- For extrude depth enter: **.425 in**.

- Click **OK**.

- Rotate the part and Verify that the tab is centered on the Front plane.

Rotated 180°

19. Modifying the recess feature:

- Locate the spacing dimension of the recess (1.375") and change to **.875"**.

- Click **Rebuild** .

- Find the final mass of the part and enter it here: _____ lbs.

20. Modifying the Revolved feature:

- <u>Edit the sketch</u> of the **Revolved2** feature.

- Add 3 new lines as indicated.

Add 3 lines

- Add the 3 dimensions (circled) to fully define this sketch.

- <u>Exit</u> the sketch or click Rebuild.

The change causes some errors in a couple of features.

- <u>Edit</u> the **Fillet1** feature and select the missing edge as noted.

Replace the Coincident with a Collinear relation

- Edit the Sketch5 under the Cut-Extrude2. Replace the relation as noted. Click Rebuild.

- Measure the final mass of the part and enter it here: _____ lbs.

21. Saving your work:

- Save your work as **Challenge1** and close the document when done.

- Use the example file from the Training Files to review the construction of the part, if needed.

Certified-SolidWorks-Professional program (CSWP)
Certification Practice for the Core-Exam

Challenge II-A: Part Configurations & Design Tables

Complete both challenges A&B within 40 minutes

(The following examples are intended to assist you in familiarizing yourself with the structures of the exams and the method in which the questions are asked).

- Modify this part in SolidWorks   - Unit: **Millimeter, 2 decimals**   - Origin: **Arbitrary**

- Drafting Standards: **ANSI**   - Material: **Alloy Steel**   - Density: **0.008 /mm^3**

1. Opening a part document:

- Browse to the Training Files, open the part document: **Challenge II-A**.

2. Setting the options:

- Change the material to **Alloy Steel**.

- Change the system options to match the settings above.

3. Switching Configuration:

- Switch to the ConfigurationManager tree, double click to activate **Configuration A**.

4. Measuring the Mass:

- Select **Tools/ Mass Properties**.

- Enter the mass in grams:

_____ grams.

<u>NOTE:</u> *Material must be selected before calculating the mass of the part.*

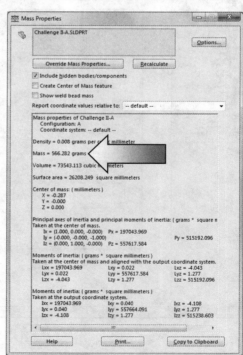

5. Adding a New Configuration:

- Create a <u>new configuration</u> named **D**, and enter the comment: **Added a 10mm hole**.

- Select the face shown below and open a new sketch.

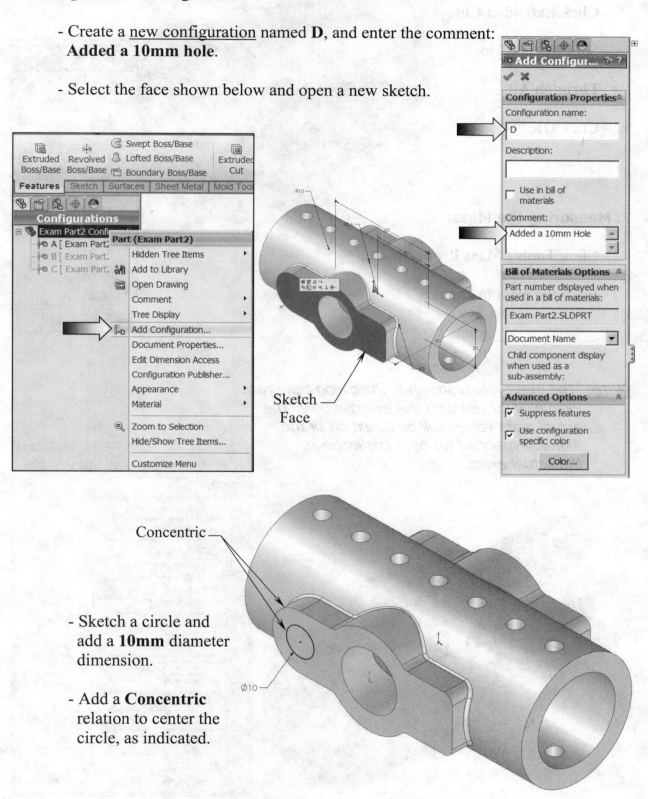

Sketch Face

Concentric

- Sketch a circle and add a **10mm** diameter dimension.

- Add a **Concentric** relation to center the circle, as indicated.

6. Extruding a cut:

- Click **Extruded Cut**.

- Set Direction1 to:

 Through All.

- Click **OK** .

Ø10

7. Measuring the Mass:

- Click **Tools / Mass Properties**.

- Enter the mass in grams:

 _____ grams.

**Note:** *The mass values shown in the dialog boxes are examples for use with this exercise only. The actual mass values will be based off of the material specified for each challenge in the actual exam.*

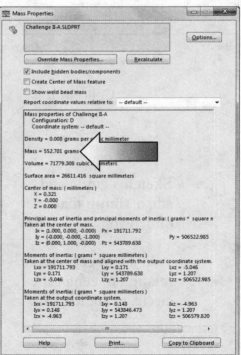

8. Switching configuration:

- Double click on **Configuration B** to make it active.

9. Measuring the Mass:

- Select **Tools/ Mass Properties**.

- Enter the new mass:

_____ grams.

Note: *Before calculating the mass, double check the material every time a configuration is changed.*

10. Creating a Design Table:

- Double click the
  configuration **B**
  to activate it.

- Go to: **Insert /
  Tables / Design Tables**.

- Select the **Auto Create** option and leave
  all other options at their default settings.

11. Adding new Configurations:

- Right click on **Row4** and select **Copy**.

- Right click on **Row7** and select **Paste**.

The Default Design Table

Copy Row No. 4

Paste to Row No. 7

Note: Instead of Copy/Paste, the parameters in
Row7 can also be entered manually, if needed.

12. Modifying the new configurations:

- Change the names of the configuration and description to **E**.

- Change the ID dimension on the body to **24**.

- Change the hole Diameter to **16**.

- Leave the Suppression States at Suppressed (S).

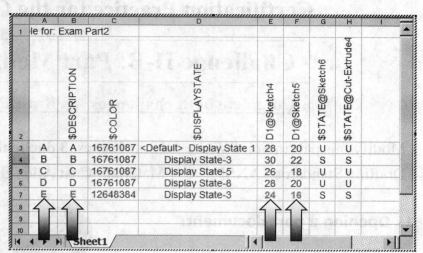

	$DESCRIPTION	$COLOR	$DISPLAYSTATE	D1@Sketch4	D1@Sketch5	$STATE@Sketch6	$STATE@Cut-Extrude4
A	A	16761087	<Default> Display State 1	28	20	U	U
B	B	16761087	Display State-3	30	22	S	S
C	C	16761087	Display State-5	26	18	U	U
D	D	16761087	Display State-8	28	20	U	U
E	E	12648384	Display State-3	24	16	S	S

- Click anywhere in the background to return to SolidWorks.

- Double click on **Configuration E** to activate. _Uncheck the Link to Display State option and click Rebuild to update the color)._

13. Measuring the final Mass:

- Select **Tools/ Mass Properties**.

- Enter the final mass: _____ grams

14. Save your work as Challenge 2-A.

Certified-SolidWorks-Professional program (CSWP)
Certification Practice for the Core-Exam

Challenge II-B: Part Modifications

Complete both challenges A&B within 40 minutes

- Modify this part in SolidWorks   - Unit: **Inches**, **3 decimals**   - Origin: **Arbitrary**

- Drafting Standards: **ANSI**   - Material: **Cast Alloy Steel**   - Density: **0.264 / in^3**

1. Opening a part document:

- Browse to the Training Files folder and open the part named **Challenge II-B**.

2. Setting the options:

- Change the material to **Cast Alloy Steel**.

- Change the system options to match the settings above.

3. Adding the 1st cut:

- Select the <u>Top</u> plane and open a new sketch.

- Sketch the profile shown below, it will be used to trim off the material on the top.

- Add the dimensions and relations needed to fully define the sketch.

- Click **Extruded Cut**.

- Set Direction 1 to: **Through All - Both**.

- Set Direction 2 also to: **Through All**.

- Enable the **Flip Side to Cut** checkbox if needed.

- Click **OK**.

4. Measuring the Mass:

- Select **Tools/ Mass Properties**.

- Enter the mass here: _____ pounds.

5. Adding the 2nd cut:

- Select the <u>Face</u> as indicated and open a new sketch.

Convert Entity

Sketch face

- Create the circle by using the
Convert Entities option.

- Extrude a cut using the
2 Directions as shown.

- Click **OK**.

6. Reversing the extruded cut:

- <u>Edit</u> the Sketch2 (under the Cut-Extude1 feature).

- Delete the coincident relation and the two dimensions as indicated.

Select the endpoint then delete the coincident symbol

Delete

- Drag the horizontal line downward, recreate the coincident relation and the two deleted dimensions.

Coincident

- The change causes some errors in the model. Click **Continue** to close the error dialog box (arrow).

7. Editing the Shell feature:

- One of the faces in the shell feature is missing due to the last change. There should be a total of <u>three faces</u> in the Faces-To-Remove selection box.

- Click inside the **Faces-to-Remove** selection box to active this option, then <u>select the planar face</u> on the right as noted.

- Click **OK** .

Remove
3 faces

Select face
to remove

8. Editing the parent sketch:

- <u>Edit</u> the Sketch1 below the Boss-Extrude1 feature.

- This is the parent sketch, changing its geometry will cause errors in some of the children features.

- Select the 3 entities noted and click the checkbox **For Construction** to convert them to centerlines.

Change these 3 entities to Construction...

Add lines

Add Relations
— Horizontal
| Vertical
Fix
Merge

The endpoint is vertical w/origin

- Add the additional <u>lines</u> and a <u>tangent arc</u>. Merge the centers of the two arc on the right

- Hold the <u>Shift</u> key and add the **5.00"** dimension that measures from the endpoint of the line to the right-quadrant of the arc. This sketch becomes fully defined.

- <u>Exit</u> the sketch.

- The change causes some errors in the model once again. Select the option: **Exit the Sketch and Rebuild anyway**.

- The right end of the model disappeared. To correct this, we need to re-select the contour of the extruded feature.

9. Editing the parent feature:

- Click the Boss-Extrude1 feature and **Edit Feature** (arrow).

- Expand the <u>Selected Contour</u> section, click inside the area as noted and click **OK**.

- The highlighted area is used as the contour for the handle body.

Click in this area

10. Correcting the dangling relations:

- The new contour causes the dependent sketch to become dangling.

- Edit the Sketch2 below the Cut-Extrude1 feature to fix this error.

Click this line

Click this point

- Click the endpoint of the line to see the dangling relation, displayed in <u>Olive-Green</u> color, under the Existing relations box.
Right click the Coincident8 and select **Delete**.

- Repeat the last step and delete the collinear relation and also the dimension **.125**, they both have the dangling color.

Replace

Coincident

Coincident

Missing face

- Re-create the Coincident relations and the dimension .125" as indicated above.

- The status of the sketch should change to Fully Defined at this point.

- **Exit** the sketch and click **continue** to close the errors dialog.

- **Edit** the **Shell** feature and re-select the Missing Face. Click **OK** to close.

11. Repairing the other errors:

- Click the **Fillet1** on the feature tree and select **Edit Feature** (arrow).

- Delete the 2 missing edges from the Edges to Fillet selection box.

- Select the 2 inner edges, behind the circular boss to replace with the missing ones.

- Click **OK** ✓.

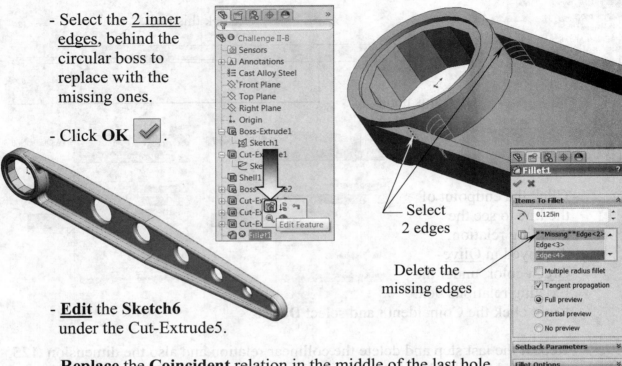

Select 2 edges

Delete the missing edges

- **Edit** the **Sketch6** under the Cut-Extrude5.

- **Replace** the **Coincident** relation in the middle of the last hole with a **Concentric** relation.

Concentric

- **Edit** the **Fillet2** and re-select all edges on the handle body.

- **Edit** the **Fillet3** and re-select any missing edges on the left end.

- There should be a total of 4 edges in this fillet.

- **Edit** the **Sketch8** under the **Cut-Extrude7** and repair the Coincident relation as noted.

12. Correcting the wall thickness:

- Select the <u>Top</u> plane and open a new sketch. (The section view is created for clarity only, use the Wireframe display mode for this sketch).

- The wall thickness needs to be corrected. Reordering the Shell feature would cause a lot of errors which will take extra time to repair. We are going to create a boss to correct this error instead.

<u>Section View</u>

- Create a sketch below and add the dimensions / relations needed to fully define it.

- Click **Extruded Boss/Base**.

- Set **Direction 1** to: **Up To Surface** and select the <u>inside face on the right</u> of the wall.

- Set **Direction 2** to: **Up To Surface** and select the <u>inside face on the left</u> of the wall.

- Click **OK**.

13. Measuring the Mass:

- Select **Tools/ Mass Properties**.

- Enter the final mass: _____ pounds.

14. Correcting the fillets:

- Some of the fillets got disconnected due to newly added features in the last few steps. One quick way to correct this is to add some new fillets to the missing edges.

- Click the **Fillet** command from the Features toolbar.

- Add the 2 fillets, **R.040** and **R.010**, as indicated in the images below.

Disconnected Fillets

Disconnected Fillets

R.010

R.040

15. Measuring the Mass:

- Select **Tools/ Mass Properties**.

- Enter the final mass: _____ pounds.

16. Saving your work:

- Click **File / Save As**.

- Enter **Challenge 2-B** for the name of the file.

- Click **Save**.

Certified SolidWorks Professional program (CSWP) Certification Practice for the Core-Exam

Challenge III: Bottom up Assembly

Complete this challenge within 90 minutes

(The following examples are intended to assist you in familiarizing yourself with the structures of the exams and the method in which the questions are asked).

1. Assemble the components using mates.
2. Create a new coordinate system in the Assem.
3. Units: IPS (Inch/Pound/Second).

4. Detect and repair all interferences.
5. Mate modifications.
6. Decimal: 3 places.

1. Opening the 1st part document:

- Open the document named: **Base** from the Challenge 3 folder.

- This part will be used as the Parent component in the main assembly.

2. Transferring the part to Assembly:

- Select **Make Assembly From Part** from the **File** pull down menu (arrow).

- Select the default **Assembly Template** and click **OK** [OK] .

- Place the component on the assembly's origin as indicated.

- The 1st component should be fixed before other components can be mated.

Place the 1st part on the origin.

3. Creating a Coordinate System:

- From the Assembly toolbar, click the Reference Geometry button and select the **Coordinate System** command – OR –

- From the pull down menu select:
**Insert / Reference Geometry /
Coordinate System**.

- Select the Corner-Vertex for **Origin** as noted.

- Select the **X** and **Y** axis as indicated. Click Reverse Direction if needed.

- Leave the Z direction blank.

- Click **OK** .

- This Coordinate System will be used to calculate the Center of Mass for all questions from here on.

Leave Z axis blank

X Axis

Origin

Y Axis

4. Inserting the 2nd component:

- From the Assembly toolbar, click the **Insert Component** command.

- Click **Browse** | Browse... | and open the component named: **Pivot**.

- Place the component approx. as shown below.

5. Adding the 1st mate:

- From the Assembly toolbar, click **Mate**.

- Select the Circular Boss and the Hole as indicated.

- The **Concentric** mate is automatically created by default.

- Click **OK** .

Select 2 faces

NOTE:

Most components will receive only 2 mates, since they were designed to move and rotate after everything is assembled.

Sometimes you may need to create the 3rd mate just to align the components. These mates should be suppressed prior to mating other components.

6. Adding the 2nd mate:

- Click **Mate** again if you are not already there.

- Select the <u>bottom face</u> of the Circular Boss and the <u>upper face</u> of the Base.

- The **Coincident** mate is added automatically.

- Click **OK** .

Coincident

7. Adding the 3rd mate:

- Click **Mate** again.

- Select the FRONT of the Base and the FRONT plane of the Pivot.

- Click the **Parallel** mate option.

- Click **OK** .

<u>NOTE:</u>
This parallel mate will align the 2 components for the time being, it will get changed to an Angle mate later on.

Parallel

8. Measuring the Center Of Mass:

- Select **Tools / Mass Properties**.

- Change the default output coordinate to:
  Coordinate System1.

- Enter the Center Of Mass (in Inches).

X = _____

Y = _____

Z = _____

NOTE:
*The center of mass shown in the dialog boxes
are examples for use with this exercise only.*

*The actual mass properties of the components
and the center of mass of the assembly depend
upon the materials and the locations specified for each component in the assembly.*

9. Creating an Angle mate:

- Expand the **Mate Group** from the bottom of the FeatureManager tree.

- Edit the **Parallel** mate, change it to **Angle** mate and enter **30.00deg**. Click **OK**.

30.00 deg.
Angle mate

10. Measuring the new Center Of Mass:

- Select **Tools / Mass Properties**.

- Use the same output **Coordinate System1**.

- Enter the Center Of Mass (in Inches).

$$X = \underline{\hspace{8cm}}$$

$$Y = \underline{\hspace{8cm}}$$

$$Z = \underline{\hspace{8cm}}$$

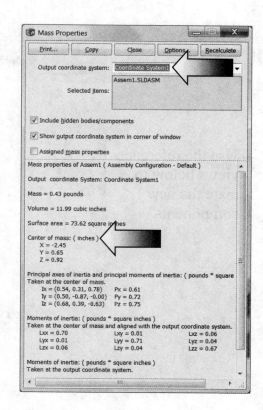

11. Inserting and mating other components:

- Click the **Insert Component** command from the Assembly toolbar.

- **Insert** and **Mate** the following components:

     * Arm   *** Probe**   *** Piston**   *** Piston Housing**

- Use the reference views below to mate the new components.

FRONT VIEW

- Use either of the Front planes on each component to center the components with Coincident mates

– OR –

use the **Width mate** option to achieve the same results.

TOP VIEW

NOTE:
If a sub-assembly is inserted into the top-level assembly it will become "Rigid", none of its components can be moved or rotated. To overcome this, right click the name of the sub-assembly and select "Flexible" at the lower right corner of the dialog box.

- Most component should have at least 1 degree of freedom left.

- You should be able to rotate the assembly back and forth, or up and down at this point.

RIGHT VIEW

12. Measuring the new Center Of Mass:

- Select **Tools / Mass Properties**.

- Use the same output **Coordinate System1**.

- Enter the Center Of Mass (in Inches).

X = _____

Y = _____

Z = _____

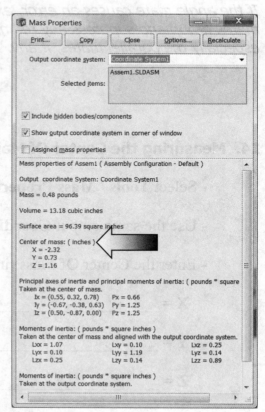

NOTE:
The current angle between the Base and the Pivot is still set at 30 degrees.

13. Changing the mate angle:

- Edit the **30deg** mate and change it to **180deg**.

- Click **Flip-Dimension** if needed.

- Click **OK** [✓].

Change the mate angle from 30 deg. to 180deg.

NOTE:
If the angle mate causes an error, expand the mates group and suppress any red mates, especially the parallel mates, if any.

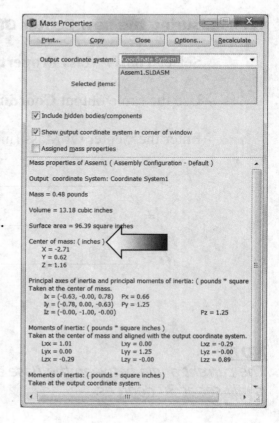

14. Measuring the Center Of Mass:

- Select **Tools / Mass Properties**.

- Use the same output **Coordinate System1**.

- Enter the Center Of Mass (in Inches).

X = _____

Y = _____

Z = _____

15. Replacing the Base:

- From the FeatureManager tree, right click the component **Base** and select: **Replace Component** (Arrow).

- Browse to the Training Files locate and open the part named: **Base B**.

- Under the Options dialog box, leave all default options as they were.

- Click **OK**.

- The Base B does not have the features needed to re-attach the existing mates. The Mated-Entities dialog appears, asking for the new entities to replace with the old ones.

16. Replacing mate entities:

- The first error shows <u>the hole</u> that was used to create the <u>concentric</u> mate is being missing.

Select a new entity
to replace this hole

- Rotate the assembly and <u>select the main hole</u> in the center of the Base B as noted.

- All components (except the Base B) got flipped 180 degrees, click the **Flip-Mate-Alignment** button (arrow) to re-align the components.

Select this hole

- The first mate error is fixed.
  A green check mark appears
  under the Mated Entities section
  indicating the condition has been satisfied.

- <u>Do not</u> click OK just yet.

- Click the second error (the red question mark) in the Mated Entities dialog box.

- The second error shows the upper face the base is missing.

Missing face

- Switch back to the Isometric view (Control + 7) and <u>select the planar face</u> as indicated to replace with the missing one.

Select this face

- The second error is corrected.

- A green check mark appears again indicating the last condition has been satisfied.

- Click **OK** .

17. Measuring the final Center Of Mass:

- Select **Tools / Mass Properties**.

- Use the same output **Coordinate System1**.

- Enter the Center Of Mass (in Inches).

X = _____

Y = _____

Z = _____

18. Saving your work:

- Click **File / Save As**.

- Enter **Challenge 3** for the name of the assembly.

- Click **Save**.

<u>NOTE:</u> When you're ready to take the actual examination, log on to:

www.solidworks.com/sw/mcad-certification-programs.htm, click on the CSWP option and select **purchase exam**. After the registration is completed, you will receive 2 emails from SolidWorks; one of them is the receipt for the purchase of the exam and the other have the instruction on how to download and take the online exam.

If you passed all 3 parts, an email will be sent to you from the Grading server notifying you of the results and instructing you on how to print out your certificate.

But if you failed, there is a 14-day waiting period, you will need to register and pay for the segment that you did not pass, and start the process over again.

Glossary

Alloys:

An Alloy is a mixture of two or more metals (and sometimes a non-metal). The mixture is made by heating and melting the substances together.
Example of alloys are Bronze (Copper and Tin), Brass (Copper and Zinc), and Steel (Iron and Carbon).

Gravity and Mass:

Gravity is the force that pulls everything on earth toward the ground and makes things feel heavy. Gravity makes all falling bodies accelerates at a constant 32ft. per second (9.8 m/s). In the earth's atmosphere, air resistance slow acceleration. Only on airless Moon would a feather and a metal block fall to the ground together.
The mass of an object is the amount of material it contains.
A body with greater mass has more inertia; it needs a greater force to accelerate.
Weight depends on the force of gravity, but mass does not.

When an object spins around another (for example: a satellite orbiting the earth) it is pushed outward. Two forces are at work here: Centrifugal (pushing outward) and Centripetal (pulling inward). If you whirl a ball around you on a string, you pull it inward (Centripetal force). The ball seems to pull outward (Centrifugal force) and if released will fly off in a straight line.

Heat:

Heat is a form of energy and can move from one substance to another in one of three ways: by Convection, by Radiation, and by Conduction.

- Convection takes place only in liquids like water (for example: water in a kettle) and gases (for example: air warmed by a heat source such as a fire or radiator). When liquid or gas is heated, it expands and become less dense. Warm air above the radiator rises and cool air moves in to take its place, creating a convection current.
- Radiation is movement of heat through the air. Heat forms a match sets molecules of air moving and rays of heat spread out around the heat source.

- Conduction occurs in solids such as metals. The handle of a metal spoon left in boiling liquid warms up as molecules at the heated end moves faster and collide with their neighbors, setting them moving. The heat travels through the metal, which is a good conductor of heat.

Inertia:

A body with a large mass is harder to start and also to stop. A heavy truck traveling at 50mph needs more power breaks to stop its motion than a smaller car traveling at the same speed.
Inertia is the tendency of an object either to stay still or to move steadily in a straight line, unless another force (such as a brick wall stopping the vehicle) makes it behave differently.

Joules:

The Joules is the SI unit of work or energy.
One Joule of work is done when a force of one Newton moves through a distance of one meter. The Joule is named after the English scientist James Joule (1818-1889).

Materials:

- Stainless steel is an alloy of steel with chromium or nickel.

- Steel is made by the basic oxygen process. The raw material is about three parts melted iron and one part scrap steel. Blowing oxygen into the melted iron raises the temperature and gets rid of impurities.

- All plastic are chemical compounds called polymers.

- Glass is made by mixing and heating sand, limestone, and soda ash. When these ingredients melt they turn into glass, which is hardened when it cools. Glass is in fact not a solid but a "supercooled" liquid, it can be shaped by blowing, pressing, drawing, casting into molds, rolling, and floating across molten tin, to make large sheets.

- Ceramic objects, such as pottery and porcelain, electrical insulators, bricks, and roof tiles are all made from clay. The clay is shaped or molded when wet and soft, and heated in a kiln until it hardens.

Machine Tools:

Are powered tools used for shaping metal or other materials, by drilling holes, chiseling, grinding, pressing or cutting. Often the material (the workpiece) is moved while the tool stays still (lathe), or vice versa, the workpiece stayed while the tool moves (mill).

Most common machine tools are: Mill, Lathe, Saw, Broach, Punch press, Grind, Bore and Stamp break.

Newton's Law:

1. Every object remains stopped or goes on moving at a steady rate in a straight line unless acted upon by another force. This is the inertia principle.
2. The amount of force needed to make an object change its speed depends on the mass of the object and the amount of the acceleration or deceleration required.
3. To every action there is an equal and opposite reaction. When a body is pushed on way by a force, another force pushes back with equal strength.

Polymers:

A polymer is made of one or more large molecules formed from thousands of smaller molecules. Rubber and Wood are natural polymers. Plastics are synthetic (artificially made) polymers.

Speed and Velocity:

- Speed is the rate at which a moving object changes position (how far it moves in a fixed time).
- Velocity is speed in a particular direction.
- If either speed or direction is changed, velocity also changed.

────────────────────── ──────────────────────

Absorbed

A feature, sketch, or annotation that is contained in another item (usually a feature) in the FeatureManager design tree. Examples are the profile sketch and profile path in a base-sweep, or a cosmetic thread annotation in a hole.

Align

Tools that assist in lining up annotations and dimensions (left, right, top, bottom, and so on). For aligning parts in an assembly.

Alternate position view

A drawing view in which one or more views are superimposed in phantom lines on the original view. Alternate position views are often used to show range of motion of an assembly.

Anchor point

The end of a leader that attaches to the note, block, or other annotation. Sheet formats contain anchor points for a bill of materials, a hole table, a revision table, and a weldment cut list.

Annotation

A text note or a symbol that adds specific design intent to a part, assembly, or drawing. Specific types of annotations include note, hole callout, surface finish symbol, datum feature symbol, datum target, geometric tolerance symbol, weld symbol, balloon, and stacked balloon. Annotations that apply only to drawings include center mark, annotation centerline, area hatch, and block.

Appearance callouts

Callouts that display the colors and textures of the face, feature, body, and part under the entity selected and are a shortcut to editing colors and textures.

Area hatch

A crosshatch pattern or fill applied to a selected face or to a closed sketch in a drawing.

Assembly

A document in which parts, features, and other assemblies (sub-assemblies) are mated together. The parts and sub-assemblies exist in documents separate from the assembly. For example, in an assembly, a piston can be mated to other parts, such as a connecting rod or cylinder. This new assembly can then be used as a sub-assembly in an assembly of an engine. The extension for a SolidWorks assembly file name is .SLDASM.

Attachment point

The end of a leader that attaches to the model (to an edge, vertex, or face, for example) or to a drawing sheet.

Axis

A straight line that can be used to create model geometry, features, or patterns. An axis can be made in a number of different ways, including using the intersection of two planes.

Balloon

Labels parts in an assembly, typically including item numbers and quantity. In drawings, the item numbers are related to rows in a bill of materials.

Base

The first solid feature of a part.

Baseline dimensions

Sets of dimensions measured from the same edge or vertex in a drawing.

Bend

A feature in a sheet metal part. A bend generated from a filleted corner, cylindrical face, or conical face is a round bend; a bend generated from sketched straight lines is a sharp bends.

Bill of materials

A table inserted into a drawing to keep a record of the parts used in an assembly.

Block

A user-defined annotation that you can use in parts, assemblies, and drawings. A block can contain text, sketch entities (except points), and area hatch, and it can be saved in a file for later use as, for example, a custom callout or a company logo.

Bottom-up assembly

An assembly modeling technique where you create parts and then insert them into an assembly.

Broken-out section

A drawing view that exposes inner details of a drawing view by removing material from a closed profile, usually a spline.

Cavity

The mold half that holds the cavity feature of the design part.

Center mark

A cross that marks the center of a circle or arc.

Centerline

A centerline marks, in phantom font, an axis of symmetry in a sketch or drawing.

Chamfer

Bevels a selected edge or vertex. You can apply chamfers to both sketches and features.

Child

A dependent feature related to a previously-built feature. For example, a chamfer on the edge of a hole is a child of the parent hole.

Click-release

As you sketch, if you click and then release the pointer, you are in click-release mode. Move the pointer and click again to define the next point in the sketch sequence.

Click-drag

As you sketch, if you click and drag the pointer, you are in click-drag mode. When you release the pointer, the sketch entity is complete.

Closed profile
Also called a closed contour, it is a sketch or sketch entity with no exposed endpoints; for example, a circle or polygon.

Collapse
The opposite of explode. The collapse action returns an exploded assembly's parts to their normal positions.

Collision Detection
An assembly function that detects collisions between components when components move or rotate. A collision occurs when an entity on one component coincides with any entity on another component.

Component
Any part or sub-assembly within an assembly

Configuration
A variation of a part or assembly within a single document. Variations can include different dimensions, features, and properties. For example, a single part such as a bolt can contain different configurations that vary the diameter and length.

ConfigurationManager
Located on the left side of the SolidWorks window, it is a means to create, select, and view the configurations of parts and assemblies.

Constraint
The relations between sketch entities, or between sketch entities and planes, axes, edges, or vertices.

Construction geometry
The characteristic of a sketch entity that the entity is used in creating other geometry but is not itself used in creating features.

Coordinate system
A system of planes used to assign Cartesian coordinates to features, parts, and assemblies. Part and assembly documents contain default coordinate systems; other coordinate systems can be defined with reference geometry. Coordinate systems can be used with measurement tools and for exporting documents to other file formats.

Cosmetic thread

An annotation that represents threads.

Crosshatch

A pattern (or fill) applied to drawing views such as section views and broken-out sections.

Curvature

Curvature is equal to the inverse of the radius of the curve. The curvature can be displayed in different colors according to the local radius (usually of a surface).

Cut

A feature that removes material from a part by such actions as extrude, revolve, loft, sweep, thicken, cavity, and so on.

Dangling

A dimension, relation, or drawing section view that is unresolved. For example, if a piece of geometry is dimensioned, and that geometry is later deleted, the dimension becomes dangling.

Degrees of freedom

Geometry that is not defined by dimensions or relations is free to move. In 2D sketches, there are three degrees of freedom: movement along the X and Y axes, and rotation about the Z axis (the axis normal to the sketch plane). In 3D sketches and in assemblies, there are six degrees of freedom: movement along the X, Y, and Z axes, and rotation about the X, Y, and Z axes.

Derived part

A derived part is a new base, mirror, or component part created directly from an existing part and linked to the original part such that changes to the original part are reflected in the derived part.

Derived sketch

A copy of a sketch, in either the same part or the same assembly, that is connected to the original sketch. Changes in the original sketch are reflected in the derived sketch.

Design Library

Located in the Task Pane, the Design Library provides a central location for reusable elements such as parts, assemblies, and so on.

Design table

An Excel spreadsheet that is used to create multiple configurations in a part or assembly document.

Detached drawing

A drawing format that allows opening and working in a drawing without loading the corresponding models into memory. The models are loaded on an as-needed basis.

Detail view

A portion of a larger view, usually at a larger scale than the original view.

Dimension line

A linear dimension line references the dimension text to extension lines indicating the entity being measured. An angular dimension line references the dimension text directly to the measured object.

DimXpertManager

Located on the left side of the SolidWorks window, it is a means to manage dimensions and tolerances created using DimXpert for parts according to the requirements of the ASME Y.14.41-2003 standard.

DisplayManager

The DisplayManager lists the appearances, decals, lights, scene, and cameras applied to the current model. From the DisplayManager, you can view applied content, and add, edit, or delete items. When PhotoView 360 is added in, the DisplayManager also provides access to PhotoView options.

Document

A file containing a part, assembly, or drawing.

Draft

The degree of taper or angle of a face, usually applied to molds or castings.

Drawing

A 2D representation of a 3D part or assembly. The extension for a SolidWorks drawing file name is .SLDDRW.

Drawing sheet

A page in a drawing document.

Driven dimension

Measurements of the model, but they do not drive the model and their values cannot be changed.

Driving dimension

Also referred to as a model dimension, it sets the value for a sketch entity. It can also control distance, thickness, and feature parameters.

Edge

A single outside boundary of a feature.

Edge flange

A sheet metal feature that combines a bend and a tab in a single operation.

Equation

Creates a mathematical relation between sketch dimensions, using dimension names as variables, or between feature parameters, such as the depth of an extruded feature or the instance count in a pattern.

Exploded view

Shows an assembly with its components separated from one another, usually to show how to assemble the mechanism.

Export

Save a SolidWorks document in another format for use in other CAD/CAM, rapid prototyping, web, or graphics software applications.

Extension line

The line extending from the model indicating the point from which a dimension is measured.

Extrude

A feature that linearly projects a sketch to either add material to a part (in a base or boss) or remove material from a part (in a cut or hole).

Face

A selectable area (planar or otherwise) of a model or surface with boundaries that help define the shape of the model or surface. For example, a rectangular solid has six faces.

Fasteners

A SolidWorks Toolbox library that adds fasteners automatically to holes in an assembly.

Feature

An individual shape that, combined with other features, makes up a part or assembly. Some features, such as bosses and cuts, originate as sketches. Other features, such as shells and fillets, modify a feature's geometry. However, not all features have associated geometry. Features are always listed in the FeatureManager design tree.

FeatureManager design tree

Located on the left side of the SolidWorks window, it provides an outline view of the active part, assembly, or drawing.

Fill

A solid area hatch or crosshatch. Fill also applies to patches on surfaces.

Fillet

An internal rounding of a corner or edge in a sketch, or an edge on a surface or solid.

Forming tool

Dies that bend, stretch, or otherwise form sheet metal to create such form features as louvers, lances, flanges, and ribs.

Fully defined

A sketch where all lines and curves in the sketch, and their positions, are described by dimensions or relations, or both, and cannot be moved. Fully defined sketch entities are shown in black.

Geometric tolerance

A set of standard symbols that specify the geometric characteristics and dimensional requirements of a feature.

Graphics area

The area in the SolidWorks window where the part, assembly, or drawing appears.

Guide curve

A 2D or 3D curve used to guide a sweep or loft.

Handle

An arrow, square, or circle that you can drag to adjust the size or position of an entity (a feature, dimension, or sketch entity, for example).

Helix

A curve defined by pitch, revolutions, and height. A helix can be used, for example, as a path for a swept feature cutting threads in a bolt.

Hem

A sheet metal feature that folds back at the edge of a part. A hem can be open, closed, double, or tear-drop.

HLR

(Hidden lines removed) a view mode in which all edges of the model that are not visible from the current view angle are removed from the display.

HLV

(hidden lines visible) A view mode in which all edges of the model that are not visible from the current view angle are shown gray or dashed.

Import

Open files from other CAD software applications into a SolidWorks document.

In-context feature

A feature with an external reference to the geometry of another component; the in-context feature changes automatically if the geometry of the referenced model or feature changes.

Inference

The system automatically creates (infers) relations between dragged entities (sketched entities, annotations, and components) and other entities and geometry. This is useful when positioning entities relative to one another.

Instance

An item in a pattern or a component in an assembly that occurs more than once. Blocks are inserted into drawings as instances of block definitions.

Interference detection

A tool that displays any interference between selected components in an assembly.

Jog

A sheet metal feature that adds material to a part by creating two bends from a sketched line. (2)

Knit

A tool that combines two or more faces or surfaces into one. The edges of the surfaces must be adjacent and not overlapping, but they cannot ever be planar. There is no difference in the appearance of the face or the surface after knitting.

Layout sketch

A sketch that contains important sketch entities, dimensions, and relations. You reference the entities in the layout sketch when creating new sketches, building new geometry, or positioning components in an assembly. This allows for easier updating of your model because changes you make to the layout sketch propagate to the entire model.

Leader
A solid line from an annotation (note, dimension, and so on) to the referenced feature.

Library feature
A frequently used feature, or combination of features, that is created once and then saved for future use.

Lightweight
A part in an assembly or a drawing has only a subset of its model data loaded into memory. The remaining model data is loaded on an as-needed basis. This improves performance of large and complex assemblies.

Line
A straight sketch entity with two endpoints. A line can be created by projecting an external entity such as an edge, plane, axis, or sketch curve into the sketch.

Loft
A base, boss, cut, or surface feature created by transitions between profiles.

Lofted bend
A sheet metal feature that produces a roll form or a transitional shape from two open profile sketches. Lofted bends often create funnels and chutes.

Mass properties
A tool that evaluates the characteristics of a part or an assembly such as volume, surface area, centroid, and so on.

Mate
A geometric relationship, such as coincident, perpendicular, tangent, and so on, between parts in an assembly.

Mate reference
Specifies one or more entities of a component to use for automatic mating. When you drag a component with a mate reference into an assembly, the software tries to find other combinations of the same mate reference name and mate type.

Mates folder
A collection of mates that are solved together. The order in which the mates appear within the Mates folder does not matter.

Mirror

(a) A mirror feature is a copy of a selected feature, mirrored about a plane or planar face.
(b) A mirror sketch entity is a copy of a selected sketch entity that is mirrored about a centerline.

Miter flange

A sheet metal feature that joins multiple edge flanges together and miters the corner.

Model

3D solid geometry in a part or assembly document. If a part or assembly document contains multiple configurations, each configuration is a separate model.

Model dimension

A dimension specified in a sketch or a feature in a part or assembly document that defines some entity in a 3D model.

Model item

A characteristic or dimension of feature geometry that can be used in detailing drawings.

Model view

A drawing view of a part or assembly.

Mold

A set of manufacturing tooling used to shape molten plastic or other material into a designed part. You design the mold using a sequence of integrated tools that result in cavity and core blocks that are derived parts of the part to be molded.

Motion Study

Motion Studies are graphical simulations of motion and visual properties with assembly models. Analogous to a configuration, they do not actually change the original assembly model or its properties. They display the model as it changes based on simulation elements you add.

Multibody part

A part with separate solid bodies within the same part document. Unlike the components in an assembly, multibody parts are not dynamic.

Native format

DXF and DWG files remain in their original format (are not converted into SolidWorks format) when viewed in SolidWorks drawing sheets (view only).

Open profile

Also called an open contour, it is a sketch or sketch entity with endpoints exposed. For example, a U-shaped profile is open.

Ordinate dimensions
A chain of dimensions measured from a zero ordinate in a drawing or sketch.

Origin
The model origin appears as three gray arrows and represents the (0,0,0) coordinate of the model. When a sketch is active, a sketch origin appears in red and represents the (0,0,0) coordinate of the sketch. Dimensions and relations can be added to the model origin, but not to
a sketch origin.

Out-of-context feature
A feature with an external reference to the geometry of another component that is not open.

Over defined
A sketch is over defined when dimensions or relations are either in conflict or redundant.

Parameter
A value used to define a sketch or feature (often a dimension).

Parent
An existing feature upon which other features depend. For example, in a block with a hole, the block is the parent to the child hole feature.

Part
A single 3D object made up of features. A part can become a component in an assembly, and it can be represented in 2D in a drawing. Examples of parts are bolt, pin, plate, and so on. The extension for a SolidWorks part file name is .SLDPRT.

Path
A sketch, edge, or curve used in creating a sweep or loft.

Pattern
A pattern repeats selected sketch entities, features, or components in an array, which can be linear, circular, or sketch-driven. If the seed entity is changed, the other instances in the pattern update.

Physical Dynamics

An assembly tool that displays the motion of assembly components in a realistic way. When you drag a component, the component applies a force to other components it touches. Components move only within their degrees of freedom.

Pierce relation

Makes a sketch point coincident to the location at which an axis, edge, line, or spline pierces the sketch plane.

Planar

Entities that can lie on one plane. For example, a circle is planar, but a helix is not.

Plane

Flat construction geometry. Planes can be used for a 2D sketch, section view of a model, a neutral plane in a draft feature, and others.

Point

A singular location in a sketch, or a projection into a sketch at a single location of an external entity (origin, vertex, axis, or point in an external sketch).

Predefined view

A drawing view in which the view position, orientation, and so on can be specified before a model is inserted. You can save drawing documents with predefined views as templates.

Profile

A sketch entity used to create a feature (such as a loft) or a drawing view (such as a detail view). A profile can be open (such as a U shape or open spline) or closed (such as a circle or closed spline).

Projected dimension

If you dimension entities in an isometric view, projected dimensions are the flat dimensions in 2D.

Projected view

A drawing view projected orthogonally from an existing view.

PropertyManager

Located on the left side of the SolidWorks window, it is used for dynamic editing of sketch entities and most features.

RealView graphics

A hardware (graphics card) support of advanced shading in real time; the rendering applies to the model and is retained as you move or rotate a part.

Rebuild
Tool that updates (or regenerates) the document with any changes made since the last time the model was rebuilt. Rebuild is typically used after changing a model dimension.

Reference dimension
A dimension in a drawing that shows the measurement of an item, but cannot drive the model and its value cannot be modified. When model dimensions change, reference dimensions update.

Reference geometry
Includes planes, axes, coordinate systems, and 3D curves. Reference geometry is used to assist in creating features such lofts, sweeps, drafts, chamfers, and patterns.

Relation
A geometric constraint between sketch entities or between a sketch entity and a plane, axis, edge, or vertex. Relations can be added automatically or manually.

Relative view
A relative (or relative to model) drawing view is created relative to planar surfaces in a part or assembly.

Reload
Refreshes shared documents. For example, if you open a part file for read-only access while another user makes changes to the same part, you can reload the new version, including the changes.

Reorder
Reordering (changing the order of) items is possible in the FeatureManager design tree. In parts, you can change the order in which features are solved. In assemblies, you can control the order in which components appear in a bill of materials.

Replace
Substitutes one or more open instances of a component in an assembly with a different component.

Resolved

A state of an assembly component (in an assembly or drawing document) in which it is fully loaded in memory. All the component's model data is available, so its entities can be selected, referenced, edited, used in mates, and so on.

Revolve

A feature that creates a base or boss, a revolved cut, or revolved surface by revolving one or more sketched profiles around a centerline.

Rip

A sheet metal feature that removes material at an edge to allow a bend.

Rollback

Suppresses all items below the rollback bar.

Section

Another term for profile in sweeps.

Section line

A line or centerline sketched in a drawing view to create a section view.

Section scope

Specifies the components to be left uncut when you create an assembly drawing section view.

Section view

A section view (or section cut) is (1) a part or assembly view cut by a plane, or (2) a drawing view created by cutting another drawing view with a section line.

Seed

A sketch or an entity (a feature, face, or body) that is the basis for a pattern. If you edit the seed, the other entities in the pattern are updated.

Shaded

Displays a model as a colored solid.

Shared values

Also called linked values, these are named variables that you assign to set the value of two or more dimensions to be equal.

Sheet format

Includes page size and orientation, standard text, borders, title blocks, and so on. Sheet formats can be customized and saved for future use. Each sheet of a drawing document can have a different format.

Shell
A feature that hollows out a part, leaving open the selected faces and thin walls on the remaining faces. A hollow part is created when no faces are selected to be open.

Sketch
A collection of lines and other 2D objects on a plane or face that forms the basis for a feature such as a base or a boss. A 3D sketch is non-planar and can be used to guide a sweep or loft, for example.

Smart Fasteners
Automatically adds fasteners (bolts and screws) to an assembly using the SolidWorks Toolbox library of fasteners.

SmartMates
An assembly mating relation that is created automatically.

Solid sweep
A cut sweep created by moving a tool body along a path to cut out 3D material from a model.

Spiral
A flat or 2D helix, defined by a circle, pitch, and number of revolutions.

Spline
A sketched 2D or 3D curve defined by a set of control points.

Split line
Projects a sketched curve onto a selected model face, dividing the face into multiple faces so that each can be selected individually. A split line can be used to create draft features, to create face blend fillets, and to radiate surfaces to cut molds.

Stacked balloon
A set of balloons with only one leader. The balloons can be stacked vertically (up or down) or horizontally (left or right).

Standard 3 views
The three orthographic views (front, right, and top) that are often the basis of a drawing.

Stereolithography
The process of creating rapid prototype parts using a faceted mesh representation in STL files.

Sub-assembly
An assembly document that is part of a larger assembly. For example, the steering mechanism of a car is a sub-assembly of the car.

Suppress
Removes an entity from the display and from any calculations in which it is involved. You can suppress features, assembly components, and so on. Suppressing an entity does not delete the entity; you can un-suppress the entity to restore it.

Surface
A zero-thickness planar or 3D entity with edge boundaries. Surfaces are often used to create solid features. Reference surfaces can be used to modify solid features.

Sweep
Creates a base, boss, cut, or surface feature by moving a profile (section) along a path. For cut-sweeps, you can create solid sweeps by moving a tool body along a path.

Tangent arc
An arc that is tangent to another entity, such as a line.

Tangent edge
The transition edge between rounded or filleted faces in hidden lines visible or hidden lines removed modes in drawings.

Task Pane
Located on the right-side of the SolidWorks window, the Task Pane contains SolidWorks Resources, the Design Library, and the File Explorer.

Template
A document (part, assembly, or drawing) that forms the basis of a new document. It can include user-defined parameters, annotations, predefined views, geometry, and so on.

Temporary axis
An axis created implicitly for every conical or cylindrical face in a model.

Thin feature
An extruded or revolved feature with constant wall thickness. Sheet metal parts are typically created from thin features.

TolAnalyst

A tolerance analysis application that determines the effects that dimensions and tolerances have on parts and assemblies.

Top-down design

An assembly modeling technique where you create parts in the context of an assembly by referencing the geometry of other components. Changes to the referenced components propagate to the parts that you create in context.

Triad

Three axes with arrows defining the X, Y, and Z directions. A reference triad appears in part and assembly documents to assist in orienting the viewing of models. Triads also assist when moving or rotating components in assemblies.

Under defined

A sketch is under defined when there are not enough dimensions and relations to prevent entities from moving or changing size.

Vertex

A point at which two or more lines or edges intersect. Vertices can be selected for sketching, dimensioning, and many other operations.

Viewports

Windows that display views of models. You can specify one, two, or four viewports. Viewports with orthogonal views can be linked, which links orientation and rotation.

Virtual sharp

A sketch point at the intersection of two entities after the intersection itself has been removed by a feature such as a fillet or chamfer. Dimensions and relations to the virtual sharp are retained even though the actual intersection no longer exists.

Weldment

A multibody part with structural members.

Weldment cut list

A table that tabulates the bodies in a weldment along with descriptions and lengths.

Wireframe

A view mode in which all edges of the part or assembly are displayed.

Zebra stripes

Simulate the reflection of long strips of light on a very shiny surface. They allow you to see small changes in a surface that may be hard to see with a standard display.

Zoom

To simulate movement toward or away from a part or an assembly.

Index

Quick Reference Guide To SolidWorks® 2014 Command Icons & Toolbars

The SKETCH TOOLS Toolbar

 Selects items for commands to act on.

 Sets up Grid parameters.

 Creates a sketch on a selected plane or face.

 Creates a 3D sketch.

 Scales/Translates/Rotates the current sketch.

 Moves or copies sketch entities and annotations.

 Scales sketch entities and annotations.

 Sketches an angle rectangle from the center.

 Sketches a parallelogram.

 Sketches a line.

 Creates a center point arc: center, start, end.

 Creates an arc tangent to a line.

 Sketches splines on a surface or face.

 Sketches a circle.

 Sketches a circle by its perimeter.

 Sketches a partial ellipse.

 Makes a path of sketch entities.

 Mirrors entities dynamically about a centerline.

 Insert a plane into the 3D sketch.

 Rotates sketch entities and annotations.

 Copies sketch entities and annotations.

 Sketches on a plane in a 3D sketch.

 Moves sketch entities without solving dimensions or relations.

The SKETCH TOOLS Toolbar (Cont.)

 Partial ellipses.

 Adds a Parabola.

 Creates sketched splines.

 Sketches a polygon.

 Sketches a rectangle.

 Sketches a parallelogram.

 Creates points.

 Creates sketched centerlines.

 Adds text to sketch.

 Converts selected model edges or sketch entities to sketch segments.

 Creates a sketch along the intersection of multiple bodies.

 Converts face curves on the selected face into 3D sketch entities.

 Mirrors selected segments about a centerline.

 Fillets the corner of two lines.

 Creates a chamfer between two sketch entities.

 Creates a sketch curve by offsetting model edges or sketch entities at a specified distance.

 Fits a spline to selected entities.

 Trims a sketch segment.

 Extends a sketch segment.

 Splits a sketch segment.

 Construction Geometry.

 Creates linear steps and repeat of sketch entities.

 Creates circular steps and repeat of sketch entities.

The Sketch Tools toolbar

Quick Reference Guide To SolidWorks® 2014 Command Icons & Toolbars

The SHEET METAL Toolbar

Inserts a FlattenBends & a ProcessBends feature, A sheet metal feature will be added.

Shows flat pattern for this sheet metal part.

Shows part without inserting any bends.

Inserts a rip feature to a sheet metal part.

Inserts a Sheet Metal Base Flange or a Tab feature.

Inserts a Sheet Metal Miter Flange feature.

Folds selected bends.

Unfolds selected bends.

Inserts bends using a sketch line.

Inserts a flange by pulling an edge.

Inserts a sheet metal corner feature.

Inserts a Hem feature by selecting edges.

Breaks a corner by filleting/chamfering it.

Inserts a Jog feature using a sketch line.

Inserts a lofted bend feature using 2 sketches.

Creates inverse dent on a sheet metal part.

Trims out material from a corner, in a sheet metal part.

Inserts a fillet weld bead.

Converts a solid/surface into a sheet metal part.

Adds a Cross Break feature into a selected face.

The SURFACES Toolbar

Deletes a face or a set of faces.

Creates mid surfaces between offset face pairs.

Patches surface holes and external edges.

The SURFACES Toolbar (cont.)

Creates an extruded surface.

Creates a revolved surface.

Creates a swept surface.

Creates a lofted surface.

Creates an offset surface.

Radiates a surface originating from a curve, parallel to a plane.

Knits surfaces together.

Creates a planar surface from a sketch or A set of edges.

Creates a surface by importing data from a file.

Extends a surface.

Trims a surface.

Generating MidSurface(s).

Deletes Face(s).

Replaces Face with Surface.

Patches surface holes and external edges by extending the surfaces.

Creates parting surfaces between core & cavity surfaces.

Inserts ruled surfaces from edges.

The WELDMENTS Toolbar

Creates a weldment feature.

Creates a structure member feature.

Adds a gusset feature between 2 planar adjoining faces.

Creates an end cap feature.

Adds a fillet weld bead feature.

Trims or extends structure members.

The DIMENSIONS/RELATIONS Toolbar

 Inserts dimension between two lines.

 Creates a horizontal dimension between selected entities.

 Creates a vertical dimension between selected entities.

 Creates a reference dimension between selected entities.

 Creates a set of ordinate dimensions.

 Creates a set of Horizontal ordinate dimensions.

 Creates a set of Vertical ordinate dimensions.

 Creates a chamfer dimension.

 Adds a geometric relation.

 Automatically Adds Dimensions to the current sketch.

 Displays and deletes geometric relations.

 Fully defines a sketch.

 Scans a sketch for elements of equal length or radius.

 Automatically recognize tolerance features.

 Creates linked, unlinked, or collection pattern feature.

 Paints faces of toleranced features in different colors.

 Adds DimXpert location dimension.

 Adds DimXpert datum.

 Copies existing tolerance scheme to current configuration.

 Adds DimXpert size dimension.

 Adds DimXpert geometric tolerance.

 Deletes all tolerance data base.

 Adds new Tol Analyst.

Did you know??
* Ctrl+Q will force a rebuild on all features of a part.
* Ctrl+B will rebuild the feature being worked on and its dependants.

The STANDARD VIEWS Toolbar

 Front view.

 Back view.

 Left view.

 Right view.

 Top view.

 Bottom view.

 Isometric view.

 Trimetric view.

 Dimetric view.

 Normal to view.

 Links all views in the viewport together.

 Displays viewport with front & right views

 Displays a 4 view viewport with 1ˢ or 3ʳ Angle of projection.

 Displays viewport with front & top views

 Displays viewport with a single view. views

The Block Toolbar

 Makes a new block.

 Edits the selected block.

 Inserts a new block to a sketch or drawing.

 Adds/Removes sketch entities to/from blocks.

 Updates parent sketches effected by this block.

 Saves the block to a file.

Explodes the selected block.

Inserts a belt.

Creates a boss feature by extruding a sketched profile.

Creates a revolved feature based on profile and angle parameter.

Creates a cut feature by extruding a sketched profile.

Creates a cut feature by revolving a sketched profile.

Creates a sweep feature by sweeping a profile along a path curve.

Creates a cut by sweeping a closed profile along an open or closed path.

Creates a cut by removing material between two or more profiles

Creates a cut by thickening one or more adjacent surfaces.

Adds a deformed surface by push or pull on points.

Creates a lofted feature between two or more profiles.

Creates a solid feature by thickening one or more adjacent surfaces.

Creates a filled feature.

Chamfers an edge or a chain of tangent edges.

Inserts a rib feature.

Scales model by a specified factor.

Creates a shell feature.

Applies draft to a selected surface.

Creates a cylindrical hole.

Inserts a hole with a pre-defined cross section.

Puts a dome surface on a face.

Puts a shape feature on a face.

Applies global deformation to solid or surface bodies.

Wraps closed sketch contour(s) onto a face.

Moves / Sizes features.

Suppresses the selected feature or component.

Un-suppresses the selected feature or component.

Flexes solid and surface bodies

Creates a linear pattern using the selected feature(s).

Creates a circular pattern using the selected feature(s).

Mirrors a feature about a plane.

Creates a Curve Driven Pattern.

Creates a Sketch Driven pattern.

Creates a Table Driven Pattern.

Inserts a split Feature.

Combines two or more solid bodies.

Joins bodies from one or more parts into a single part in the context of an assembly.

Deletes a solid or a surface.

Inserts solid(s) or surface(s) into an existing open document.

Inserts a part from file into the active part document.

Moves/Copies solid and surface bodies or moves graphics bodies.

Merges short edges on faces

Pushes solid / surface model by another solid / surface model

Moves face(s) of a solid

Area fills faces or bodies into one or more contours.

Inserts holes into a series of parts.

Returns suppressed items with dependents to the model.

Cuts a solid model with a surface.

Adds material between profiles in two directions to create a solid feature.

Cuts a solid model by removing material between profiles in two directions.

Did you know??

* Right-mouse drag a component in an assembly rotates it.
* Left- mouse drag a component in an assembly moves it.

The MOLD TOOLS Toolbar

 Extracts core(s) from existing tooling split

 Constructs a surface patch

 Moves face(s) of a solid

 Finds & creates mold shut-off surfaces

 Inserts cavity into a base part.

 Scales a model by a specified factor.

 Applies draft to a selected surface.

 Inserts a split line feature.

 Creates an offset surface.

 Creates parting lines to separate core & cavity surfaces

 Creates a planar surface from a sketch or
A set of edges.

 Knits surfaces together.

 Analyzes draft angles of faces, based on a mold
pull direction.

 Inserts ruled surfaces from edges.

 Creates parting surfaces between core & cavity surfaces

 Creates multiple bodies from a single body.

 Inserts a tooling split feature.

 Identifies faces that form undercuts.

 Creates parting surfaces between the core & cavity.

 Inserts surface body folders for mold operation.

The SELECTION FILTERS Toolbar

 Turns selection filters on and off.

 Clears all filters.

 Selects all filters.

Inverts current selection.

The SELECTION FILTERS cont.

 Allows selection of edges only.

 Allows selection of faces only.

 Adds filter for Surface Bodies.

 Adds filter for Solid Bodies.

 Adds filter for Axes.

 Adds filter for Planes.

 Adds filter for Sketch Points.

 Adds filter for Sketch Segments.

 Adds filter for Midpoints.

 Adds filter for Center Marks.

 Adds filter for Centerline.

 Adds filter for Dimensions and Hole Callouts.

 Adds filter for Surface Finish Symbols.

 Adds filter for Geometric Tolerances.

 Adds filter for Notes / Balloons.

 Adds filter for Weld Symbols.

 Adds filter for Datum Targets.

 Adds filter for Cosmetic Threads.

 Adds filter for blocks.

 Adds filter for Dowel pin symbols.

 Adds filter for connection points.

 Allows selection filter for vertices only.

 Allows selection of weld symbols only.

 Allows selection of blocks only.

 Adds filter for routing points.

The FLYOUT Toolbar

 2D to 3D.

 Align.

 Annotation.

 Assemblies.

 Curves.

 Dimensions / Relation.

 Drawings.

 Features.

 Fonts.

 Line Formats.

 Macros.

 Molds.

 Reference Geometry.

 Quick snap filters.

 Selection Filters.

 Sheet Metal.

 Simulation.

 Sketch.

 SolidWorks Office.

 Splines.

 Standard.

 Standard Views.

 Surfaces.

 Tools.

 View.

 Web.

 Weldments.

 Block commands.

 Explode sketch commands.

 Table commands.

 Fastening feature commands.

 Creates a rounded internal or external fillet.

 Linear Patterns Features, Faces and Bodies.

 Creates various corner treatments.

 Displays Deletes geometric relations.

 Creates dimensions for one or more entities.

 Adds an existing part or assembly.

 Linear Patterns components in assembly.

 Moves components in assembly.

 Adds section view with a section line.

 Creates various assembly features.

 Toggles various view settings.

The SCREEN CAPTURE Toolbar

 Copies the current graphics window to the clipboard.

 Records the current graphics window to an AVI file.

 Stops recording the current graphics window to an AVI file.

The Explode Line Sketch Toolbar

 Adds a route line that connect entities.

 Adds a jog to the route lines.

The LINE FORMAT Toolbar

Changes layer properties.

Changes line color.

Changes line thickness.

Changes line style.

Hides a visible edge.

Shows a hidden edge.

Changes line display mode.

The 2D-To-3D Toolbar

Makes a Front sketch from the selected entities.

Makes a Top sketch from the selected entities.

Makes a Right sketch from the selected entities.

Makes a Left sketch from the selected entities.

Makes a Bottom sketch from the selected entities.

Makes a Back sketch from the selected entities.

Makes an Auxiliary sketch from the selected entities.

Creates a new sketch from the selected entities.

Repairs the selected sketch.

Aligns a sketch to the selected point.

Creates an extrusion from the selected sketch segments, starting at the selected sketch point.

Creates a cut from the selected sketch segments, optionally starting at the selected sketch point.

The ALIGN Toolbar

Aligns the left side of the selected annotations with the leftmost annotation.

Aligns the right side of the selected annotations with the rightmost annotation.

Aligns the top side of the selected annotations with the topmost annotation.

Aligns the bottom side of the selected annotations with the lowermost annotation.

Evenly spaces the selected annotations horizontally.

Evenly spaces the selected annotations vertically.

Centrally aligns the selected annotations horizontally.

Centrally aligns the selected annotations vertically.

Compacts the selected annotations horizontally.

Compacts the selected annotations vertically.

Aligns the center of the selected annotations between The nearest selected horizontal or vertical line.

Creates a group from the selected items

Deletes the grouping between these items

Aligns & groups selected dimensions along a line or an arc

Aligns & groups dimensions at a uniform distances

The SIMULATION Toolbar

Stops Record or Playback.

Records Simulation.

Replays Simulation.

Resets Components.

Adds Linear Motor.

Adds Rotary Motor.

Adds Spring.

Adds Gravity.

The MACRO Toolbar

Runs a Macro.

Stops Macro recorder.

Records (or pauses recording of) actions to create a Macro.

Launches the Macro Editor and begins editing a new macro.

Opens a Macro file for editing.

Creates a custom macro.

The TABLE Toolbar

 Adds a hole table of selected holes from a specified origin datum.

 Adds a Bill of Materials.

 Adds a revision table.

 Displays a Design table in a drawing.

 Adds a weldments cuts list table.

 Adds a Excel based of Bill of Materials

 Adds a general table to a drawing sheet.

The REFERENCE GEOMETRY Toolbar

 Adds a reference plane

 Creates an axis.

 Creates a coordinate system.

 Adds a reference point

 Specifies entities to use as references using SmartMates.

The SPLINE TOOLS Toolbar

 Adds a point to a spline.

 Displays points where the concavity of selected spline changes.

 Displays minimum radius of selected spline.

 Displays curvature combs of selected spline.

 Reduces numbers of points in a selected spline.

 Adds a tangency control.

 Adds a curvature control.

 Adds a spline based on selected sketch entities & edges.

 Displays all handles of selected splines.

 Displays the spline control polygon.

The ANNOTATIONS Toolbar

 Inserts a note.

 Inserts a surface finish symbol.

 Inserts a new geometric tolerancing symbol.

 Attaches a balloon to the selected edge or face.

 Adds balloons for all components in selected view.

 Inserts a stacked balloon.

 Attaches a datum feature symbol to a selected edge / detail.

 Inserts a weld symbol on the selected edge / face / vertex.

 Inserts a datum target symbol and / or point attached to a selected edge / line.

 Selects and inserts block.

 Inserts annotations & reference geometry from the part / assembly into the selected drawing view

 Adds center marks to circles on model.

 Inserts a Centerline.

 Inserts a hole callout.

 Adds a cosmetic thread to the selected cylindrical feature.

 Inserts a Multi-Jog leader.

 Selects a circular edge or and arc for Dowel pin symbol insertion.

 Toggles the visibility of annotations & dimensions.

 Inserts latest version symbol.

 Adds a cross hatch patterns or solid fill.

 Adds a weld symbol on a selected entity.

 Adds a weld bead caterpillar on an edge.

The "Feathers"

 Lightweight component.

 Out-of-Date component.

 Hidden Lightweight component.

 Hidden, Out-of-Date and Lightweight.

The DRAWINGS Toolbar

Updates the selected view to the model's current stage.

Creates a detail view.

Creates a section view.

Inserts an aligned section using the selected line or section line.

Unfolds a new view from an existing view.

Generates a standard 3-view drawing (1˚ or 3˚ angle).

Inserts an auxiliary view of an inclined surface.

Adds an Orthogonal or Named view based on an existing part or assembly.

Adds a Relative view by two orthogonal faces or planes.

Adds a Predefined orthogonal projected or Named view with a model.

Adds an empty view.

Adds vertical break lines to selected view.

Crops a view.

Creates a Broken-out section.

Inserts an Alternate Position view.

The QUICK SNAP Toolbar

Snap to points.

Snap to center points.

Snap to midpoints.

Snap to quadrant points.

Snap to intersection of 2 curves.

Snap to nearest curve.

Snap tangent to curve.

Snap perpendicular to curve.

Snap parallel to line.

Snap horizontally / vertically.

Snap horizontally / vertically to points.

Snap to discrete line lengths.

Snap to grid points.

Snap to angle.

The LAYOUT Toolbar

Creates the assembly layout sketch.

Sketches a line.

Sketches a rectangle.

Sketches a circle.

Sketches a 3 point arc.

Rounds a corner.

Trims or extends a sketch.

Adds sketch entities by offsetting faces, Edges curves.

Mirrors selected entities about a centerline.

Adds a relation.

Creates a dimension.

Displays / Deletes geometric relations.

Makes a new block.

Edits the selected block.

Inserts a new block to the sketch or drawing.

Adds / Removes sketch entities to / from a block.

Saves the block to a file.

Explodes the selected block.

Creates a new part from a layout sketch block.

Positions 2 components relative to one another.

Moves a component within the degrees of freedom defined by its mates.

The CURVES Toolbar

Projects sketch onto selected surface.

Inserts a split line feature.

Creates a composite curve from selected edges, curves and sketches.

Creates a curve through free points.

Creates a 3D curve through reference points.

Helical curve defined by a base sketch and shape parameters.

The VIEW Toolbar

Displays a view in the selected orientation.

Reverts to previous view.

Zooms out to see entire model.

Zooms in by dragging a bounding box.

Zooms in or out by dragging up or down.

Zooms to fit all selected entities.

Dynamic view rotation.

Scrolls view by dragging.

Displays image in wireframe mode.

Displays hidden edges in gray.

Displays image with hidden lines removed.

Controls the visibility of planes.

Controls the visibility of axis.

Controls the visibility of parting lines.

Controls the visibility of temporary axis.

Controls the visibility of origins.

Controls the visibility of coordinate systems.

Controls the visibility of reference curves.

Controls the visibility of sketches.

Controls the visibility of 3D sketch planes.

Controls the visibility of 3D sketch dimensions.

Controls the visibility of all annotations.

Controls the visibility of reference points.

Controls the visibility of routing points.

Controls the visibility of lights.

Controls the visibility of cameras.

Controls the visibility of sketch relations.

Redraws the current window.

Rolls the model view.

Turns the orientation of the model view.

Dynamically manipulate the model view in 3D to make selection.

Changes the display style for the active view.

Displays a shade view of the model with its edges.

Displays a shade view of the model.

Toggles between draft quality & high quality HLV.

Cycles through or applies a specific scene.

Views the models through one of the model's cameras.

Displays a part or assembly w/different colors according to the local radius of curvature.

Displays zebra stripes.

Displays a model with hardware accelerated shades.

Edits the real view appearance of entities in the model.

Applies a texture to entities in a model.

Changes the visibility of items in the graphics area.

Controls visibility of the sketch grid.

The **TOOLS** Toolbar

 Calculates the distance between selected items.

 Adds or edits equation.

 Calculates the mass properties of the model.

 Checks the model for geometry errors.

 Inserts or edits a Design Table.

 Evaluates section properties for faces and sketches that lie in parallel planes.

 Reports Statistics for this Part/Assembly.

 Deviation Analysis.

 Runs the SimulationXpress analysis wizard Powered by SolidWorks Simulation.

 Checks the spelling.

 Import diagnostics.

 Runs the DFMXpress analysis wizard.

 Runs the DriveWorkXpress wizard.

 Runs the SolidWorksFloXpress analysis wizard.

The **ASSEMBLY** Toolbar

 Creates a new part & inserts it into the assembly.

 Adds an existing part or sub-assembly to the assembly.

 Creates a new assembly & inserts it into the assembly.

 Turns on/off large assembly mode for this document.

 Hides / shows model(s) associated with the selected model(s).

 Toggles the transparency of components.

 Changes the selected components to suppressed or resolved.

 Toggles between editing part and assembly.

 Inserts a belt.

Inserts a new part into an assembly.

 Smart Fasteners.

 Positions two components relative to one. another.

 External references will not be created.

 Moves a component.

 Rotates an un-mated component around its center point.

 Replaces selected components.

 Replaces mate entities of mates of the selected components on the selected Mate group.

 Creates a New Exploded view.

 Creates or edits explode line sketch.

 Interference detection.

 Changes assembly transparency.

 Shows or Hides the Simulation toolbar.

 Patterns components in one or two linear directions.

 Patterns components around an axis.

 Toggles the transparency of components Between 0 and 75 percent.

 Toggles between editing a Part and Assembly.

 Adds fasteners to the assembly using Toolbox.

 Displays statistics and check the health of The current assembly.

 Patterns components relative to an existing Pattern in a part.

 Shows hidden components.

 Toggles large assembly mode for this document.

 Checks assembly hole alignments.

 Mirrors subassemblies and parts.

To add or remove an icon
to or from the toolbar, first select:

Tools/Customize/Commands
Next select a **Category**, click a button to see its description and then drag / drop the command icon into any toolbar.

Rotate the model

* Horizontally or Vertically: _____ Arrow keys

* Horizontally or Vertically 90°: _____ Shift + Arrow keys

* Clockwise or Counterclockwise: _____ Alt + left or right Arrow

* Pan the model: _____ Ctrl + Arrow keys

* Zoom in: _____ **Z** (shift + Z or capital Z)

* Zoom out: _____ **z** (lower case z)

* Zoom to fit: _____ **F**

* Previous view: _____ Ctrl+Shift+Z

View Orientation

View Orientation Menu: _____ Space bar

* Front: _____ Ctrl+1

* Back: _____ Ctrl+2

* Left: _____ Ctrl+3

* Right: _____ Ctrl+4

* Top: _____ Ctrl+5

* Bottom: _____ Ctrl+6

* Isometric: _____ Ctrl+7

Selection Filter & Misc.

_____ **e**

Filter Vertices: _____ **v**

* Filter Faces: _____ **x**

* Toggle Selection filter toolbar: _____ **F5**

* Toggle Selection Filter toolbar (on/off): _____ **F6**

* New SolidWorks document: _____ **F1**

* Open Document: _____ Ctrl+O

* Open from Web folder: _____ Ctrl+W

* Save: _____ Ctrl+S

* Print: _____ Ctrl+P

* Magnifying Glass Zoom _____ **g**

* Switch between the SolidWorks documents _____ Ctrl + Tab

SolidWorks 2014 Quick-Guide©
Customized Keyboard Shortcuts

SW 2014 Sample Customized Hot Keys

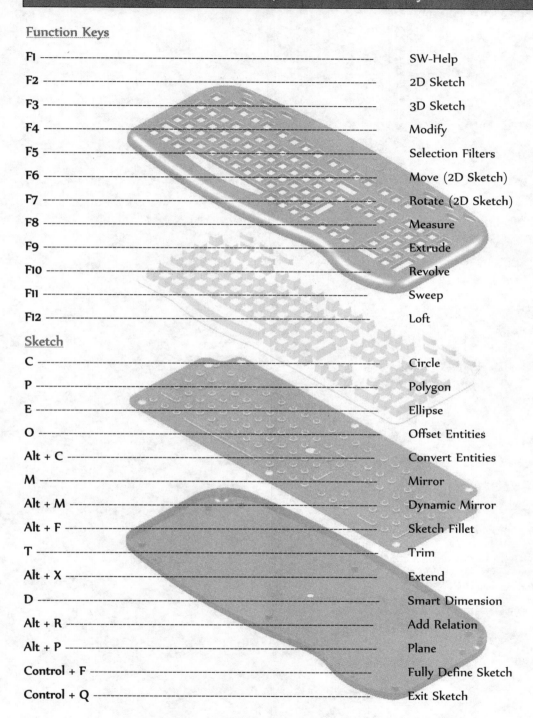

Function Keys

F1	SW-Help
F2	2D Sketch
F3	3D Sketch
F4	Modify
F5	Selection Filters
F6	Move (2D Sketch)
F7	Rotate (2D Sketch)
F8	Measure
F9	Extrude
F10	Revolve
F11	Sweep
F12	Loft

Sketch

C	Circle
P	Polygon
E	Ellipse
O	Offset Entities
Alt + C	Convert Entities
M	Mirror
Alt + M	Dynamic Mirror
Alt + F	Sketch Fillet
T	Trim
Alt + X	Extend
D	Smart Dimension
Alt + R	Add Relation
Alt + P	Plane
Control + F	Fully Define Sketch
Control + Q	Exit Sketch

Part of SolidWorks 2014 – Basic Tools and Advanced Techniques

SolidWorks® Quick-Guide by Paul Tran – Sr. Certified SolidWorks Instructor
© Issue 10 / Jan-2014 - Printed in The United State of America – All Rights Reserved